LEGENDARY LOCALS

OF

YARMOUTH

MASSACHUSETTS

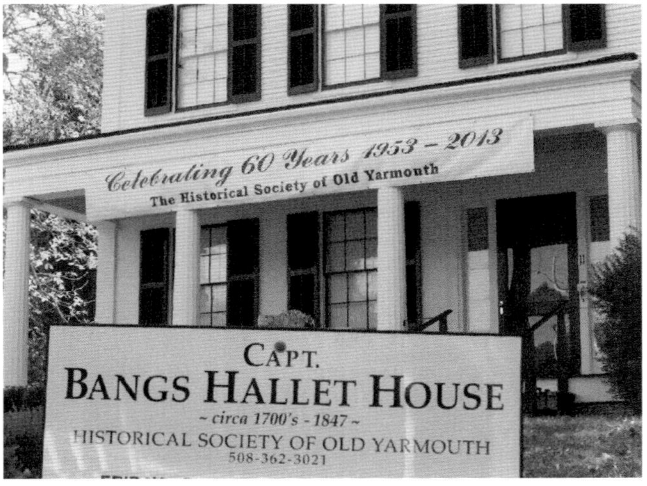

I0806120

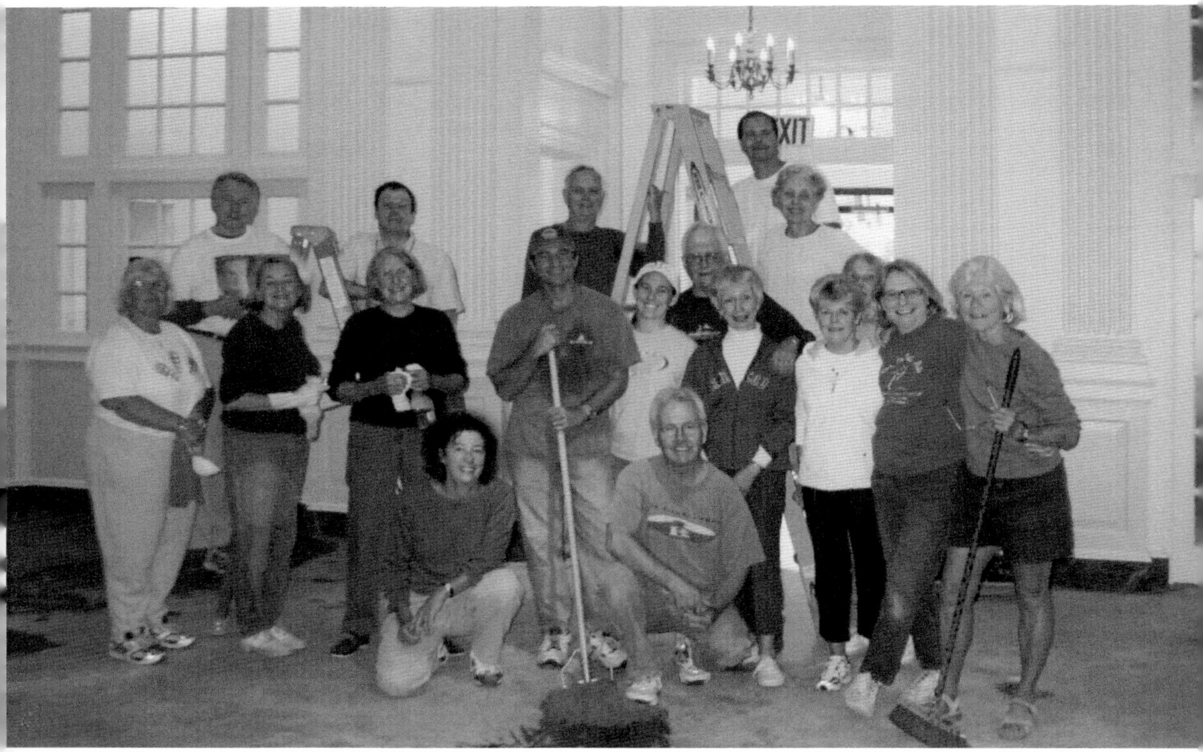

Volunteers of the Cultural Center of Cape Cod
Not a single person, but a collection of people operating under the motto "All the Arts for All of Us," the Cultural Center of Cape Cod has become a hub for music, the visual arts, dance, drama, and much more.

Located on Old Main Street in the Bass River section of South Yarmouth, the Cultural Center of Cape Cod occupies a building that began life as the Bass River Savings Bank in the 1930s. Vacant by the 1990s, the brick building, with its bank vault intact, might have fallen to the wrecking ball if not for a group of determined people who envisioned a center for the arts unlike anything that existed on Cape Cod. By early 2007, the Cultural Center of Cape Cod opened its doors and soon became the busiest place in Yarmouth as well as a model for other arts-related organizations on Cape Cod and elsewhere.

This photograph shows a group of volunteers cleaning up prior to the Cultural Center of Cape Cod's grand opening. They are, from left to right, (first row) Marion Broidrick and Robert Nash; (second row) Keran Lockhart, Patricia Garry, Sally Churchill, James Saben, JoAnna Watson, Charles Adams, Barbara Adams, Carol Ann Morris, Tabitha Ballard, Caryn Ritchie, and Patsy Chappell; (third row) Robert Lindquist, John Basile, Richard McGarr, Michael Tranchita, and Suzanne Packer. (Photograph by Robert Nash.)

Page 1: Bangs Hallet House
Today, the Greek Revival–style Capt. Bangs Hallet House at 2 Strawberry Lane on the Yarmouth Port Common stands as the headquarters for the Historical Society of Old Yarmouth. The house was built in 1840 by Thomas C. Thacher, who sold it to Capt. Allen H. Knowles, who in turn traded the house to Capt. Bangs Hallet, his good friend. For Hallet and his wife, Anna, the house was their retirement home. Upon their deaths, their heirs sold the house back to the Thacher family, bringing its ownership full circle. In 1956, the Thachers gave the house to the fledgling Historical Society of Old Yarmouth, which maintains the house as a museum and gathering place. (Photograph by author.)

LEGENDARY LOCALS
OF
YARMOUTH
MASSACHUSETTS

JOHN A. BASILE

LEGENDARY LOCALS

ISBN 978-1-4671-0147-9

Legendary Locals is an imprint of Arcadia Publishing
Charleston, South Carolina

Printed in the United States of America

Library of Congress Control Number: 2013955331

For all general information, please contact Arcadia Publishing:
Telephone 843-853-2070
Fax 843-853-0044
E-mail sales@arcadiapublishing.com
For customer service and orders:
Toll-Free 1-888-313-2665

Visit us on the Internet at www.arcadiapublishing.com

Dedication
This book is dedicated to the people of Yarmouth, past and present, whose life stories are also the story of this seaside town.

On the Front Cover: From left to right:
Marguerite E. Small, teacher (author's collection; see page 39), Keith Reed, baseball player (courtesy of Baltimore Orioles; see page 118), Suzanne Packer, artist (photograph by Robert Nash; see page 32), Edward Gorey, artist, illustrator, and writer (courtesy of Edward Gorey House; see page 29), Ben Muse, antiquarian bookseller (courtesy of the *Register*; see page 72), Elizabeth Gray Thacher, Thacher family matriarch (courtesy of Lawrence Perera; see page 18), Cpl. Nicholas G. Xiarhos, Marine Corps (courtesy of Xiarhos family; see page 51), Daniel Burbank, astronaut (courtesy of NASA; see page 42), Robert Lawton, town administrator (Courtesy of the *Register*; see page 43).

On the Back Cover: From left to right:
Dr. Marjorie Rice Fallows, college sociology professor and trustee of the South Yarmouth Library Association (courtesy of the *Register*; see page 94); Cultural Center of Cape Cod volunteers (photograph by Robert Nash; see page 2).

CONTENTS

ACKNOWLEDGMENTS

This book could not have been completed without the help of many people. Duncan Oliver at the Historical Society of Old Yarmouth offered perspective and direction on many occasions. He also was the key to locating some important images. Mary LaBombard at Cape Cod Community College assisted by pointing out sources of Yarmouth's early history and images of some of Yarmouth's earliest settlers. Lawrence Thacher Perera generously shared his family history and insight into how Yarmouth has evolved. Zabelle D'Amico shared her knowledge of West Yarmouth's people and history. Thanks also go to all those who generously shared their stories and photographs. Erin Vosgien and Kris McDonagh kept the project on track. Kathryn Basile always listened and nudged the author in the right direction.

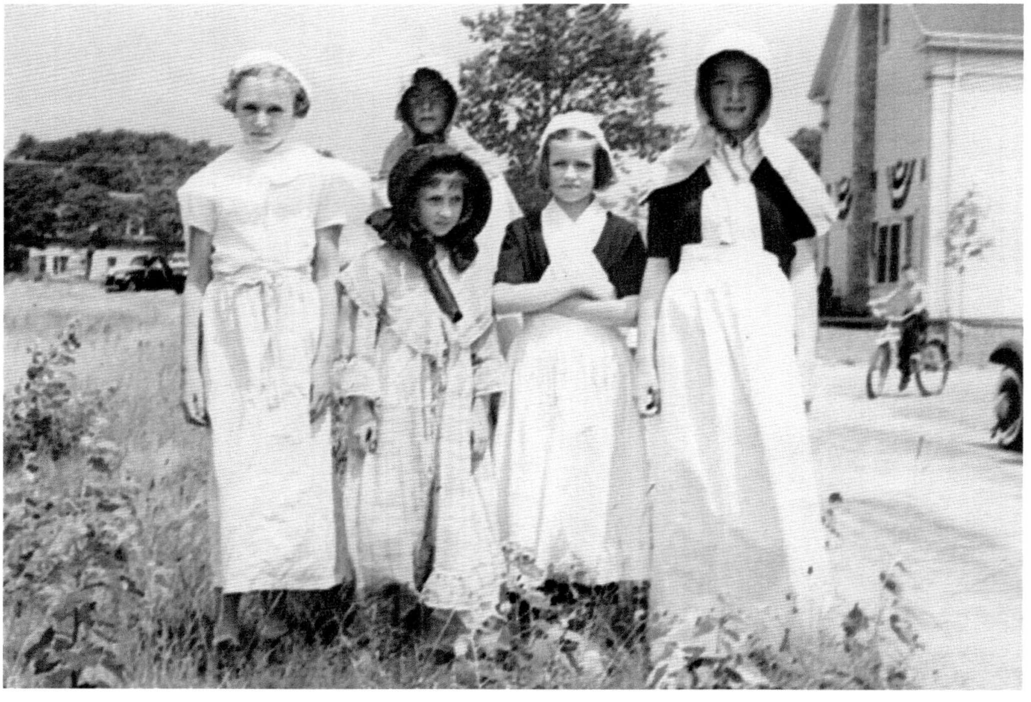

300th Anniversary
On July 30 and August 2, 1939, Yarmouth's 300th-anniversary celebration included musical events, religious services, a scholarly gathering, and a traditional fireworks display over the Bass River. It was an event rooted in hometown pride and involved nearly every resident.

The girls dressed in historic costumes, are, from left to right, (first row) Frances Salter, Dorcus Donley, Verna Morgan Bear, and Florence Whitehead Basset; (second row) Florence Boese. (Courtesy of the Historical Society of Old Yarmouth.)

INTRODUCTION

With roots as deep as any town in the United States, Yarmouth, Massachusetts, has a long and colorful history that is still being written.

When Stephen Hopkins built his home with permission from the court of Plymouth Colony on the land then called Mattacheese and now called Yarmouth, he became part of an area that already had a long history of native people. When Antony Thacher, John Crowe, and Thomas Howes received land grants, they set in motion events that resulted in the town we know today.

The land known by the natives as Mattacheese or Mattachesset, which indicated the area's close proximity to water, was bounded by the Atlantic Ocean to the north and south and had an abundance of ponds with a tidal river cutting into its dense woodlands.

It was no surprise that many Yarmouth people made their living from the sea as ship's captains, salt makers, and merchants of various kinds. It was not unusual for boys to go to sea to learn seamanship under the watchful eye of an experienced captain. Those same boys carried on the tradition as they rose to become captains themselves.

Yarmouth, as it is now configured, resulted from a split in 1793 in which the eastern portion of the town became the town of Dennis. The Bass River, running north to south, became a natural border dividing the towns that now share a regional school district.

Yarmouth sent an organized militia to Boston as the American Revolution began. Since then, Yarmouth has sent soldiers to serve in every war in the nation's history and has lost several sons in war.

The 1800s saw Yarmouth develop a thriving business community. Churches came into being along the north and south sides as families established themselves. Quakers, Congregationalists, Methodists, and Swedenborgians dominated the early years of the town's religious life. Later, Baptists, Catholics, and Episcopalians established their own churches within the town.

By the early years of the 20th century, Yarmouth was a haven for summer tourists who eyed the town's proximity to the ocean, not as the early settlers did as a place to make a living, but as a place for recreation and entertainment. Still, many made their living from a relationship with the sea; but by this time, a shift had occurred. While the days of the great sea-going captains were past, now many turned to accommodating those who wanted to spend time by the sea in Yarmouth.

The development of Hyannis Park at the town's southwestern corner was an early sign that the town had much to offer visitors. Trains brought people by the thousands to enjoy the seaside and perhaps settle in as summer or permanent residents.

This tourism-related growth was fuel for increasing commerce along busy Route 28. By the 1930s, the state road along the town's south side had become the main thoroughfare, supplanting the King's Highway, now Route 6A, along the north side as the town's business center.

Motels, restaurants, saloons, skating rinks, taffy stands, music halls, and other forms of entertainment sprang up and operated for generations. While the mix of businesses has changed, Route 28 is still the center of the town's commercial life.

Many who live in Yarmouth today first came to the town as visitors. By the latter part of the 20th century, the town's population was growing dramatically, driven by an influx of former summer visitors who wanted second homes, permanent residences, or retirement homes.

Underlying all this growth was, and still is, a reverence for history. Yarmouth has a thriving community of volunteers devoted to historical preservation. They keep history alive at the Bangs Hallet House, the Taylor-Bray Farm, and other sites.

Certain family names remain strong in Yarmouth. The Thacher, Hallet, Bray, Simpkins, Perera, Sears, Baker and Crowell families date back to the town's early years and are still prominent. Many whose families were not part of the original fabric of the town have made Yarmouth home and contributed to the town's ethnic and cultural diversity.

For all of the changes it has seen, Yarmouth remains a collection of villages and neighborhoods.

People identify themselves as being from Bass River, South Yarmouth, Captains Village, West Yarmouth, Yarmouth Port, or just Yarmouth, as a way of describing their home.

Places like Packet Landing, the Quaker Meetinghouse, Peter Homer Park, the Judah Baker Windmill, Taylor-Bray Farm, Seagull Beach, Ancient Cemetery, and the Village Green have links to the past but remain very much part of Yarmouth's present.

The access to ocean, inland waters, and woodlands that made Yarmouth so attractive to settlers in the 1600s remains. Through foresight and generous donations, Yarmouth has preserved large tracts of land as open space, protecting it from development and ensuring that much of the town's rural character will remain. The center of the town, between the extensive north side and south side beaches, while dotted with subdivisions, also includes many walking trails and woodlands that offer recreation for the human population and a haven for wildlife.

In recent years, South Yarmouth has become a center for the arts with the opening of the Cultural Center of Cape Cod in the old Bass River village. The Cultural Center of Cape Cod, occupying the former Bass River Savings Bank building and the site of the former Owl Club next door, has quickly become a regional home to first-class visual arts, musical performances, and educational events.

Educators, poets, painters, philanthropists, businesspeople, artists, merchants, and ordinary folks made the history of Yarmouth. This same mix of people and new ones yet to come on the scene will move the town forward in ways yet to be imagined.

—John A. Basile
March 2014

CHAPTER ONE

Founders and Families

This chapter introduces native people and English settlers who were part of the colony at Plymouth but sought a place of their own apart from the established settlement 40 miles to the north along Cape Cod Bay.

Quakers, sea captains, farmers, merchants, and businessmen of many kinds all left their marks on early Yarmouth. They endured as the town was split in half (becoming the towns of Yarmouth and Dennis), as industries grew and faded, and as development shifted along the town's major roads.

Monuments placed around Yarmouth acknowledge just some of those who made the town grow and thrive, citing war veterans, local heroes, and the earliest people.

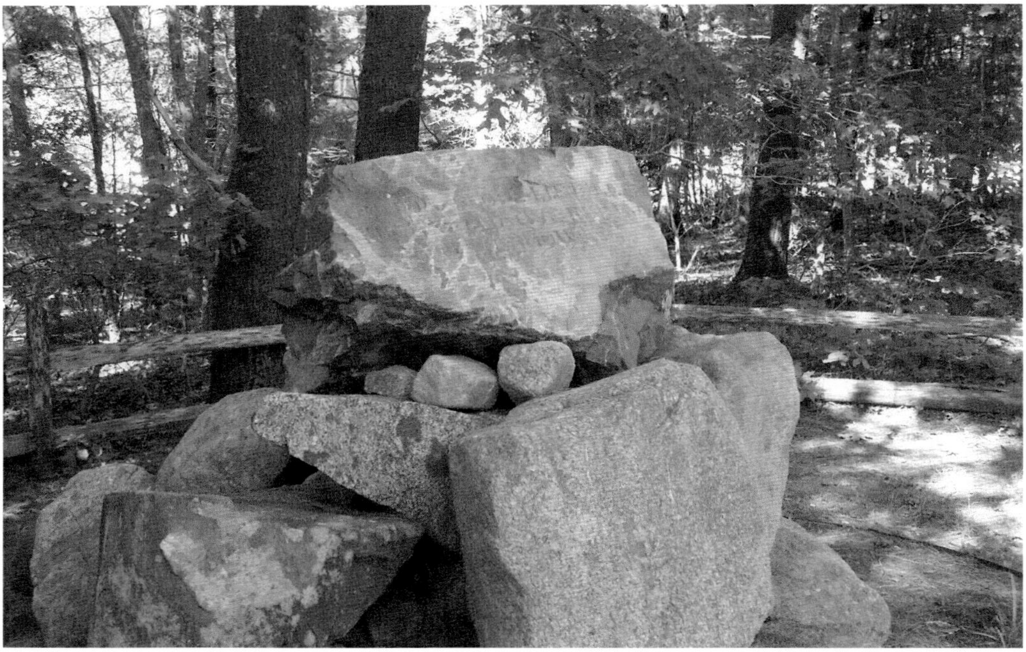

Native People and Settlers

Yarmouth as a town inhabited by English settlers who were part of the Pilgrim colony at Plymouth dates officially to 1638. It was in that year that the Plymouth Colony court granted to Stephen Hopkins, a member of the *Mayflower*'s company, permission to "erect a house at Mattacheese, and cut hay to winter his cattle, provided it be not to withdraw him from the town of Plymouth." Later that same year, the court granted permission to Gabriel Whelden and Gregory Armstrong to locate in what is now Yarmouth.

In 1639, land grants were given to Anthony Thacher, John Crowe, and Thomas Howes. The first mention of Yarmouth as the name of a town appears in the land grants to those three men, and their surnames live on in Yarmouth today.

The name of the town probably came from Yarmouth, a busy seaport in England from which many ships traveled to Holland, but there are no documents proving this link. This may be because the documents of Yarmouth's first 37 years as a town were destroyed in a fire at the town clerks' house in 1676.

The Pilgrims who made their settlement at Plymouth slightly to the north of Cape Cod might have chosen Mattacheese for their home had they seen it. In his *History of Old Yarmouth*, published in 1884, Charles F. Swift writes that "our harbor" on the north side "was passed without recognition, owing to a severe snow-storm," as a party from the *Mayflower* searched for a site on which to settle. If not for that covering of snow, Swift writes, "It is within the bounds of probability that the settlement of New England, with all its attendant consequences, might have been within the limits of Mattacheese."

By 1622, early in the Pilgrims' settlement in Plymouth, a group led by Governor Bradford visited Mattacheese "to procure food for the famishing colonists," according to Swift. They left with corn and beans grown by natives. This is one of many early contacts between English settlers and native people, which were mostly peaceful, although preliminary and sometimes marked by lack of communication.

Swift describes misunderstandings and ugly incidents between the English and their native hosts in the years before the colonists established a permanent settlement at what is now Yarmouth. Following the "slaughter" (Swift's term) by Capt. Miles Standish and his men of some native leaders and their tribesmen, the remaining Native Americans and sachem Iyannough fled the area in fear; Iyannough contracted a disease after being forced from his home and died. This photograph of Yarmouth's Indian Memorial represents the town's acknowledgment of the people who resided there long before the Pilgrims' arrival. (Photograph by author.)

Rev. Simeon Crowell (1778–1848)

Descended from two prominent Cape Cod families, Simeon Crowell was the son of Abner and Ruth (Nickerson) Crowell. His father died aboard a ship before Simeon was born, leaving the family in poverty. Simeon went to sea early in life and rapidly rose to master; however, he was bound for other careers.

At age 36, in 1814, he gave up his career as a ship captain to start a business manufacturing salt in Yarmouth. That same year, he also became an ordained Baptist minister. Ten years later, he was associated with the newly organized Baptist church in South Yarmouth. (Courtesy of Cape Cod Community College.)

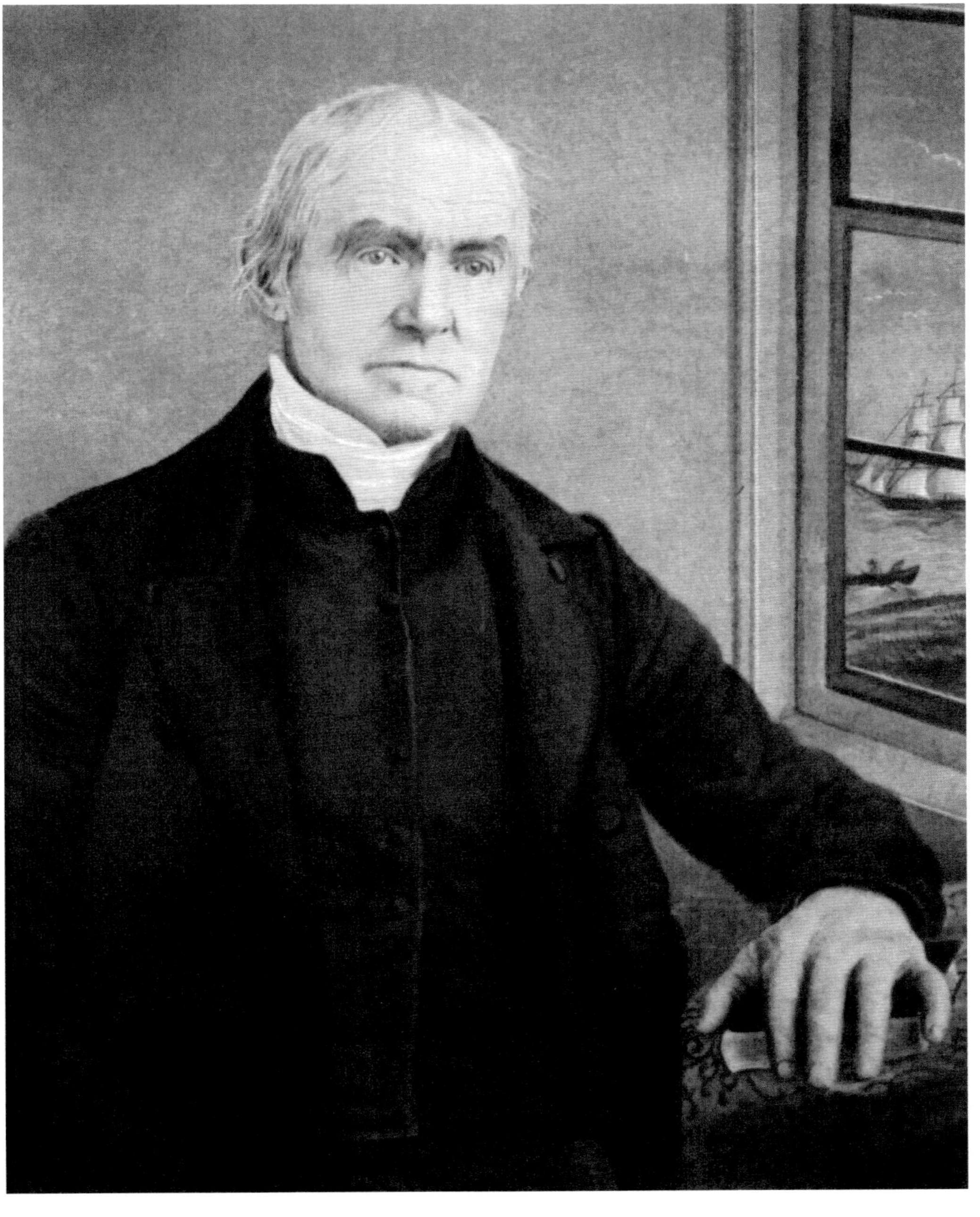

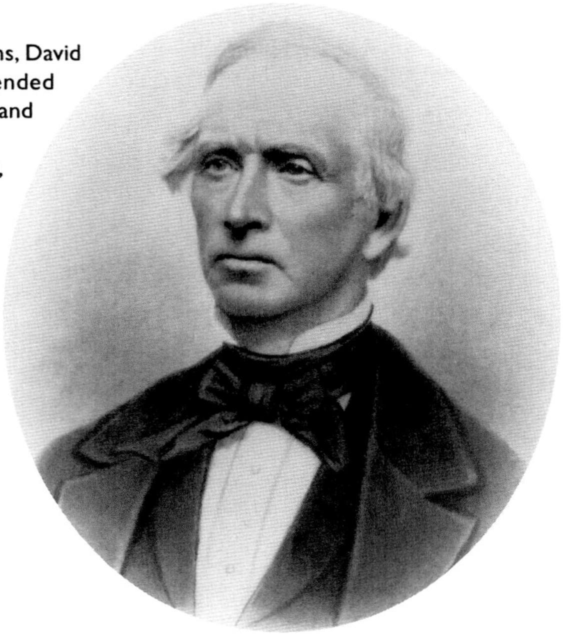

Capt. David Matthews (1801–1877)
Another of Yarmouth's well-known ship captains, David Matthews, like Simeon Crowell, was descended from two old Cape Cod families, the Halletts and Matthewses.

In *The History of Barnstable County, Massachusetts*, published in 1890 and edited by Simeon L. Deyo, C.F. Swift wrote of Captain Matthews: "He was an active, enterprising master, respected for his integrity and beloved for his thoughtful kindness in contributing to the happiness of others as a husband, brother and friend." (Courtesy of Cape Cod Community College.)

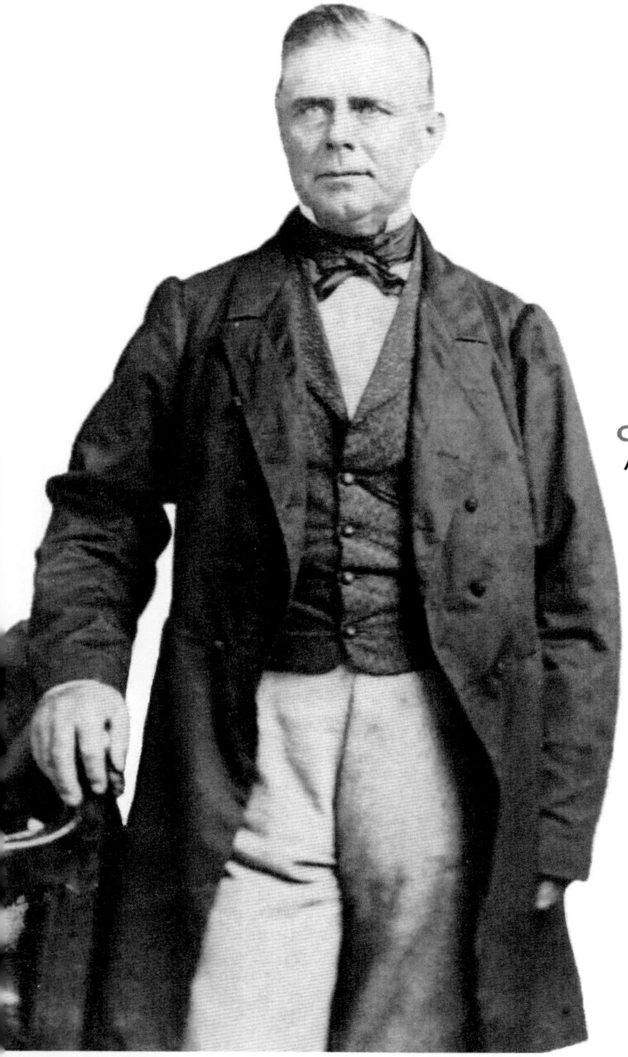

Capt. Higgins Crowell Jr. (1809–1872)
Another of Yarmouth's ship's captains, Higgins Crowell Jr. was descended from a family of seafaring men and married into one as well. His wife was Abigail Sears, the daughter of Capt. Winthrop Sears. Their children were Odlin, Susan, Abbie, Winthrop, and Mary Crowell.

Captain Crowell built a home along the main road in West Yarmouth, near what is today Berry Avenue, in an area where several other members of the Crowell family lived.

After retirement from the sea, he served as postmaster. Today, a major road in Yarmouth, with its terminus near the site of his home, is named for him. (Courtesy of the Historical Society of Old Yarmouth.)

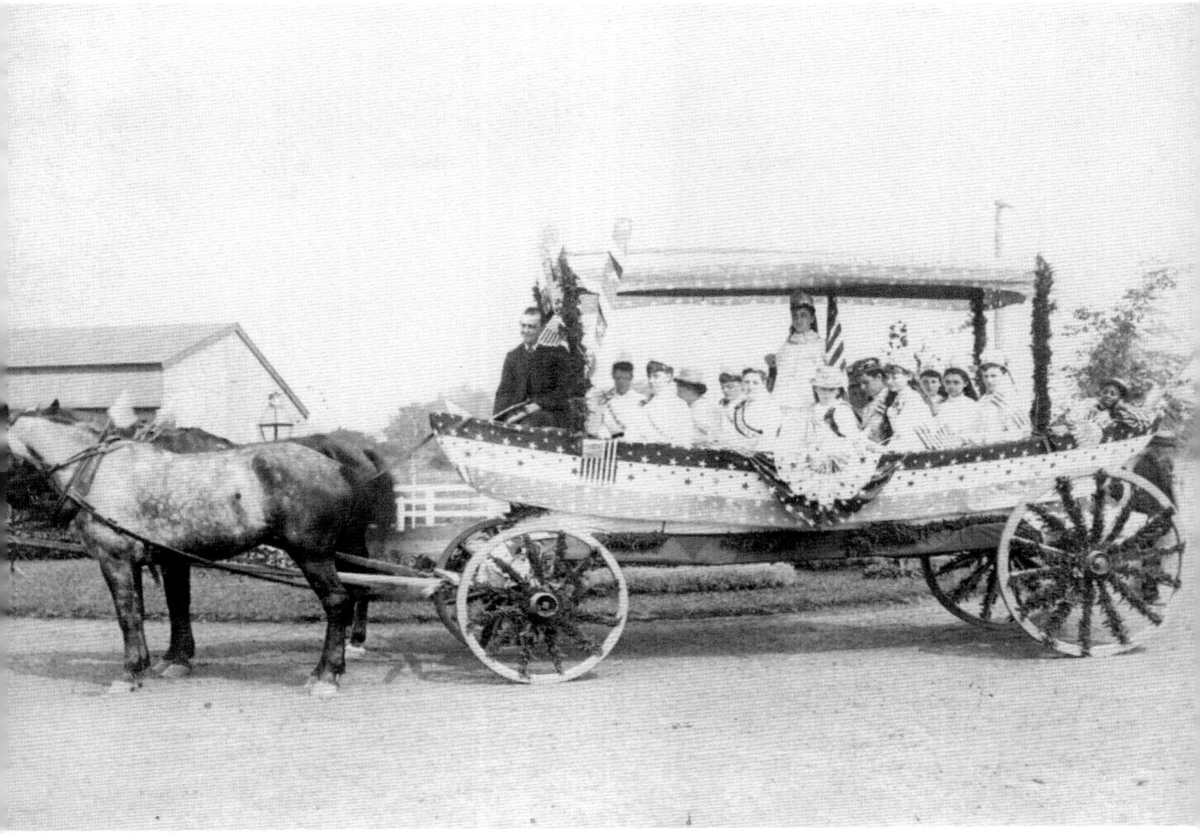

250th Anniversary
Yarmouth celebrated its 250th anniversary in grand style. Beginning on Sunday, September 1, 1889, the community got together for a commemorative service at the Congregational Church in Yarmouth Port. The Rev. John Dodge delivered a historical sermon in the morning that was followed by an afternoon service, at which visiting pastors brought greetings from their congregations around Yarmouth. Pastors from neighboring towns also delivered messages of congratulations.

More ceremonies were held on September 3. A procession along Hallet Street, likely including this wagon, brought visitors who had arrived by train. Philip Howes Sears, known as "The Pilgrim," was the orator of the day

A field day featuring sporting events preceded a historical exhibition at the church. Accounts of the day report that a caterer from Boston served dinner to a thousand people, with a band providing musical accompaniment. The evening concluded with a massive fireworks display. (Courtesy of the Historical Society of Old Yarmouth.)

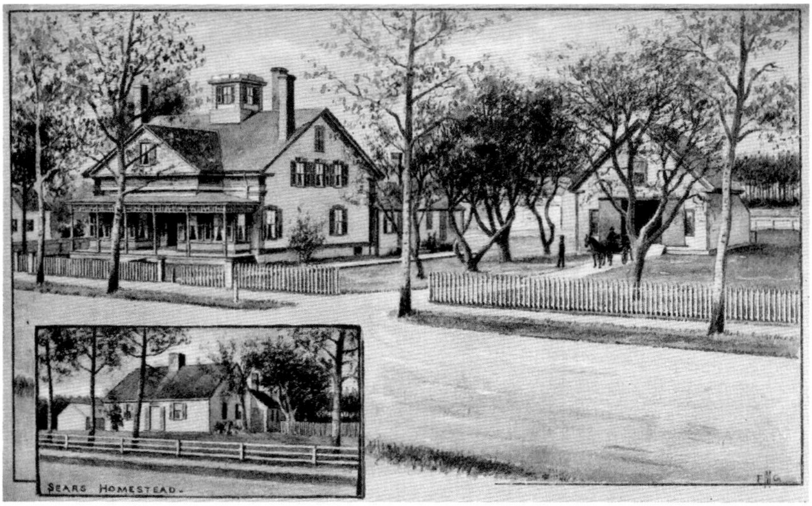

Sears Family

Perhaps no family has as long a history in Yarmouth as the Sears family. From the earliest days of the town, people named Sears have been part of the story, and they remain so today.

The Barnabas Sears homestead on Old Main Street, called the "crooked house" because of its irregular beams and floors, was said to date to around 1660. John Kelley moved it to Old Main Street in 1753. This was before South Yarmouth had been established as a village, and the house would have been adjacent to what was then Indian lands, according to *Images in Time*, published by the Historical Society of Old Yarmouth. A smallpox epidemic broke out among the Indians in the 1750s, and Elizabeth Pollard Kelley, John's wife, used the front rooms of the house as an infirmary to nurse the sick and dying.

The house came into the Sears family when the Kelleys' grandniece Hannah Crocker, who was raised there, married Barnabas Sears.

The house inspired poetry by one of Barnabas Sears's sons, Stephen Sears. His poem reads in part:

What if no paper on the walls
Nor carpet on the floor?
What if no brilliant lighted halls
No knocker on the door?
We'd softest beds whereon to rest
And clothing without spare
And then to make our lot more blest
We had a mother's care
Our father, faithful; in his sphere
Did full supplies provide
Our constant mother evernear
No matter what betide
Our rooms were known as east and west
With kitchen in the rear. And closets, to each room annexed
Supplied with relics dear

The original house was destroyed by fire in 1984, and a reproduction was built in its place. Today, John Sears III, an 11th-generation Sears, is considered an expert on Yarmouth history, particularly that of his family. He is a former selectman, was the master of ceremonies of the town's 300th-anniversary celebration, and operates a landscaping business based on the same street on which his ancestors lived. (Courtesy of Cape Cod Community College.)

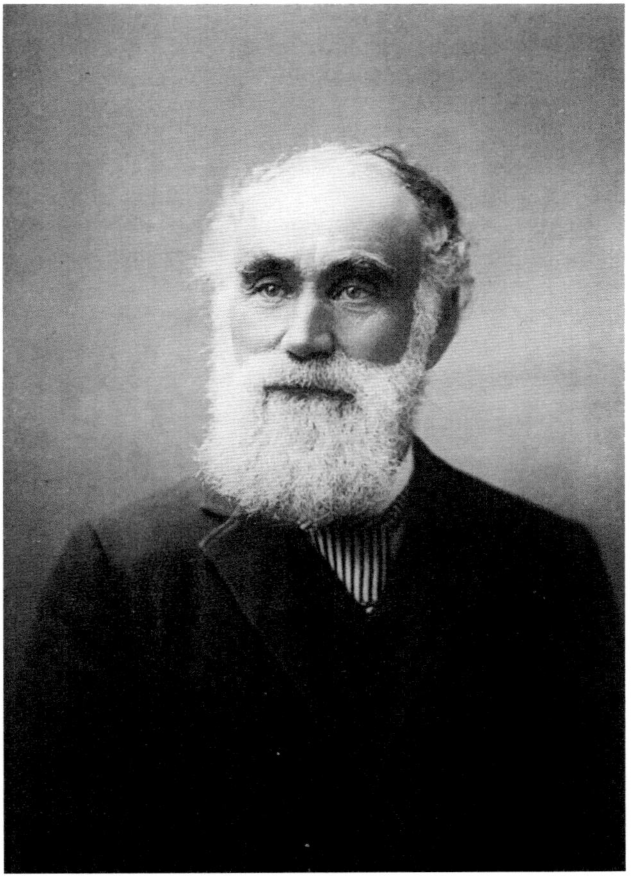

Stephen Sears (1822–1907)
Stephen Sears was a businessman, leader in the Masons, and theatrical entrepreneur in South Yarmouth. In 1888, Sears and Sturgis Crowell purchased the building then known as Eureka Hall on Main Street in South Yarmouth near the Sears homestead.

Under Sears and Crowell's ownership, the Standish Opera House was expanded to accommodate traveling theater productions, medicine shows, and other entertainments. (Courtesy of Cape Cod Community College.)

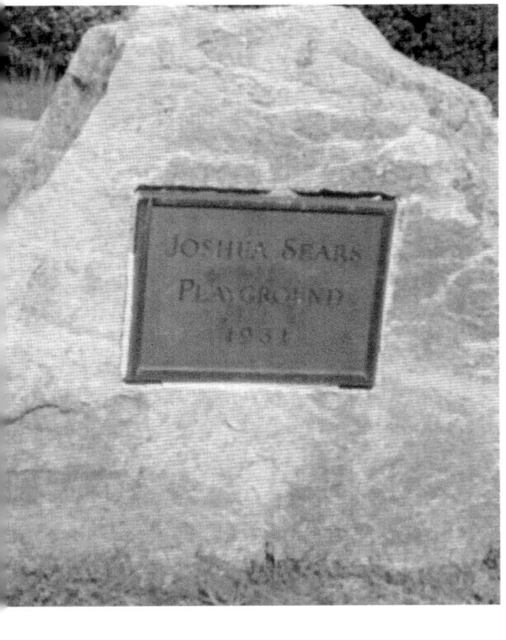

Joshua Sears Monument, South Yarmouth
This monument to Joshua Sears was placed to honor a man who was raised in Yarmouth but made his fortune elsewhere. Educated at a private academy in Yarmouth, according to Charles F. Swift's *History of Old Yarmouth*, Joshua Sears went to Boston, "with all his worldly goods packed in a silk handkerchief; and it was not long before he had taken his position as one of the leading merchants of the city."

Upon his death in 1857, he left $15,000 to the town to establish a nautical school. The school was never built, however, and after years of legal maneuvering, the funds were dedicated to the support of playgrounds in Yarmouth.

The monument stood at the playground of the school that served Yarmouth for many years. By coincidence, another Joshua Sears is memorialized a short distance away at the Yarmouth youth baseball field. The younger Joshua Sears died at age 17, and an annual blood drive is conducted in his name at the Masonic hall in South Yarmouth. (Photograph by author.)

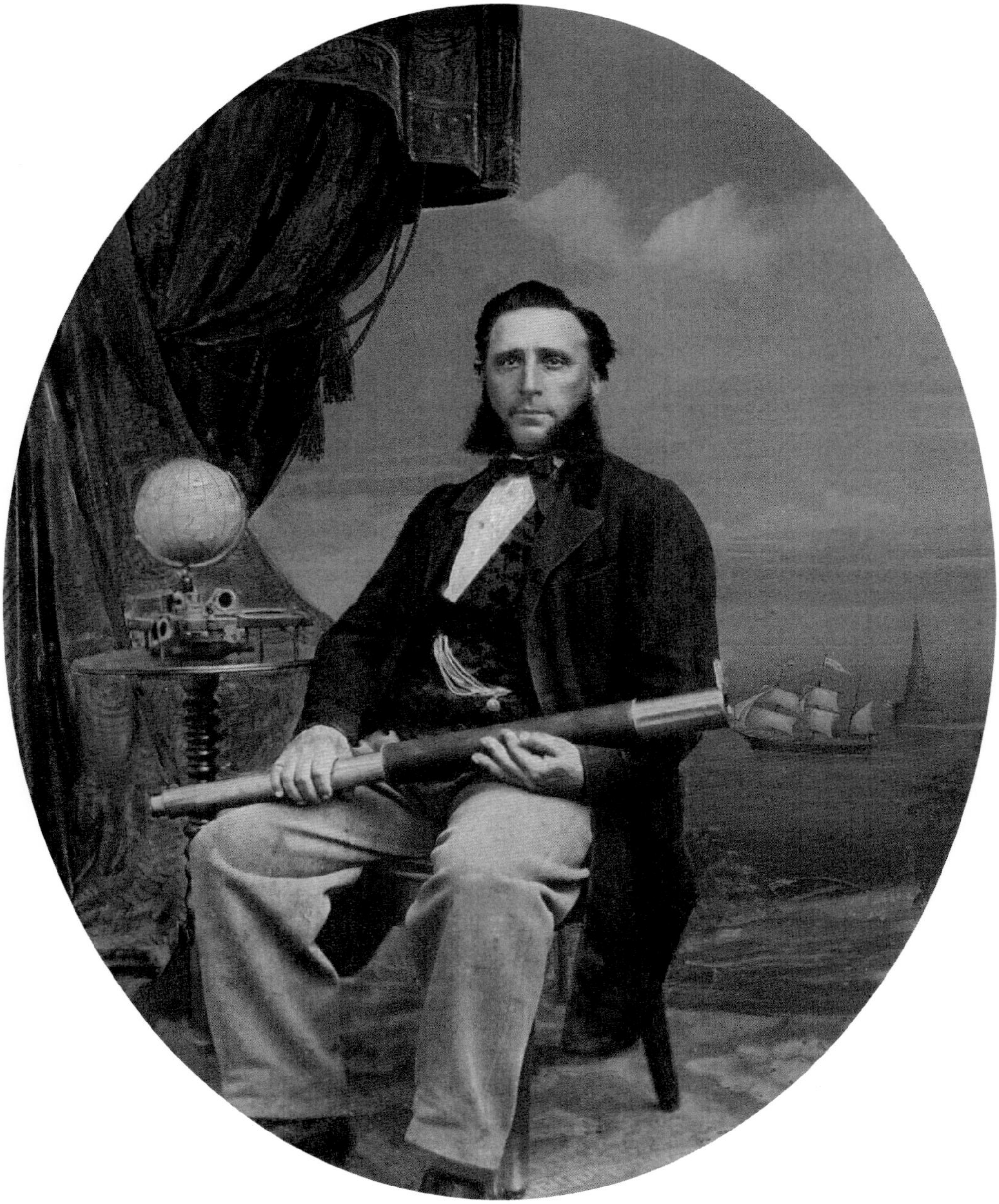

Capt. Augustus Hallet (1824–1895)

Capt. Augustus Hallet was among Yarmouth's many sea captains; however, *Images in Time* reports that although he "commanded many fine ships," his time at sea was short. His early retirement was forced due to his poor eyesight.

It is perhaps an ironic note that the best-known portrait of Augustus Hallet, shown here, depicts him in a grand setting against a backdrop of a sailing ship and surrounded by trappings of life at sea as he holds a spyglass. (Courtesy of the Historical Society of Old Yarmouth.)

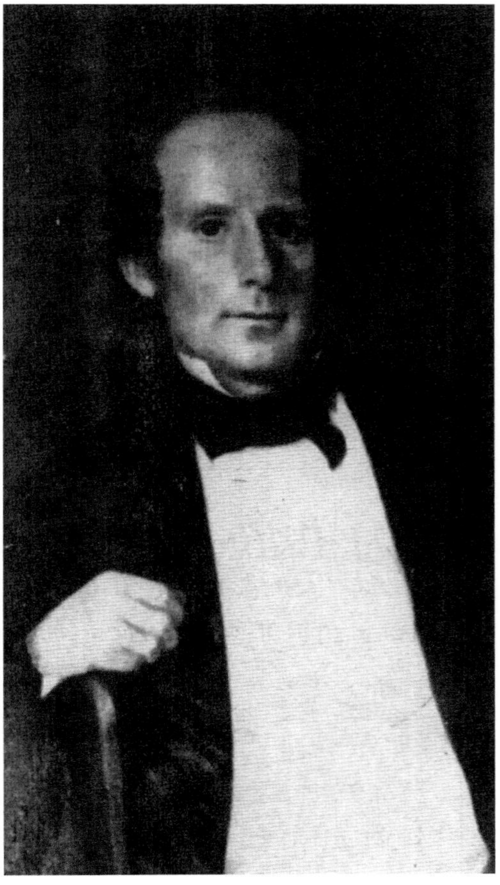

Capt. Bangs Hallet (1807–1893)
Bangs Hallet was among the many Yarmouth men who went to sea, commanding ships named *Herbert*, *Burlington*, and *Pilgrim*. A respected shipmaster, he famously taught seamanship to others who themselves became captains. He also notably commanded a ship that was struck by lightning and caught fire while at sea. An account of the incident by Lewis Lovell described Hallet as, "a thorough seaman, a skillful navigator, a man in whom the officers and men placed the most implicit confidence." (Author's collection.)

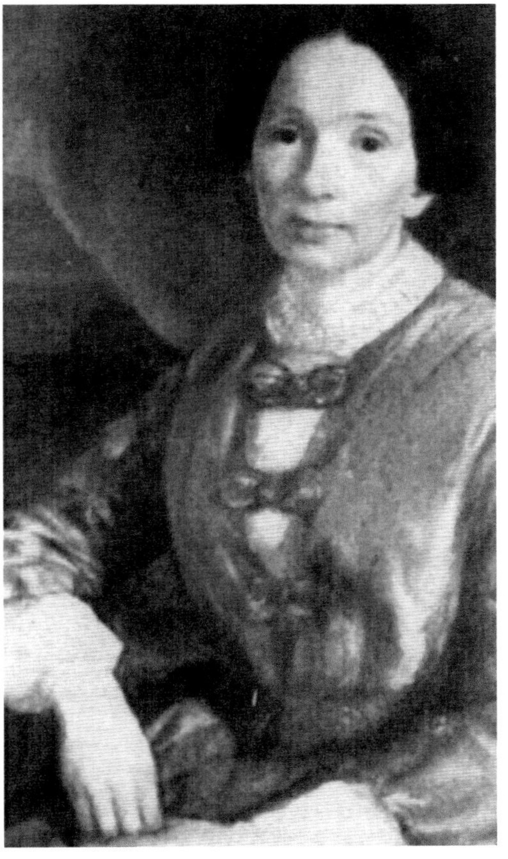

Anna Hallet (1809–1887)
Anna Eldridge Hallet was from a family of seafaring men. Her marriage to Bangs Hallet produced nine children, of whom seven died before their parents. Anna was a typical sea captain's wife in the 19th century; she kept the home together while corresponding with her husband. In 1977, Margaret Milliken wrote that Anna's letters included, "news of friends, neighbors and relatives, local tragedies and scandals, church activities, reports on the house and garden, business affairs, Thanksgiving and Christmas celebrations, much about the grandchildren and always the tender, intimate messages of a loyal, loving wife to her equally loving, absent husband." (Author's collection.)

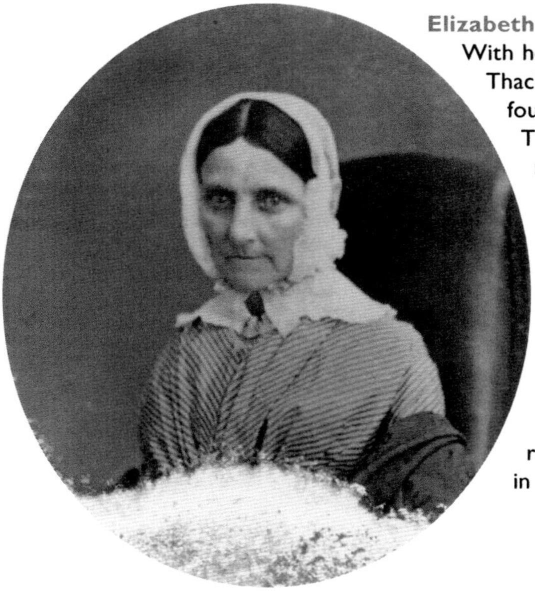

Elizabeth Gray Thacher (1786–1846)

With her husband Henry Thacher, Esq., Elizabeth Gray Thacher started the Thacher Store, which became the foundation of the Thacher family business interests. The store would have several locations around the north side of Yarmouth. Elizabeth and Henry's sons Thomas and Hency C. Thacher ultimately moved the family business to Boston, where they became merchants dealing mainly in wool and other commodities.

Elizabeth was also among the earliest people in Yarmouth to begin reading the works of Emanuel Swedenborg, organizing reading groups to discuss Swedenborg's Christian mystic message. Her early work bringing Swedenborg's message to Cape Cod resulted in the building of a Swedenborgian church in Yarmouth Port. (Courtesy of Lawrence Perera.)

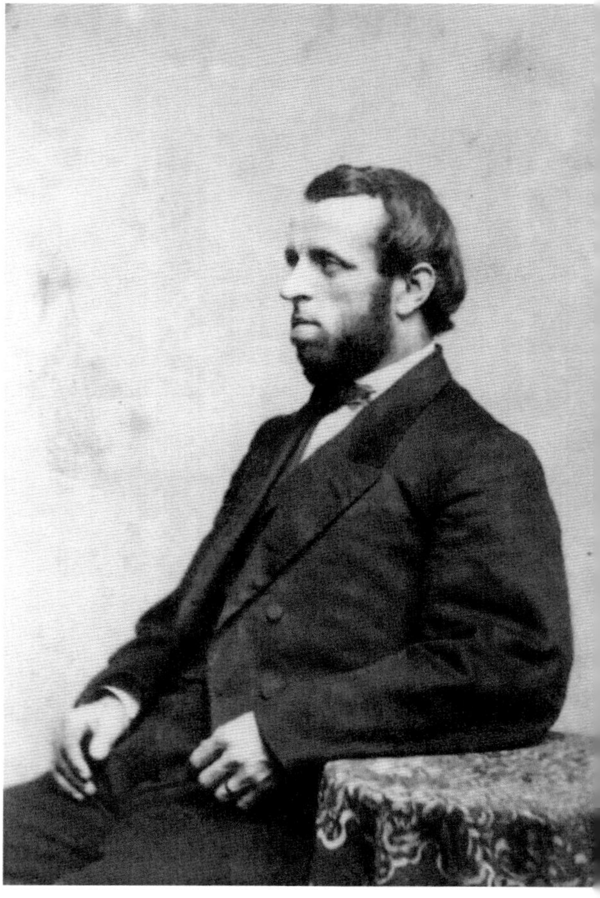

Henry C. Thacher (1829–1900)

Instrumental in moving the Thacher family business to Boston, Henry C. Thacher nevertheless spent every free moment in Yarmouth Port.

A successful businessman, both on Cape Cod and in Boston, in December 1855, Thacher married Martha Bray, a cousin and descendant of another prominent Yarmouth family. Rev. John P. Perry performed their wedding ceremony in the Swedenborgian New Church tradition, according to Lawrence Thacher Perera's *The Homestead Saga*.

When his brother Thomas's business failed, Henry came to his rescue and assumed a more prominent role in the family. He and Martha had seven children, including Thomas C. Thacher, who would become a member of Congress. (Courtesy of Lawrence Perera.)

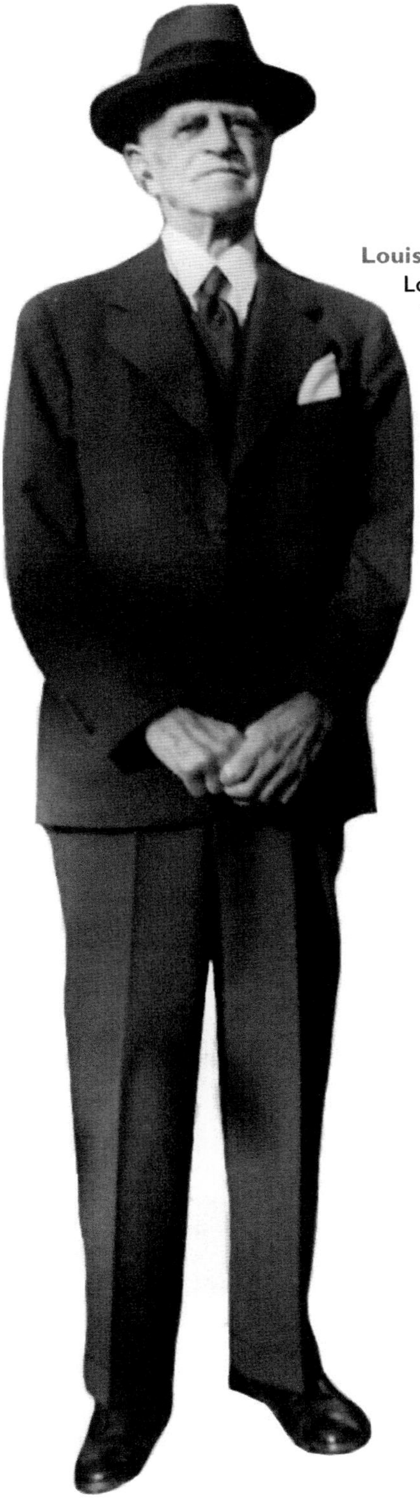

Louis B. Thacher (1867–1953)
Louis B. Thacher was a member of the generation of Thachers who gave much to Yarmouth. As chairman of Yarmouth's 300th-anniversary committee in 1939, he helped to organize the town-wide celebration.

He was also the key figure in the Thacher family's donation to the Boy Scouts of America of a large parcel of lakefront land that remains today as a Boy Scout camp. (Courtesy of Lawrence Perera.)

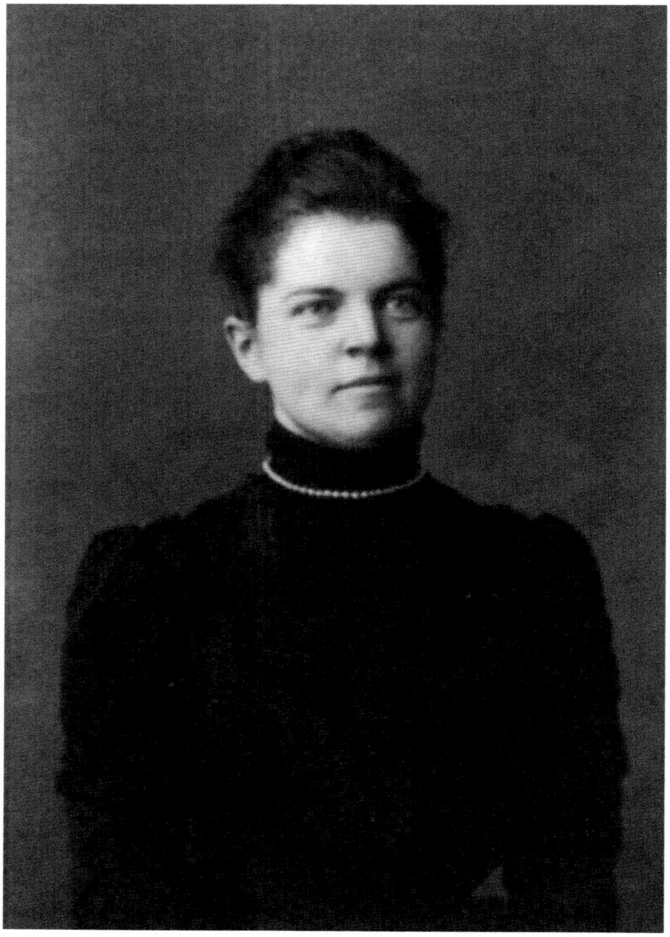

Mary B. Thacher (1868–1956)

Mary B. Thacher has been called by Historic New England, an organization responsible for preserving antiquities, "an independent and civic-minded philanthropist with a great interest in history and antiques."

Mary Thacher was born in 1868 to Henry C. and Martha Thacher. She never married and dedicated much of her time and money to preserving Cape Cod history despite the fact that she was born and educated in Boston.

After the deaths of her parents and her sister Martha, Mary, according to Historic New England, "decided that she wanted a home of her own," and in 1921, she bought a house that belonged to her ancestor Col. John Thacher at the corner of Thacher Lane and Route 6A in Yarmouth Port.

Mary became an expert in early American furnishings and acquired many, filling her house with them. Needing more space, she bought another old residence, the Winslow Crocker House, which stood in West Barnstable, and had it taken apart and moved in 1935 and 1936 to Route 6A in Yarmouth Port where it was reassembled.

During her lifetime, Mary Thacher made arrangements for both the Winslow Crocker House and the Col. John Thacher House to become museums upon her death; today, both are owned and operated as historic sites by Historic New England.

The antiques in her former homes, while not necessarily artifacts of her illustrious Yarmouth family, continue to provide an education about earlier days on Cape Cod for those who visit. (Courtesy of Lawrence Perera.)

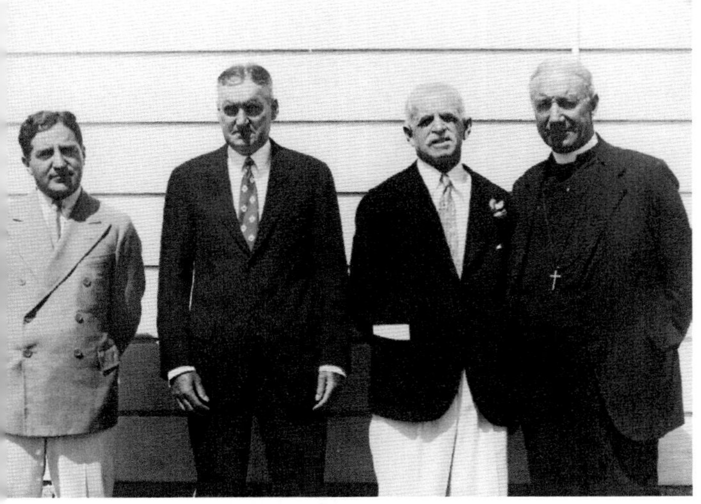

Anniversary Celebration
A prominent extended family, the Thachers and Pereras were well represented when Yarmouth observed its 300th anniversary in 1939. Pictured from left to right are celebration committee vice chairman Guido Perera, guest speaker Henry Kittredge, chairman Louis B. Thacher, and chaplain ZeBarney T. Phillips. The Thacher, Perera, and Phillips families were joined by marriage and prominent in Yarmouth from the town's earliest days. (Courtesy of Lawrence Perera.)

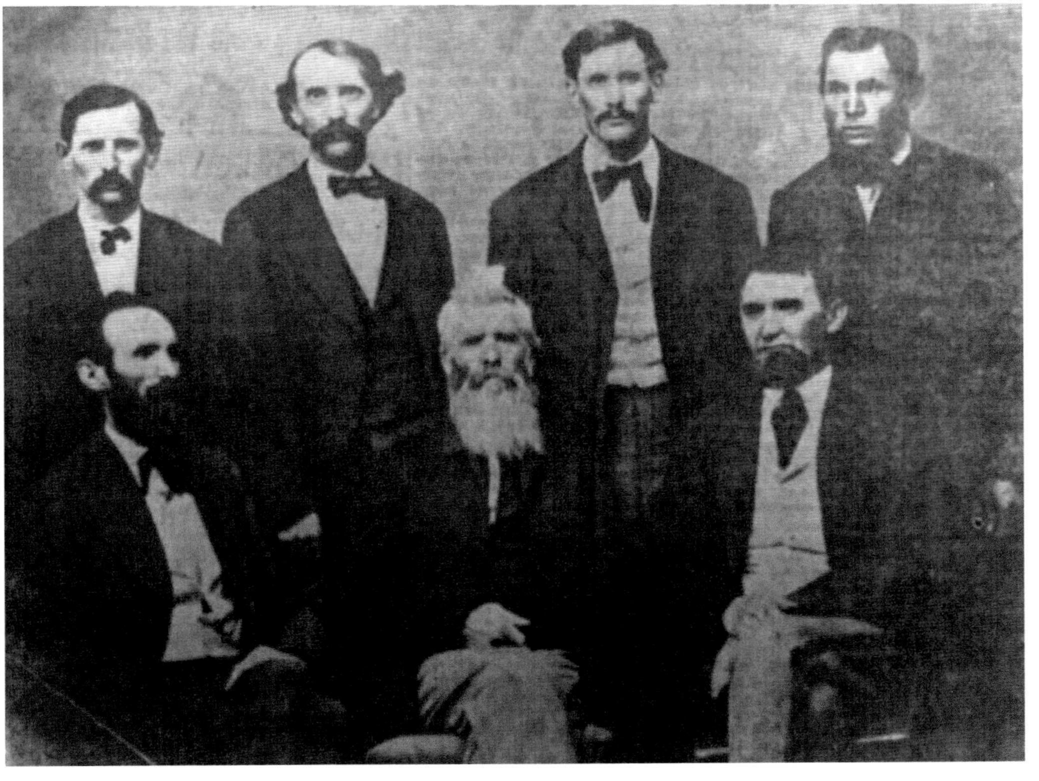

Pulsifer Family Doctors
Dr. Thomas Benton Pulsifer (1842–1912), second from right in the second row, is pictured with his father, Dr. Moses Rust Pulsifer, at center in the first row, and members of the Pulsifer and Dunn families, almost all of whom were doctors.

Thomas Benton Pulsifer, originally from Maine, was wounded while serving in the Union army in the Civil War and came to Yarmouth Port to practice medicine in 1873. He married Annie Gorham, the daughter of Benjamin Gorham of Yarmouth Port. (Courtesy of Matthew Pulsifer.)

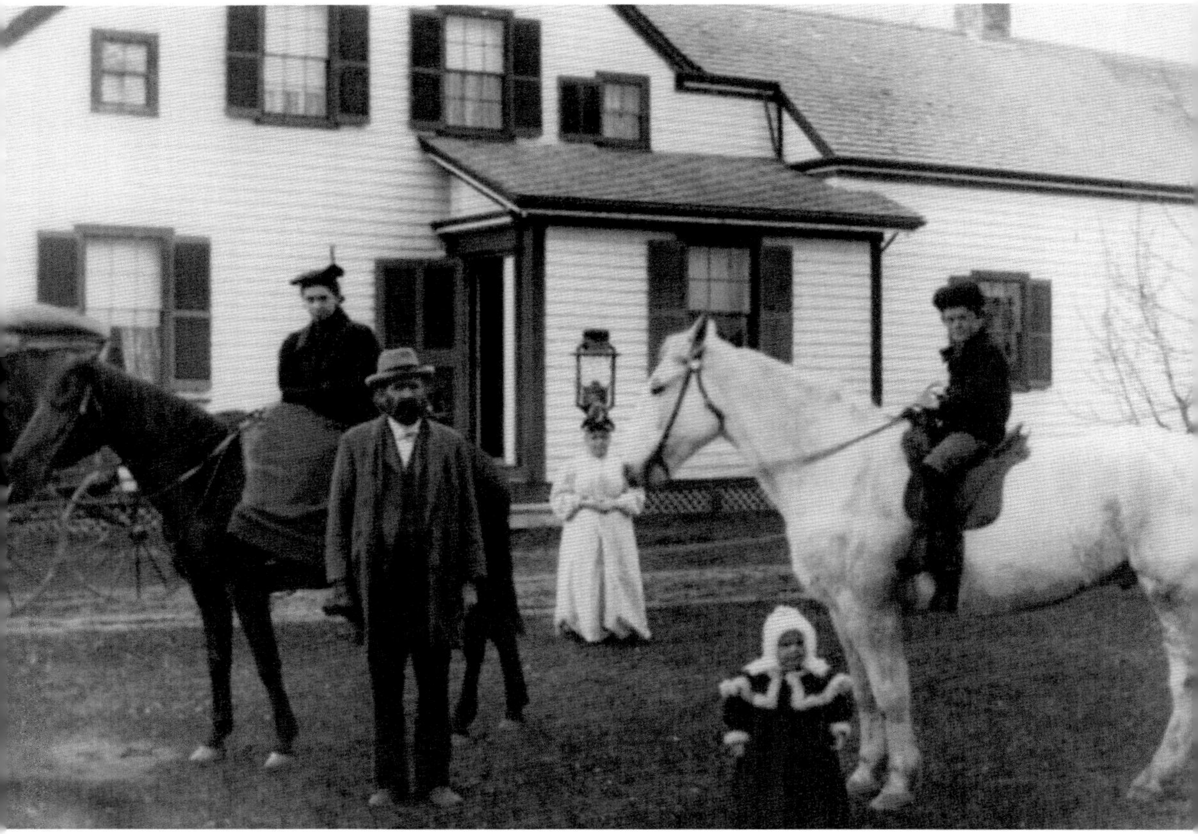

Pulsifer Family

Pictured around 1895 in Yarmouth Port, Dr. Thomas Benton Pulsifer stands with members of his family, including children Gorham, on the horse at right, and Caroline, on the horse at left. His wife, Annie (Gorham), is standing in the background, and his daughter Helen is standing in the foreground. The Pulsifer and Gorham families, prominent in business and medicine in early Yarmouth, have many descendants in the town.

Dr. Pulsifer had one of the first telephones in Yarmouth. His daughter Helen Dolan told the story, reported in Marion Vuilleumier's *The Town of Yarmouth, Massachusetts: A History 1639–1989*, that Benton's patients in Dennis, where he also practiced, paid for the installation so that they could reach the doctor quickly in case of emergency. (Courtesy of Matthew Pulsifer.)

CHAPTER TWO

Creative Minds

Yarmouth has had its share of people who devoted their lives to the arts. Writers and artists of all kinds have been part of the scene for decades, and in contemporary times, the town possibly boasts more creative people than at any time in its history.

Perhaps the most notable person to call Yarmouth home is the late illustrator and writer Edward Gorey. His often macabre, but always funny, illustrations have entertained millions. Lou Colombo brought the sound of jazz to many. Set designers Helen Pond and Herbert Senn brought style and whimsy to town, and the poet Conrad Aiken crafted some of his finest work not far from the banks of the Bass River.

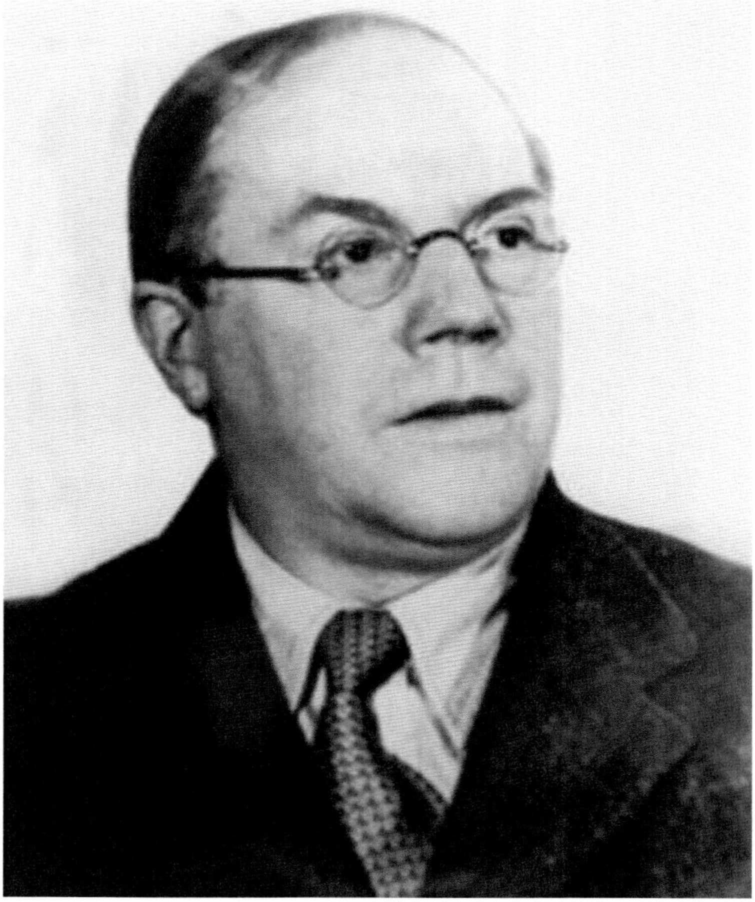

Conrad Aiken (1889–1973)
With Quaker roots in South Yarmouth, it was not surprising that the poet, novelist, and essayist Conrad Aiken should choose Yarmouth for a summer home.

After a traumatic early life during which his father killed his wife and then himself, young Conrad went to live with an aunt in Cambridge, Massachusetts, and later attended Harvard University there.

Aiken's grandfather had been a preacher in Sandwich on Cape Cod and taught school in South Yarmouth. His mother's Quaker ancestors were buried in the graveyard at the Quaker meetinghouse a short distance from where Aiken and his first wife, Jessie, bought a house, and where they spent summers with their children. This cottage was described by Edward Butscher in *The Poet of White Horse Vale* as "a sturdy white clapboard structure with a red roof set amid tall silverleaf poplars near the Bass River that flowed through the town and into the sea." The house was near the home of his good friend of Quaker descent Lucien Bainbridge Crist, the composer and teacher of music.

Butscher writes that Aiken's novel *Conversation*, published in 1939, describes his years in South Yarmouth and the disintegration of his second marriage.

In 1940, with his third wife, Aiken would build another Cape Cod home, located in Brewster on the north side of the Cape.

Aiken never achieved the fame that should have come his way. His *Selected Poems* won the Pulitzer Prize in 1930, and his *Collected Poems* won the National Book Award in 1954, but it was perhaps Aiken's refusal to do public readings that contributed to his relative obscurity despite critical acclaim. (Courtesy of the Poetry Foundation.)

Lucien Bainbridge Crist (1883–1969)

Lucien Bainbridge Crist was a composer, conductor, teacher, and lecturer. He dropped his given first name, Lucien, when publishing music. He called South Yarmouth home for much of his adult life.

Born in Indiana, he first trained as a lawyer and practiced law in Boston for six years while composing music in his spare time.

In 1912, Crist traveled to Europe to study music theory and orchestration. His studies took him to Berlin and London. Returning to the United States, he taught singing in Boston from 1915 to 1921 and in Washington, DC, from 1922 to 1923, when he returned to Europe not as a student, but as a teacher, until 1927.

Crist moved his family back to Washington, where he taught until 1939, when the family moved to Pleasant Street in the Bass River section of South Yarmouth, a short distance from the home of his friend Conrad Aiken.

Nearly 200 of Crist's works were published, many of which were for orchestras but often incorporating voice. He also composed choral music.

The *New Grove Dictionary of American Music* cites Crist's vocal pieces as "noteworthy for the skillful handling of the voice, the sensitivity of the melodic line and the aptness and variety of harmony."

His musical compositions were broadcast often and performed widely, many times with Crist conducting. He published the book *The Art of Setting Words to Music* in 1944.

In this picture, Crist conducts the band at Yarmouth's 300th-anniversary celebration in 1939. The concert was staged along the banks of the Bass River, a short distance from the Crist home where his descendants continue to live. (Courtesy of Anne Whitaker.)

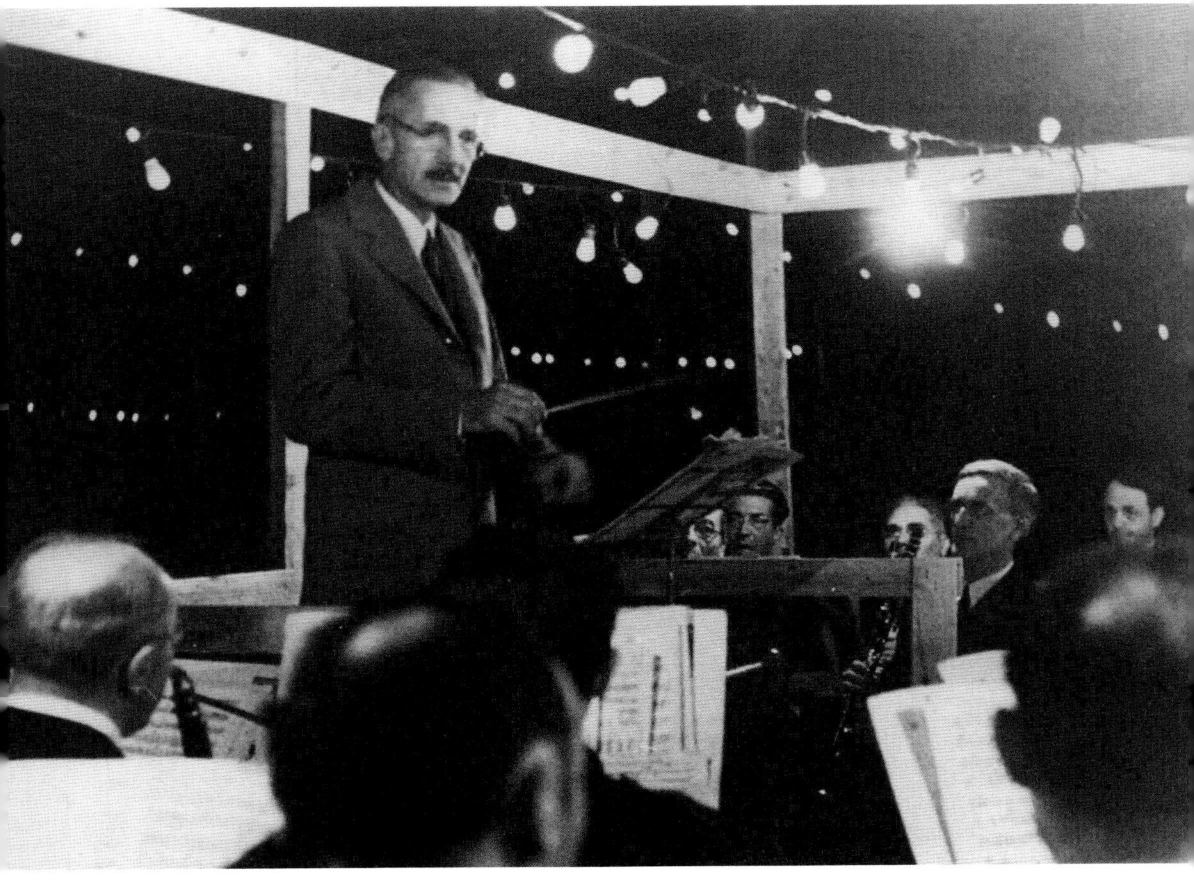

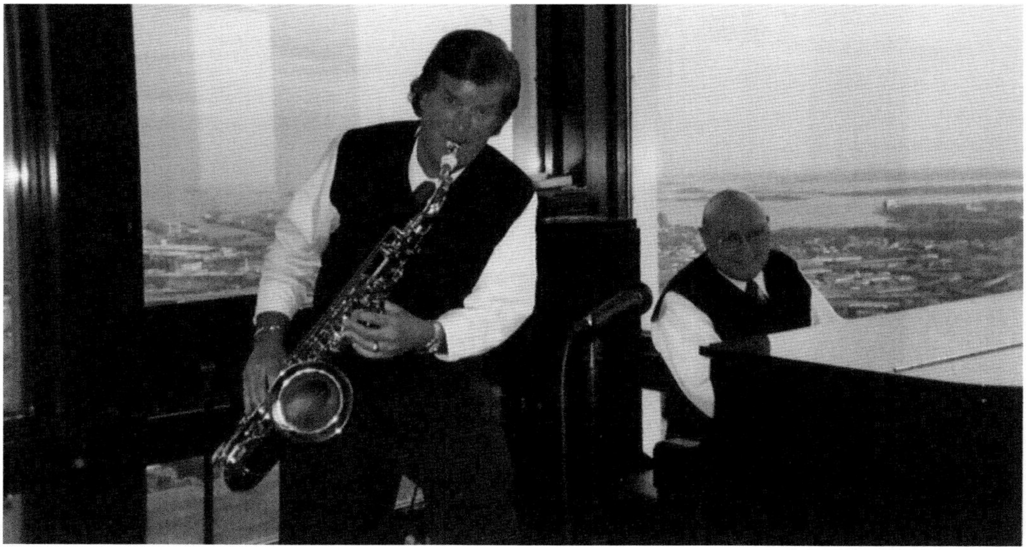

Lee Childs (1946–2012)

Lee Childs made people smile with his music. As a saxophone and clarinet player, he could perform in any jazz style, but was especially well known for playing swing and Dixieland jazz with his band the Bourbon Street Paraders.

Childs was born in Wellesley, Massachusetts, and was leading a Dixieland band by the age of 12. He attended Cornell University and graduated from the Berklee College of Music in Boston.

By the early 1980s, Childs and his family were living in Yarmouth Port, and he was an in-demand performer on the New England jazz circuit and a particular favorite on Cape Cod, where his musical contemporaries included Lou Colombo, Dave McKenna, and others in what became a golden age of jazz on Cape Cod.

Childs and his band had one of the more unusual regular gigs; they performed for years at Jordan's Furniture in Framingham, Massachusetts, where entertainment was part of the shopping experience. Childs performed on a regular basis at the Top of the Hub in the Prudential Building in Boston, where this photograph was taken, as well as anywhere the jazz life took him. He was a particular favorite on cruises along the Cape Cod Canal, where his easygoing style of jazz sounded just right.

Childs's family and friends, including many of the musicians he performed with, remembered him at a musical memorial get-together on Cape Cod a year after his untimely death. (Courtesy of JoAnne Childs.)

Paul Nossiter

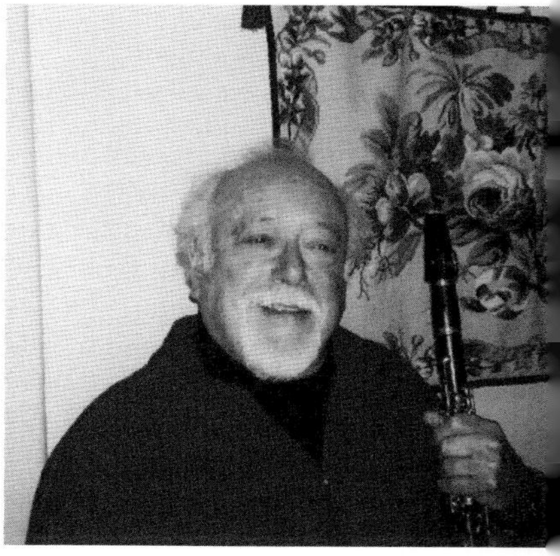

Paul Nossiter is a musician and music educator whose specialty is traditional jazz. As a clarinetist and saxophonist, Nossiter is a regular part of the Cape Cod musical scene and a tireless advocate for the music he loves.

Among Nossiter's many career highlights is a stint as co-owner with George Wein of Storyville Cape Cod, a jazz nightclub that booked all the top artists of the late 1950s and early 1960s.

Performing in bands both small and large, Nossiter's bandmates often included Marie Marcus, Lou Colombo, and many others. He is often called upon to spread the word of jazz to schools and community groups, where he shares his encyclopedic knowledge of the music and the people who play it. (Author's collection.)

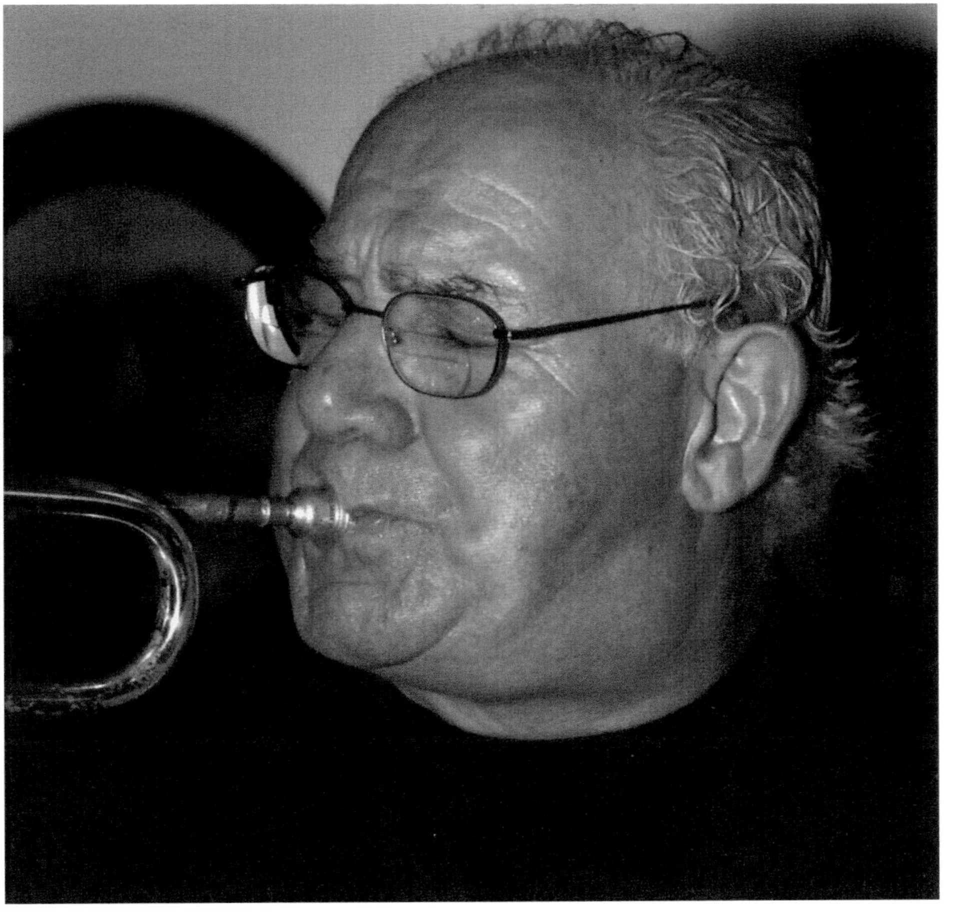

Lou Colombo (1928–2012)
Born in Brockton, Massachusetts, but an adopted son of Yarmouth, Lou Colombo specialized in a joyous brand of jazz.

A talented baseball player as a youth, he was signed by the Brooklyn Dodgers and played in the Minor Leagues until injury ended his career. But his true calling was the trumpet, and Colombo came up through the ranks of New England–based bands.

In the early 1970s, he was booked to perform seven nights a week at the Mill Hill Club in West Yarmouth, a plum gig for any jazz musician. Liking what he saw, Colombo moved his family to Yarmouth.

In his long career, Colombo worked with many top musicians on the Cape and elsewhere and was a favorite of fellow trumpet player Dizzy Gillespie. Colombo also played in the Artie Shaw Orchestra when Colombo's close friend and frequent musical partner Dick Johnson led the band.

While his music was first class, so was his commitment to his community. When a charitable organization was holding a fundraiser, more often than not Lou Colombo supplied the music. He devoted many hours to visiting senior centers and nursing homes for no pay, simply to spread the joyful sound of jazz. He died in a car crash in Florida minutes after completing a gig at a restaurant his family owned. Colombo was so revered as a musician that he was given a New Orleans–style funeral parade in Hyannis on Cape Cod, at which many jazz musicians joined in and many hundreds of jazz fans turned out to pay their respects.

In this picture, Colombo performs at The Roadhouse in Hyannis, a restaurant owned by his son and where he performed regularly. (Courtesy of David Colombo.)

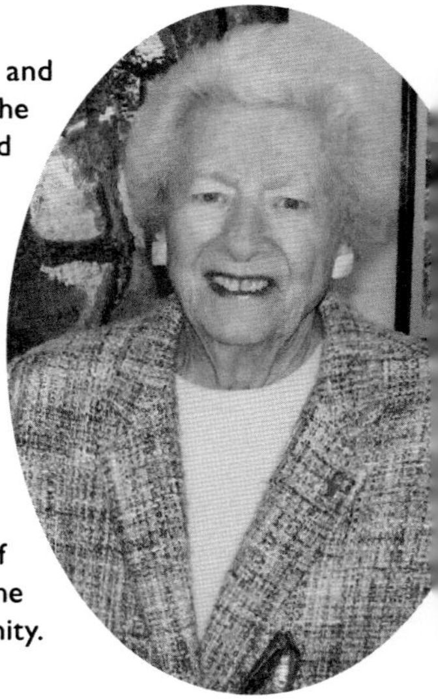

Joan Shostak

Joan Shostak is the public face of the Education Foundation for Dennis and Yarmouth, the organization responsible for raising funds that supplement the local school system's budget to provide educational opportunities that would otherwise not be available to local students.

Shostak's first career was in education, as a kindergarten teacher in Scarsdale, New York. In the mid-1960s, she became the education manager for the Creative Playthings store in New York City. In New York, she met her future husband, Jerry Shostak, who was then working for the federal government in education. The two moved to Yarmouth Port in 1983, and shortly thereafter, Jerry organized the Education Foundation for Dennis and Yarmouth as an adjunct to the public school system's budget, which is often stressed to the point where educational opportunities can be lost. After Jerry's untimely death in 1996, Joan took on his work at the foundation and has worked tirelessly since on its behalf, helping to raise hundreds of thousands of dollars, which become mini-grants for teachers and people in the community who want to pursue educational ideas that benefit the community. (Photograph by author.)

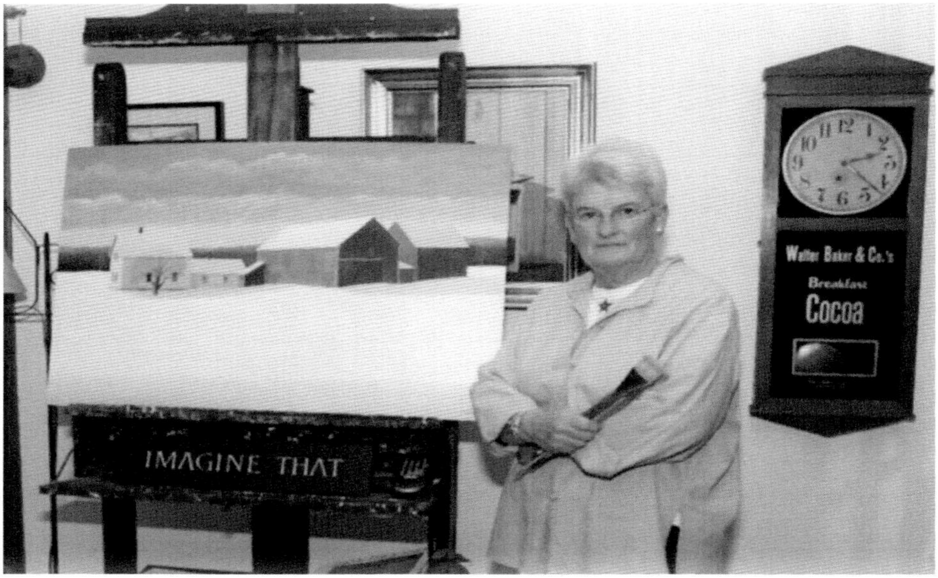

Marieluise Hutchinson

An artist with a distinctly New England style, Marieluise Hutchinson captures still-life scenes with clarity and charm.

Hutchinson is a self-taught artist who has risen to the top ranks of her profession. She is a Copley Artist at the Copley Society of Boston, a Master Artist of the Cape Cod Art Association, and a member of the Cape Cod Museum of Art, where her work appears in the permanent collection. Her work is often shown in prestigious shows and has been chosen by the Amica Insurance Company and the Red Cross to appear on their holiday greeting cards. Hutchinson often donates her work for use by nonprofit organizations as fundrasiers.

Her work in most cases does not include human figures, but she says the human presence is felt by the appearance of a snowman in a yard, a light left burning in a window, clothes on a clothesline, or smoke rising from a farmhouse chimney. (Courtesy of Marieluise Hutchinson.)

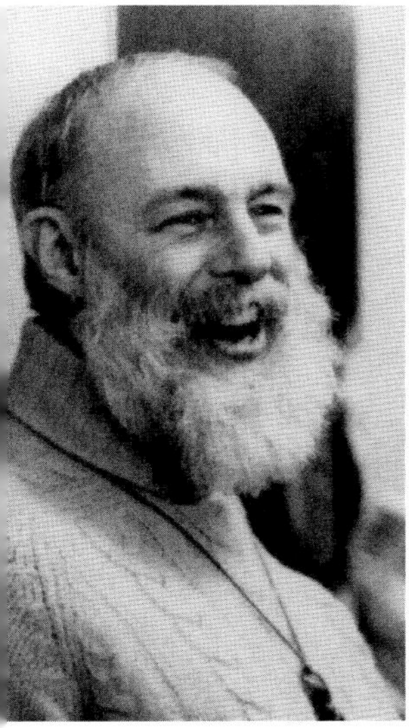

Edward Gorey (1925–2000)

Artist, illustrator, author, set designer, and costume designer Edward St. John Gorey is best known for his illustrations used in the opening credits of the PBS television series *Mystery!*, but his often grisly yet always humorous pen-and-ink drawings also graced more than a hundred works.

Titles including *The Gashlycrumb Tinies*, *The Doubtful Guest*, and *The Vinegar Works* have become staples of American literature. Gorey illustrated not only his own books but also works by authors including Charles Dickens, Samuel Beckett, John Updike, Virginia Woolf, and others.

Gorey was born in Chicago and moved to Yarmouth later in life, but he quickly became a fixture along the north side, dining each morning at Jack's Outback Restaurant operated by his friend Jack Braginton-Smith, a noted raconteur. Active in the Cape Cod arts community, he volunteered as a cameraman on local cable access television productions while continuing to produce innovative works ranging from puppet shows to a screenplay.

Educated at Harvard University, from which he graduated in 1950, and briefly at the Art Institute of Chicago, Gorey usually set his works in Victorian or Edwardian England. (Courtesy of the Edward Gorey House.)

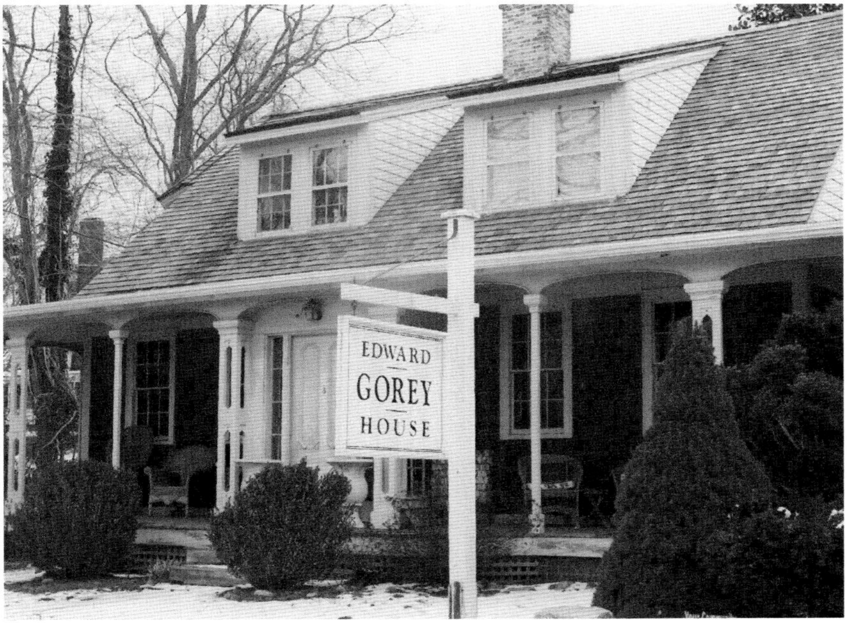

Edward Gorey House

A house with a history, the property known today as the Edward Gorey House was built in the early 1800s. It stands on Strawberry Lane overlooking the Yarmouth Port Common and was owned in the 1830s by Nathaniel Stone Simpkins, a prominent businessman in Yarmouth.

Simpkins and his descendants lived in the house for many years, and Gorey bought it in 1979. He renamed it the Elephant House, reflecting his interest in animal welfare, and filled the place with his quirky collections of interesting objects and as many as six cats at a time.

After Gorey's death, his house was converted to a museum celebrating his life and work. Today, the Edward Gorey House is open to the public and serves to keep his work in the public eye as new audiences come to enjoy his visual and linguistic wit. The Gorey House has become a regular stop for Gorey fans from around the world. (Photograph by author.)

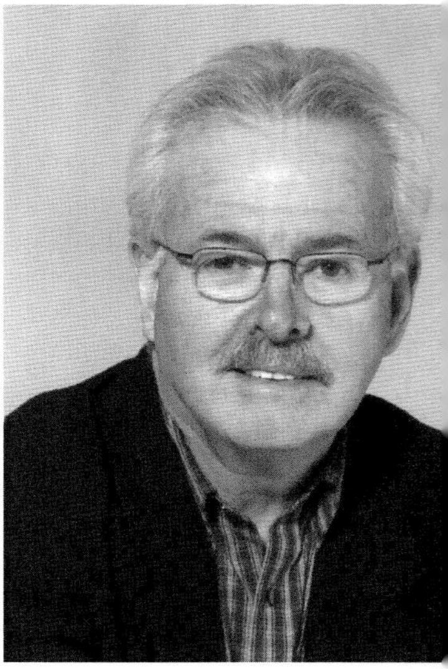

Robert Nash

Bob Nash discovered his talent for photography while serving in the Air Force in Germany in the 1960s. Borrowing a friend's camera, he shot some photographs and was immediately captivated by the images that emerged in the darkroom.

He went on to a successful 30-year career as a commercial photographer based in Worcester, Massachusetts, while maintaining a home in Yarmouth. As plans began to take shape for the Cultural Center of Cape Cod, Nash became involved in renovating the former Bass River Savings Bank building on Old Main Street in South Yarmouth, and when the Cultural Center of Cape Cod was ready to open, he was named its executive director, and he and his wife, Susan, became part of the Yarmouth scene full time.

In 2014, Nash was busy overseeing the Cultural Center of Cape Cod's expansion into a second building adjacent to its original site, a replica of the former Owl Club, which stood on the site for many years. (Courtesy of Robert Nash.)

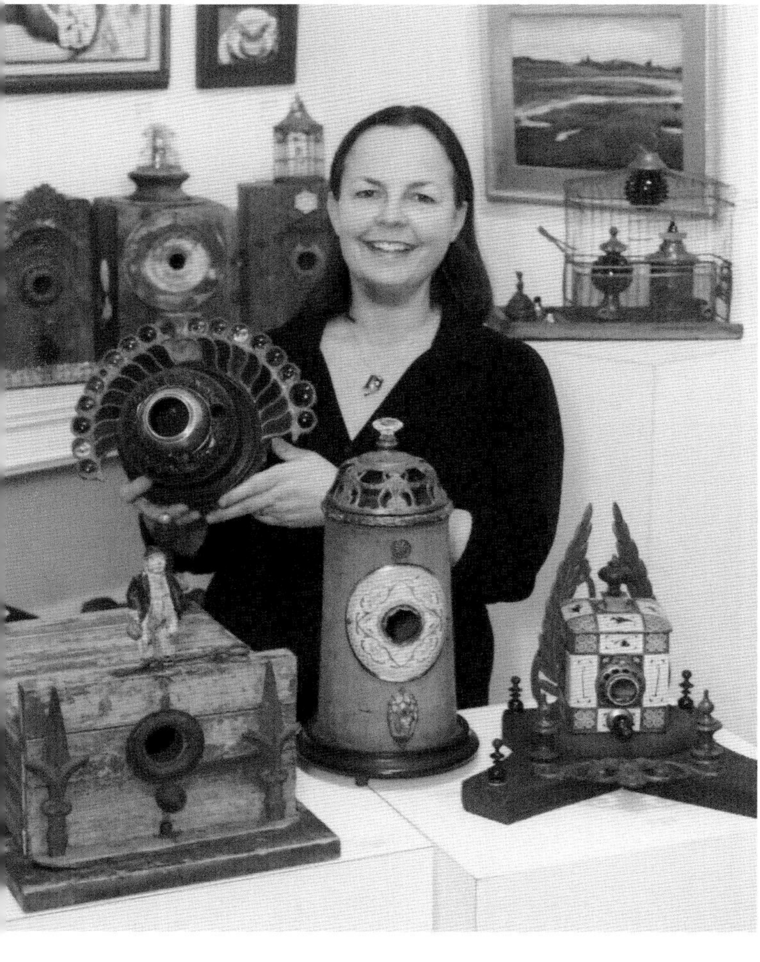

Lauren Wolk

Lauren Wolk enjoys a varied and challenging career in the arts.

A published novelist and poet, former book editor, and in recent years, an assemblage and mixed-media artist, she finds many ways to tell stories.

She says that she "attempts to create layers" in her visual art and to tell "visual stories" in her poetry and fiction. She uses a wide range of materials in her art, from paints to "antique oddments," just as she uses a range of narrative techniques in her written work.

Lauren quickly became part of the Yarmouth community as associate director of the Cultural Center of Cape Cod, where she stages art exhibits, poetry readings, musical performances, and other cultural events. (Courtesy of the *Register.*)

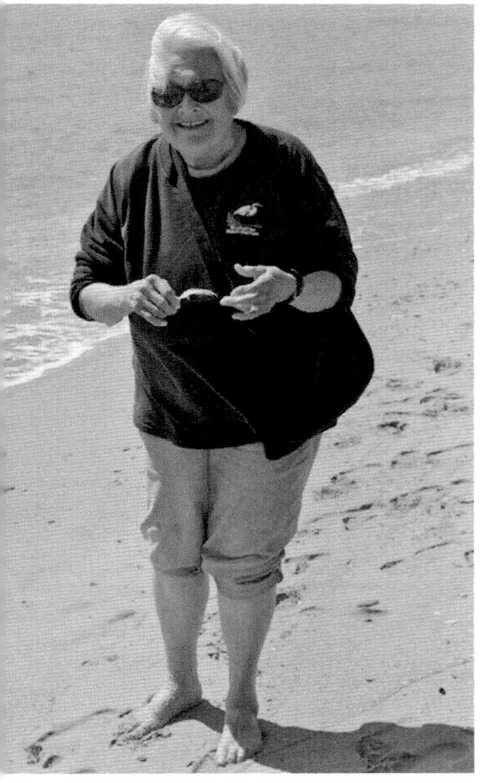

Maria King Constantinidis (1927–2012)
Maria King Constantinidis will be remembered as the woman who was instrumental in creating one of Yarmouth's, and Cape Cod's, places for the arts to flourish.

An antiques dealer, in 2000, Constantinidis made the key donation that allowed the former Bass River Savings Bank building, which had been vacant and in disrepair for years, to be converted into the Cultural Center of Cape Cod. Constantinidis's sizeable donation, which she insisted be anonymous while she was alive, allowed a committee to acquire the building and begin to plan what would become a major cultural institution, opening its doors in 2007. That same year, Constantinidis moved permanently to Greece, where she had maintained a home for many years, to be closer to her family.

Everyone who participates in the many events held at the Cultural Center, where the main gallery now bears her name, appreciates her foresight and generosity. (Courtesy of the Cultural Center of Cape Cod.)

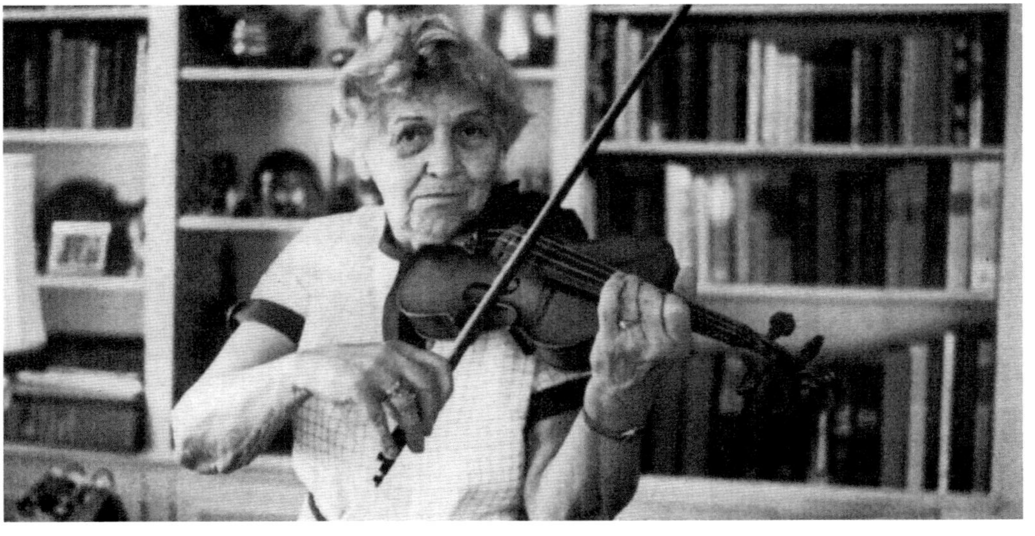

Helena Sibley (1904–1998)
Helena Sibley brought music to Yarmouth. Trained at the New England Conservatory, Sibley performed with the Cape Cod Symphony Orchestra from 1970 to 1983, taught violin at the Cape Cod Conservatory, and performed with the Bayberry String Quartet.

In 1988, her friends honored her with a gathering celebrating her contribution to the local music community and her lifelong commitment to music. (Courtesy of the *Register.*)

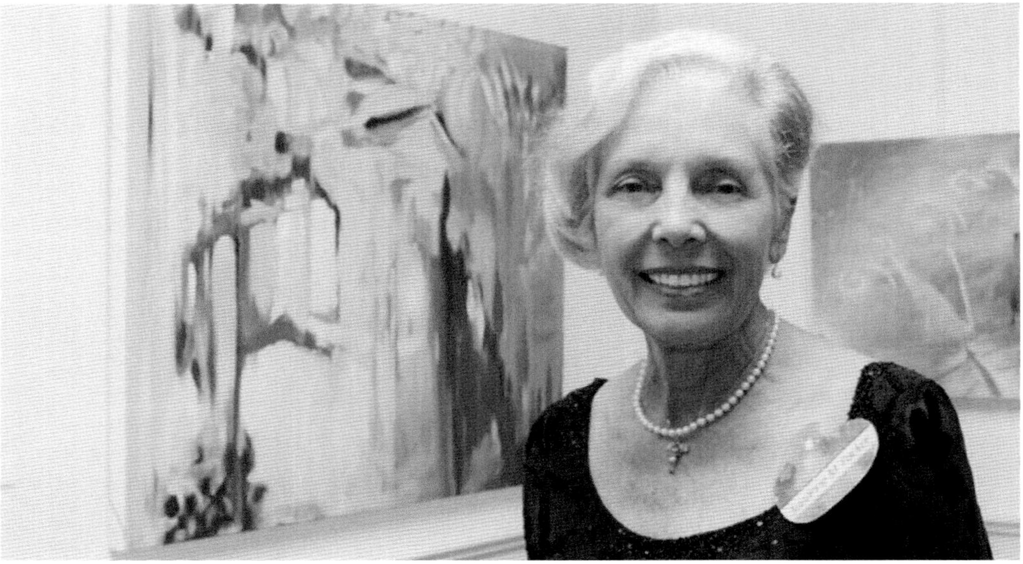

Suzanne Packer
Even in a community of many artists, Suzanne Packer stands out.

A lifelong painter, she exhibited her first work in San Francisco at age five and has not stopped painting. Educated at the Rhode Island School of Design, the Art Students League in New York, and Harvard University, her paintings have been exhibited as far away as Pakistan and Greece.

Packer's travels brought her to South Yarmouth in 1983, when she came to Cape Cod to become the founding director of the Cape Museum of Fine Arts. Her work is not confined to painting. She was a founder of the Cultural Center of Cape Cod and a founder of Women Creating, a multimedia exhibition celebrating the creative women of Cape Cod. Her many endeavors include the presidency of the Cape Cod branch of the National League of American Pen Women.

Packer has extended her art into another area, creating white line woodblock prints and teaching the technique. (Courtesy of Robert Nash.)

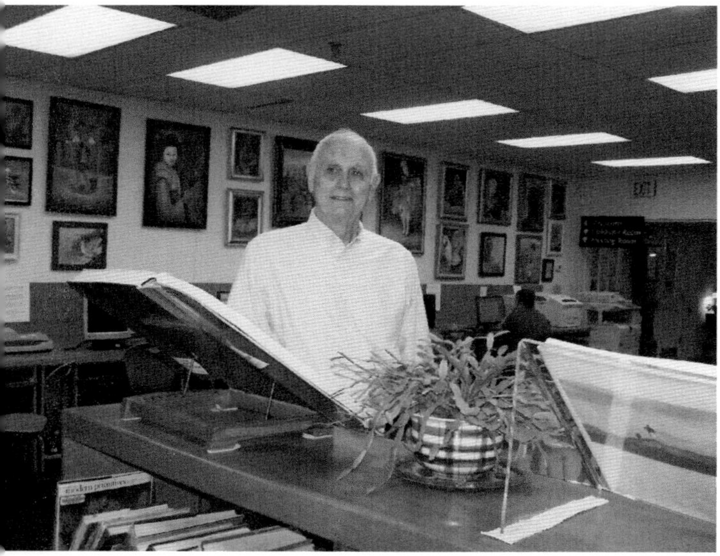

Richard McGarr
Richard McGarr was born in Norwalk, Connecticut, lived his early years in East Providence, Rhode Island, and had a career that took him to Africa and Washington before he retired to South Yarmouth to follow his avocation as an artist.

Since then, he has studied art extensively, training with several top artists, exhibited in art galleries throughout the Cape, served as a docent at the Cape Cod Museum of Art, and entered his art in many exhibitions with other artists and solo. His work is often abstract in watercolor and acrylic. (Photograph by author.)

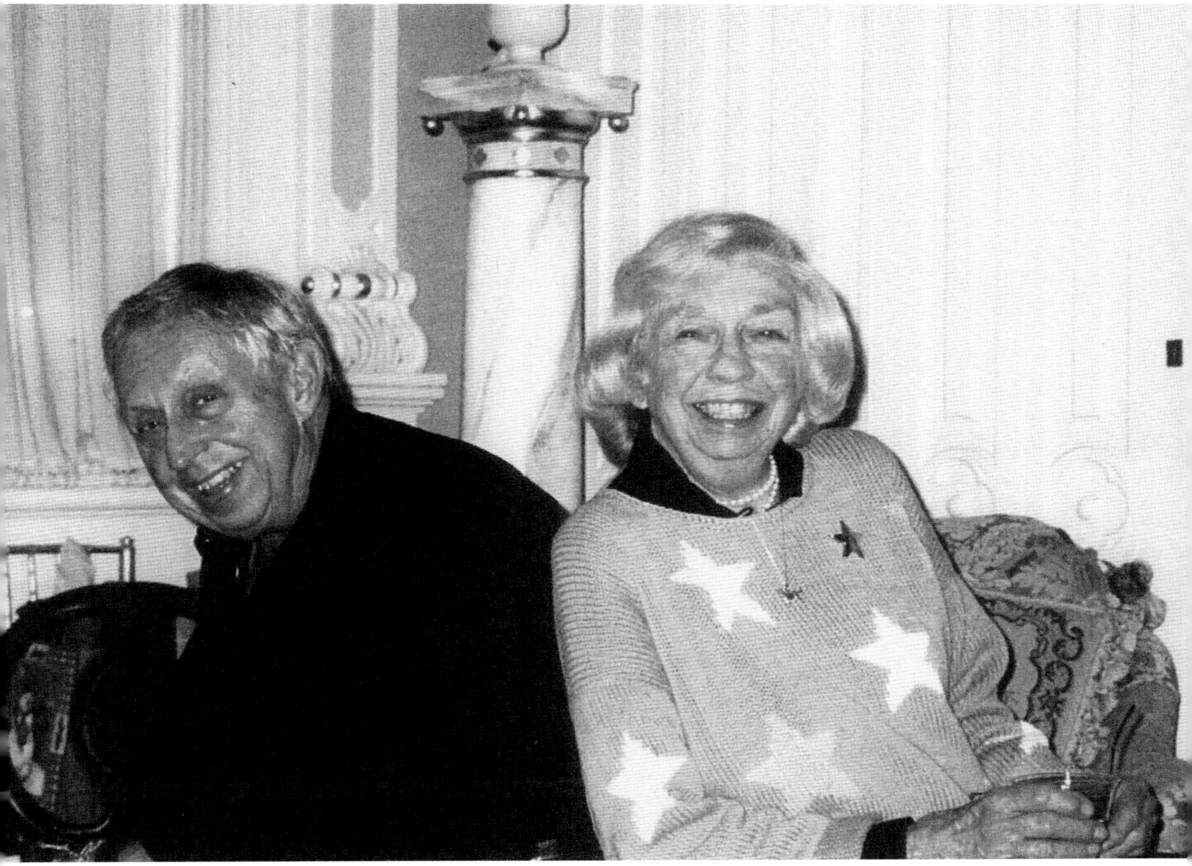

Helen Pond and Herb Senn
For four decades, Helen Pond and Herb Senn, who died in 2003, produced imaginative sets for stages in New York, Boston, and their adopted home of Cape Cod.

The couple met while attending Columbia University in New York, where they were studying dramatic arts.

Their work graced many productions, including works by writers as diverse as Shakespeare and Noel Coward. Their sets for the Boston Ballet's production of *The Nutcracker* are considered classics. The Boston Ballet's production designer Philip Jordan called them "great model makers" in a 1996 interview.

With numerous sets for opera productions in Boston to their credit, H&H, as they were known to friends, also created many works for the Cape Playhouse in Dennis, a couple of miles from their home in a converted Unitarian church, which they named Strawberry Hill, in Yarmouth Port.

Their sets are considered old-school in the most complimentary way. They carved, painted, and built them by hand.

"Pond and Senn hark back to a tradition of theatrical design that depended on beautifully painted scenery to delight audiences rather than an abstract suggestive mode of depiction," the *Boston Phoenix* said of the team in 2001.

H&H helped to keep the arts scene on Cape Cod vital. Neighbors waited for the ringing of the church bell at Strawberry Hill each New Year's Eve. (Courtesy of Helen Pond.)

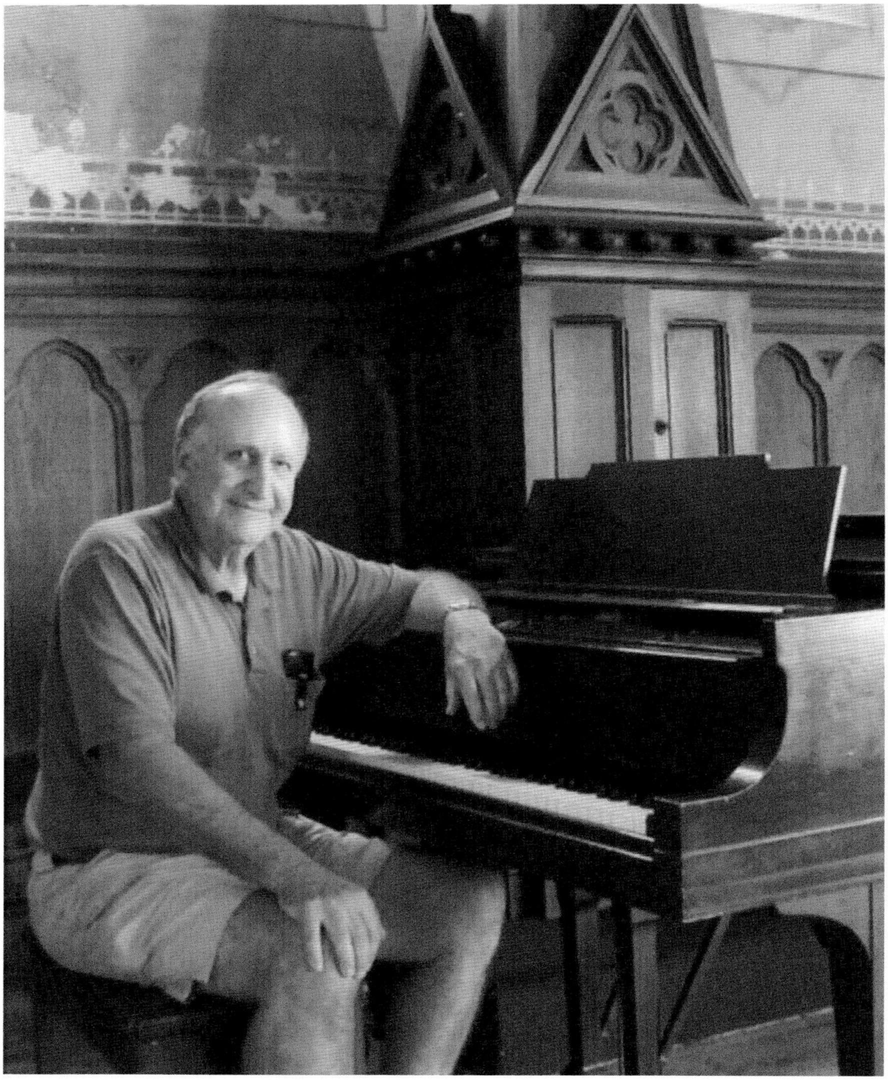

Ronald Perera

Composer Ronald Perera has written choral works, orchestral pieces, and electronic music, often linking literary works with his musical ideas. His works highlight the writings of authors including ee cummings, Emily Dickinson, William Shakespeare, and Herman Melville.

Perera is descended from the Thacher family and taught composition at Smith College in Western Massachusetts for 30 years before his retirement in 2002.

In 2012, he presented his choral work *North Country* in the former Swedenborgian Church, now a performance venue in Yarmouth Port, a short distance from Perera's ancestral home. The work brought to musical life poems by Robert Frost and was sung by the Copley Singers under the direction of Brian Jones, emeritus director of music and organist at Trinity Church in Boston and a longtime friend and musical associate of Perera. (Courtesy of the *Register.*)

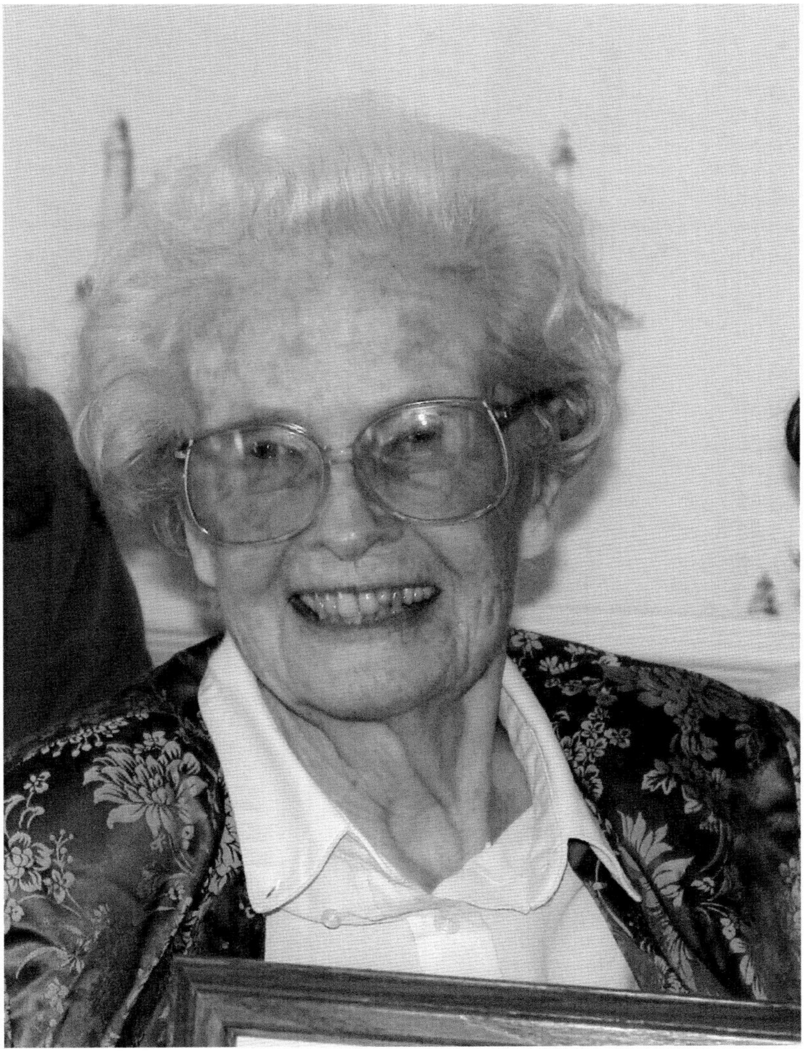

Marion Vuilleumier (1918–2013)
Marion Rawson Vuilleumier was never far from books and writing, publishing her first article at age 12 and continuing to write throughout her life.

Born in Worcester, Massachusetts, and educated at Gordon College where she received a degree in theology, she married a minister, Pierre Vuilleumier, with whom she was active in developing housing projects on Cape Cod in Mashpee and Sandwich before they helped to create Mayflower Place in West Yarmouth, a retirement community, and where Vuilleumier lived the latter part of her life.

She was a book reviewer for the *Cape Cod Times* and an adjunct professor at Cape Cod Community College, while also finding time to publish 20 books on a variety of topics including local history and religion. Vuilleumier's book *The Town of Yarmouth, Massachusetts: A History 1639–1989*, was published by the Historical Society of Old Yarmouth.

As a member of the Twelve O'Clock Scholars writers' group and a founder of the Cape Cod Writers' Center and the longtime host of its cable television program *Books and the World*, Vuilleumier helped to promote the careers of hundreds of writers. Local and nationally known authors were given a forum in which to present their work to a wide audience. (Courtesy of the Writers' Center of Cape Cod.)

Garry Mitchell

Equal parts teacher and performer, Garry Mitchell has had a successful career on a global stage in the business world and success on the theatrical stage as well.

Mitchell's consulting firm, GM Training Specialists, creates courses to help companies improve negotiation, sales, presentation, and management skills. He has been a consultant to the United Nations on negotiating and training skills and has traveled the world working with businesses.

An in-demand public speaker, Mitchell has also been a tenured professor at Nassau College in New York and holds a doctorate from New York University.

He achieved success in the business world after putting aside his original career choice, the theater, for a while. Early in his career, Mitchell performed on Broadway, off Broadway, and in various national tours and regional productions. His credits include television, films, and television commercials.

After retiring from the business world, Mitchell returned to the theater on Cape Cod, with many roles to his credit, both dramatic and comedic. (Courtesy of Garry Mitchell.)

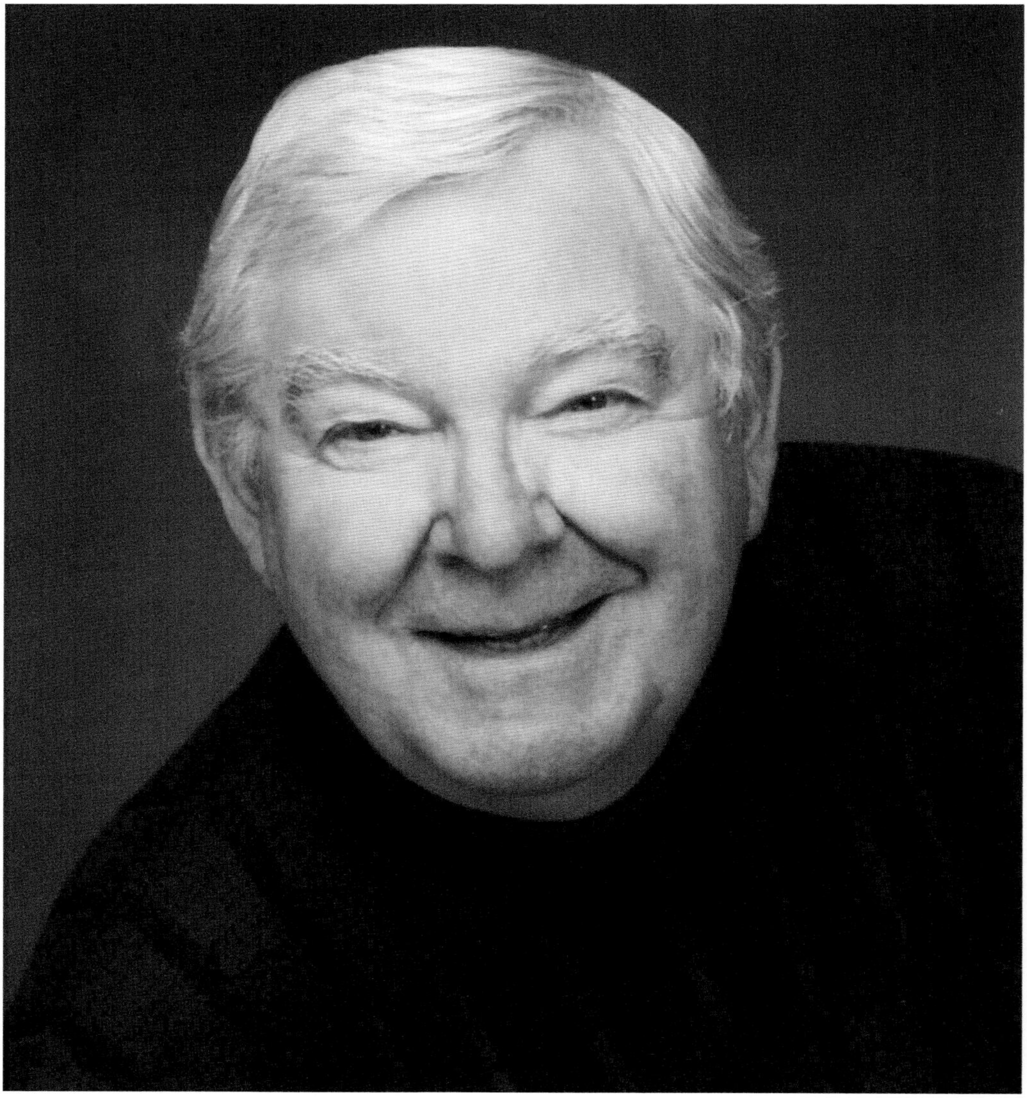

CHAPTER THREE

Public Service

This chapter's focus is on those politicians, public servants, and volunteers who give their time and talents to make Yarmouth a better place.

The town was fortunate to have Bob Lawton as its town manager for more than three decades. His steady leadership is fondly remembered. Thomas George served the town as its moderator and as state representative. Joel Wolfson was a longtime selectman, helping to set policy for the town at a time of fast growth. At the time of his death, he and his wife, Pearl, were working on a plan to create more affordable housing in Yarmouth, a project Pearl carries on with her son Michael.

Yarmouth has a long history of educators who have made a difference in many lives. They include Marguetite E. Small, Laurence MacArthur, Chuck Liberty, and Michael McCaffrey.

Police and fire chiefs, who brought Yarmouth into modern times, and people who served in unofficial, yet vital, ways are included in this chapter.

And, those who sacrificed their lives for their country are remembered here. Yarmouth has suffered losses in nearly every war, the most recent coming when Marine corporal Nicholas Xiarhox died while serving in Afghanistan in 2009.

Joel Wolfson (1932–2000)

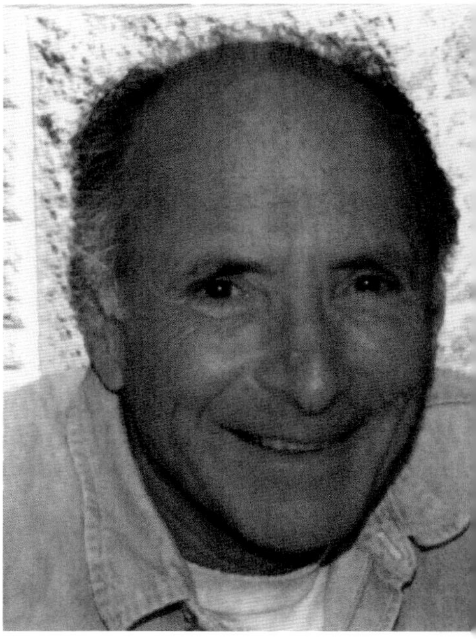

As a teacher, camp counselor, and builder, Joel Wolfson was a man noted for his foresight and generosity.

Educated at Harvard University, Wolfson declined to go into the family paper business, opting to become a schoolteacher and camp counselor. In his early 20s, with his friend David Silverman, he founded Camp Kirkland in Yarmouth, which quickly became a popular summer camp for kids that still operates.

Wolfson found time to serve as president of the Cape Cod Synagogue and as a member of the committee that built Cape Cod Regional Technical High School. He served as a selectman in Yarmouth from 1975 to 1991, among the longest-tenured people to serve in that role.

Shortly before his death in 2000, Wolfson and his wife, Pearl, formed Our First Home Inc., a nonprofit organization dedicated to building affordable housing. (Courtesy of Pearl Wolfson.)

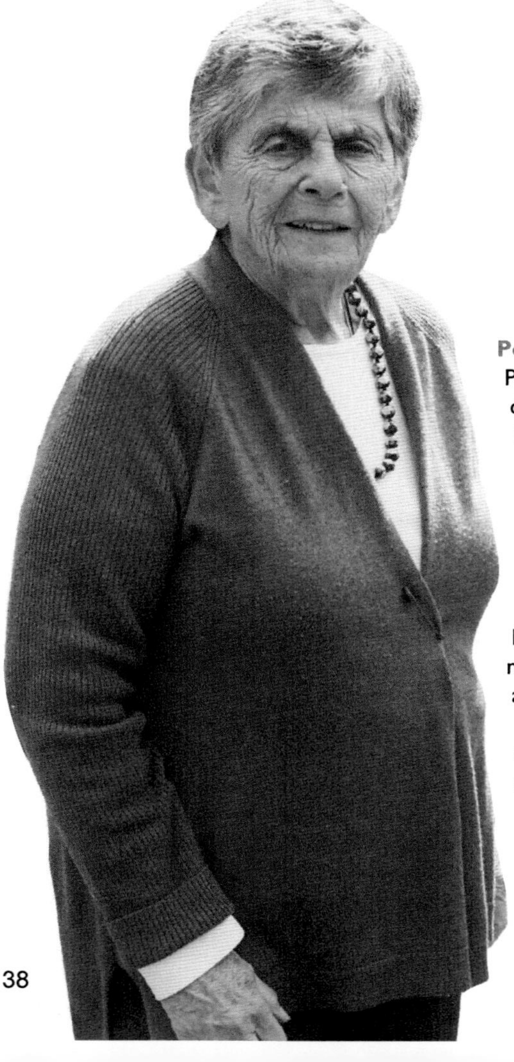

Pearl Wolfson

Pearl Wolfson knows how to get things done. As a driving force behind Our First Home Inc., she has helped to create affordable housing for people who otherwise would not be able to own a home.

Started as a retirement project with her husband, Joel, responsibility for Our First Home Inc. soon landed on Pearl alone when Joel died unexpectedly in 2000. With Joel and Pearl's son Michael stepping up as a licensed building contractor and using innovative funding mechanisms, the organization has taken on building and rehab projects throughout Yarmouth.

"It's giving back to the town that was really very supportive of us and hoping young people will be able to live in Yarmouth," Wolfson told a reporter in 2011. (Photograph by author.)

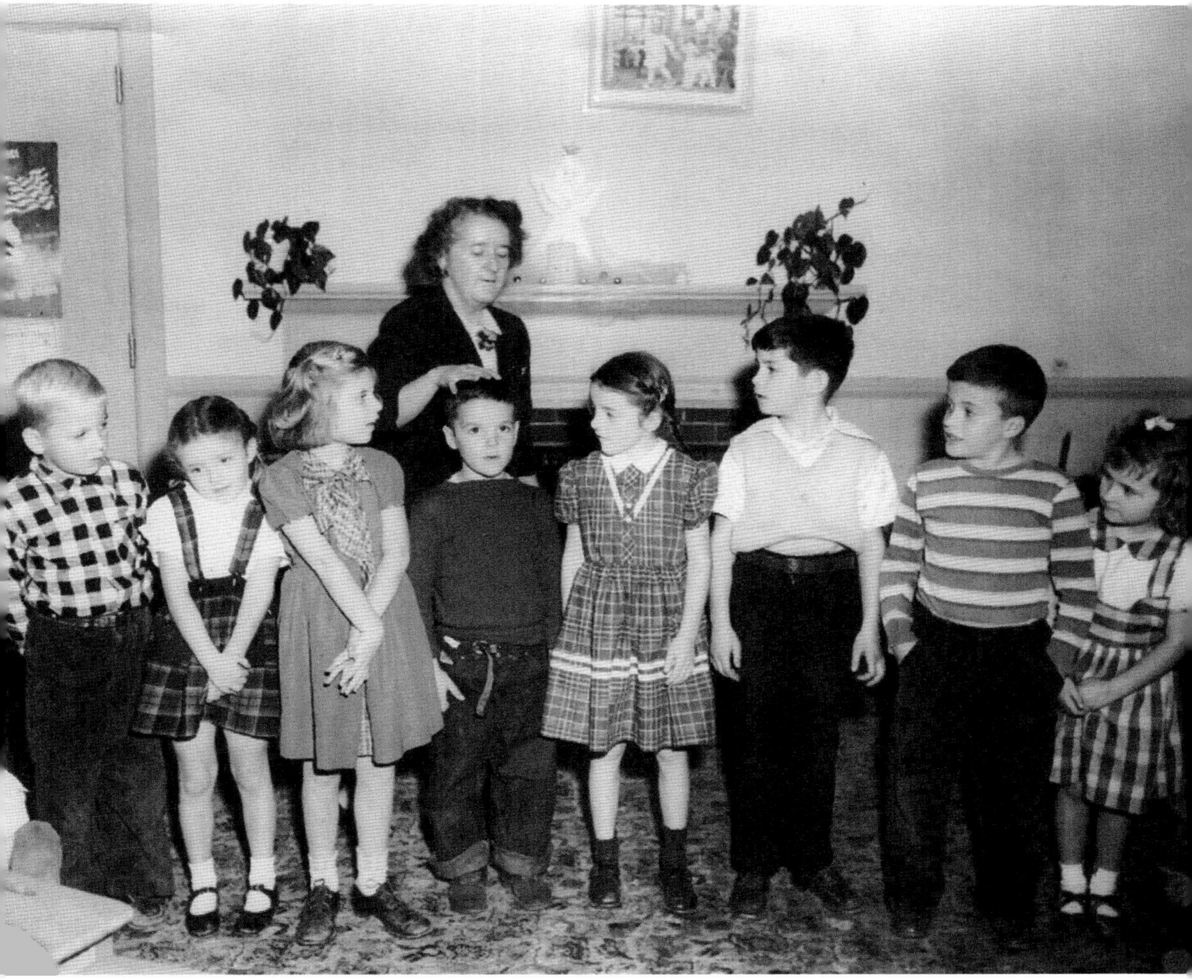

Marguetite E. Small (1911–1999)
How many people are so admired as teachers that they have a school named after them while they are still alive? Marguerite E. Small was one of that select few.

Marguerite E. Small's family moved to Yarmouth when she was a small child. Her father was superintendent of the Yarmouth schools. Her mother, grandfather, and brother were also teachers, so it was no surprise when Marguerite earned a teaching degree and began her career. After teaching in New Salem, Massachusetts, she came back to Yarmouth to teach second grade in 1935. She was first assigned to the South Yarmouth Elementary School, and when a new school was built in West Yarmouth, she taught there, eventually becoming assistant principal, then principal. Upon her retirement in 1975, the West Yarmouth Elementary School was renamed for her.

Small married for the first time after her retirement, and with her husband, Merton Young, she later moved to Florida.

In Small's obituary, the words of a former student were quoted: "I don't remember what I learned in your classroom. But I remember you loved flowers, you liked to sing and the room was always full of sunshine." (Author's collection.)

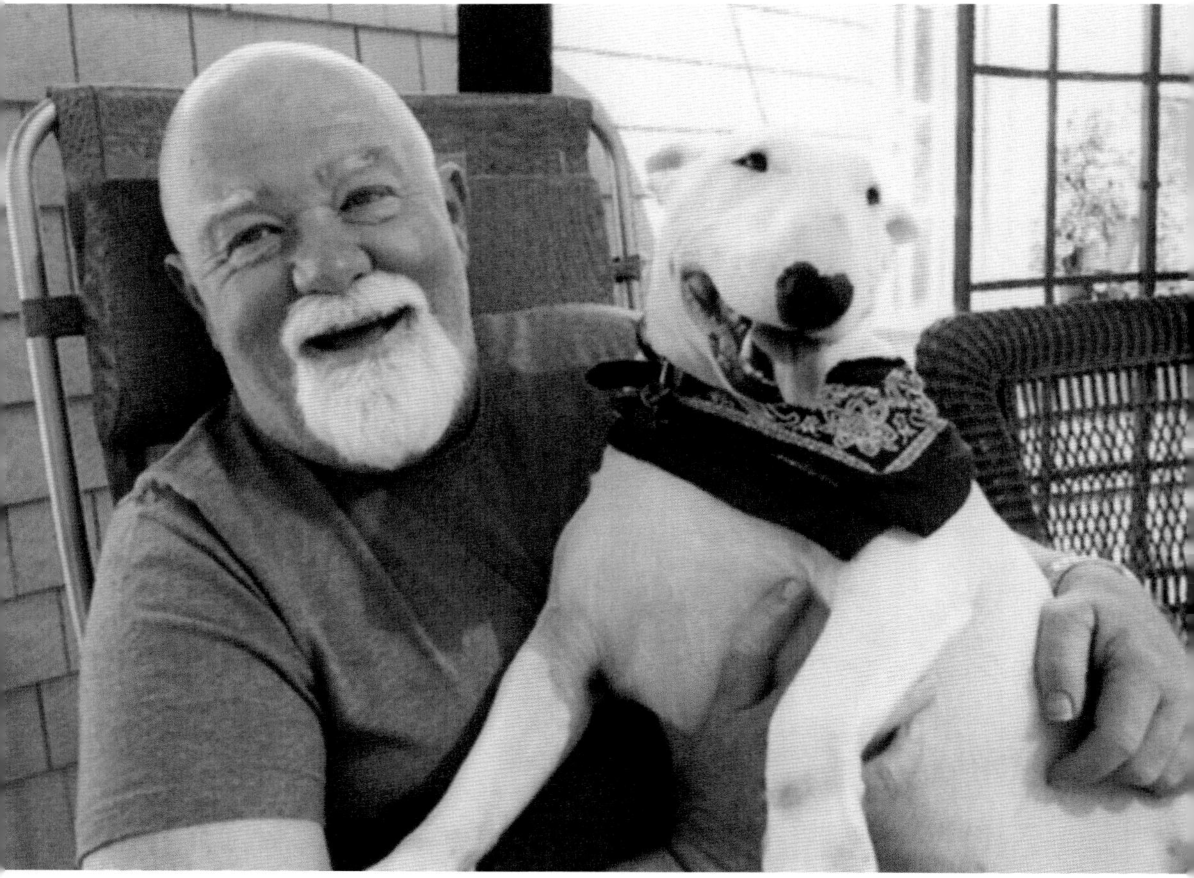

Jerry Sullivan (1950–2012)
Jerry Sullivan was a native son of Yarmouth and a prominent businessman as the owner of Jerome Sullivan Insurance. After selling his insurance business, he learned web-page design and devoted himself to flying his airplane.

What set him apart was his commitment to serving his town as a member of the zoning board of appeals and other committees and most prominently as a selectman. He stepped down from the board of selectmen to devote more time to family and business, but after three years away from town government, Sullivan ran again for the town's highest office and easily won a seat. He was reelected in 2007, saying that his last campaign "was the hardest I've run in a long time."

Sullivan was known as someone who could be relied upon to supply the historical perspective to issues that came before the selectmen, and he earned a reputation for reaching consensus and compromise. He served until 2010 when deteriorating health forced him to give up his seat. His courage while battling cancer was remarkable as he underwent an experimental treatment that extended his life by several years. Known as an avid Red Sox fan who was not averse to wrapping up selectmen's meetings so that he could get home to watch the game, Sullivan found it humorous that when the Red Sox came to Yarmouth each summer in the 1960s for a day of relaxation they stayed at the Yankee Motor Inn. (Courtesy of the *Register.*)

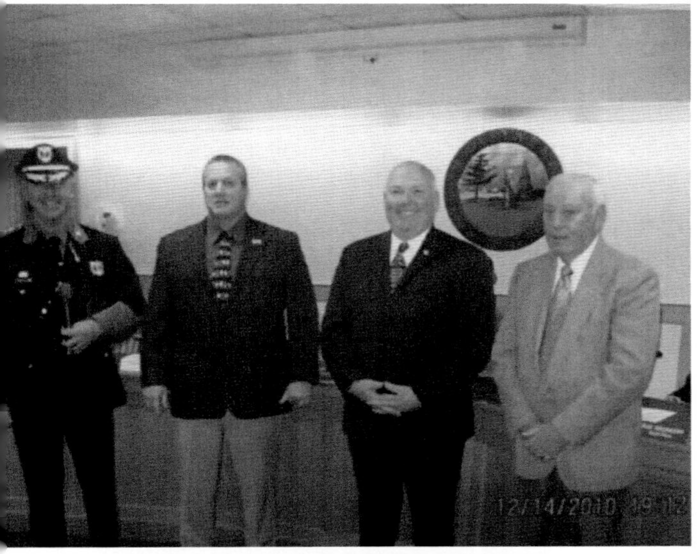

Four police chiefs
In 2010, when Frank Frederickson, left, was named chief of police in Yarmouth, his three predecessors, from left to right, Michael Almonte, Peter Carnes, and Robert Chapman, joined him at Yarmouth Town Hall. Frederickson worked his way through the ranks of the Yarmouth Police Department, as did Almonte. (Courtesy of the Yarmouth Police Department.)

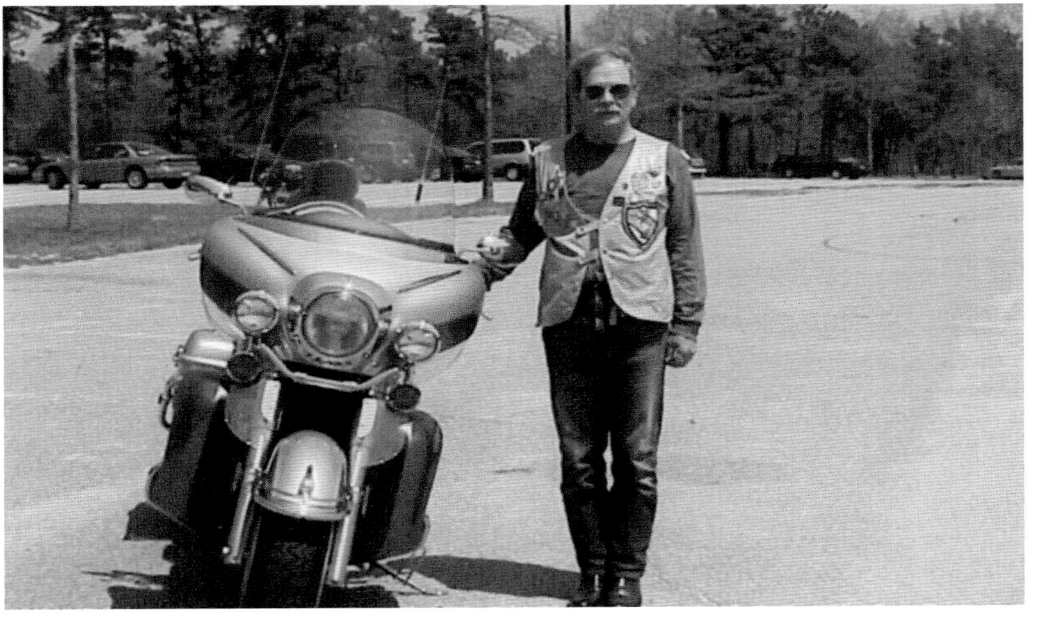

Brad Erickson (1940–2000)
Brad Erickson was known in Yarmouth as the officer who could solve any kind of problem he might be asked to handle in the course of his work. His good nature earned him many friends.

Erickson was the only Yarmouth Police Department officer to be killed in the line of duty when a truck struck him while he was directing traffic at a construction site. The outpouring of emotion for the 28-year police force veteran was impressive; police officers from around New England attended his funeral, with a 150-car procession through town.

At the time of Erickson's death, Yarmouth's new police station was being constructed. The road leading to the station is now called Brad Erickson Way.

As this picture shows, Erickson was active in the Blue Knights, a motorcycle club made up of police officers and dedicated to public service. (Courtesy of the Blue Knights Massachusetts.)

Daniel Burbank

Daniel C. Burbank has seen his adopted hometown in a way that most people never will—from space.

Burbank, a retired US Coast Guard captain and NASA astronaut, was born in Manchester, Connecticut, but considers Yarmouth Port, where he lives with his wife and children when he is not on NASA business, home.

Burbank took flight training while in the Coast Guard and became an aircraft commander and flight instructor. In 1992, he was assigned to Coast Guard Air Station Cape Cod, about 20 miles from Yarmouth. In 1996, NASA selected him as an astronaut. He served as a mission specialist, flight engineer, and commander on various NASA missions and has logged 188 days in space and more than seven hours of spacewalk time. (Courtesy of NASA.)

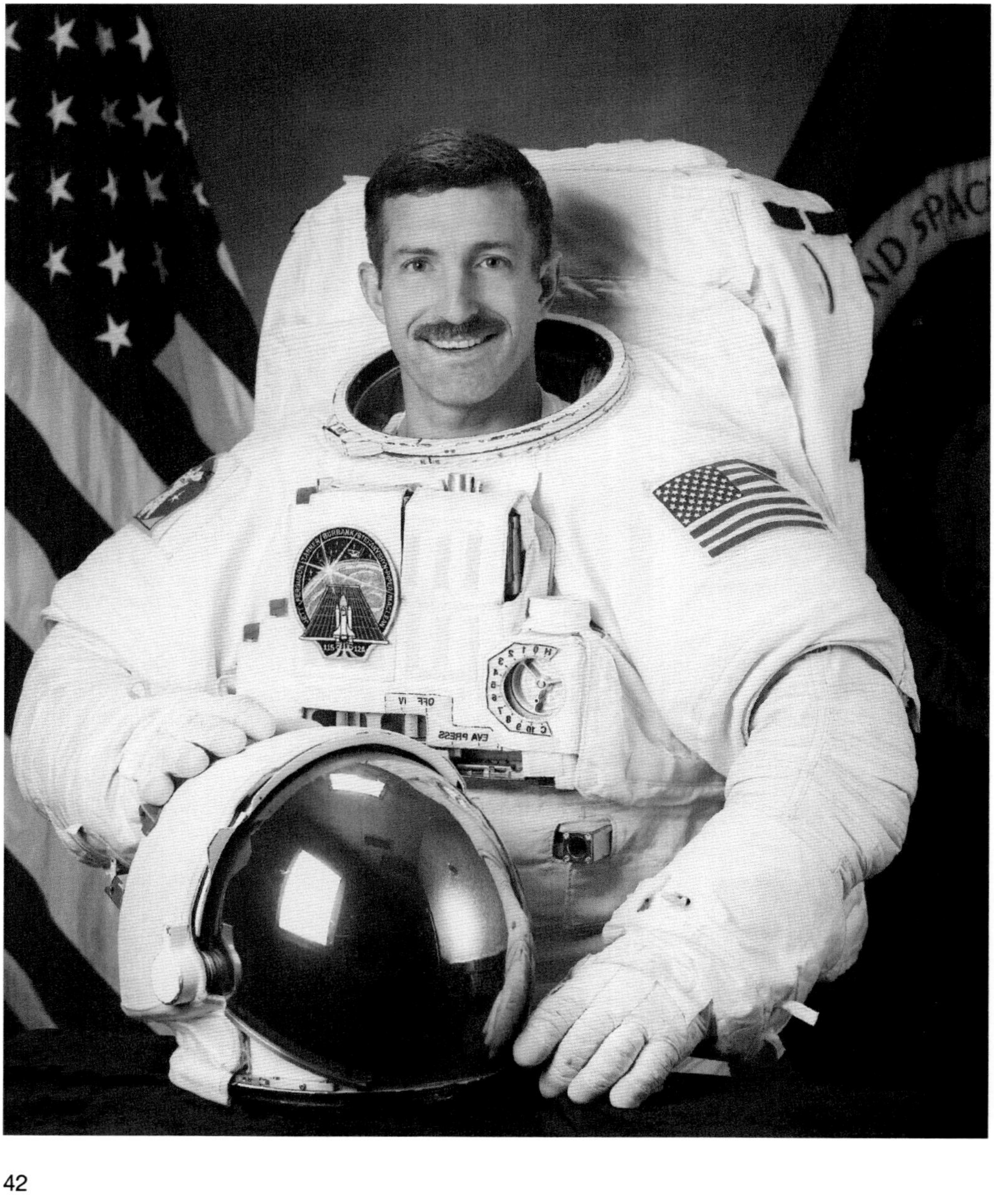

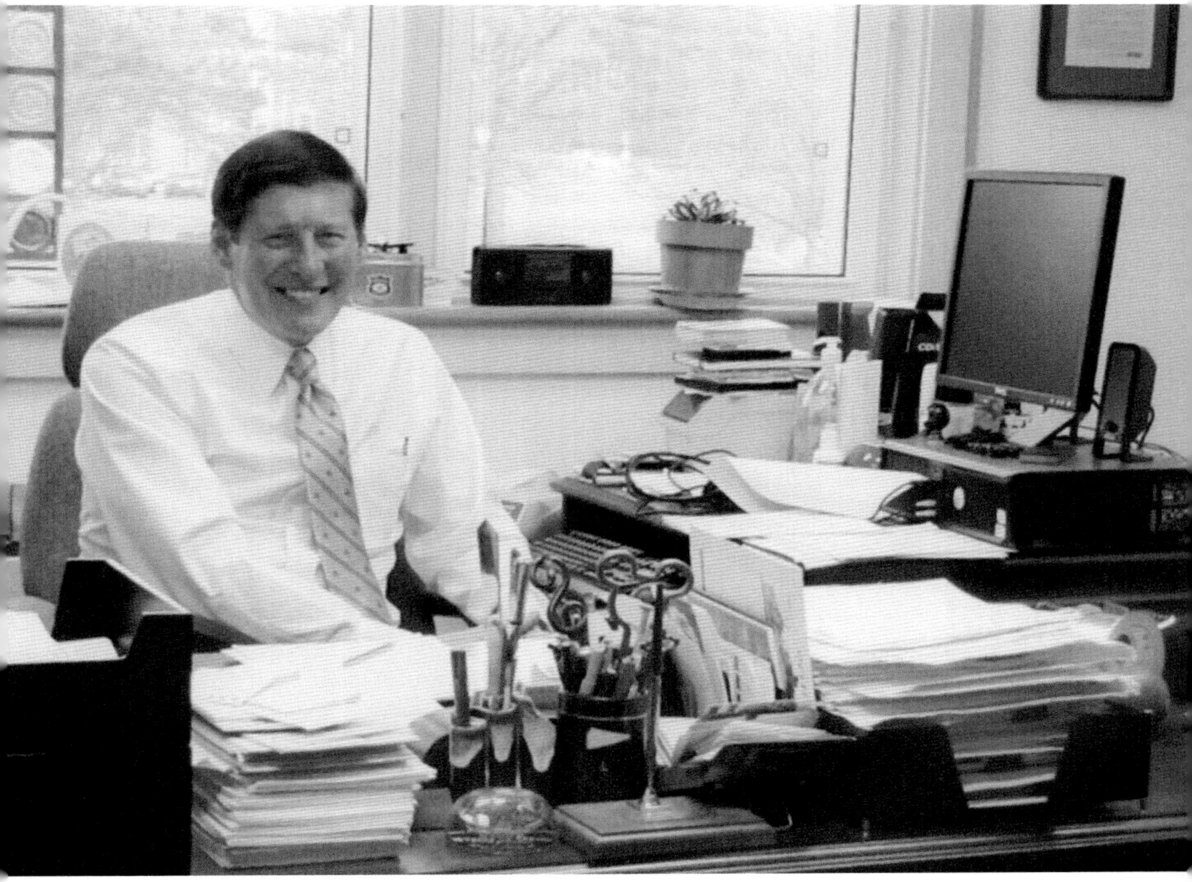

Robert Lawton
Bob Lawton came to Yarmouth from neighboring Dennis in 1978 and ended up staying 32 years.

Lawton was Yarmouth's first and only town administrator until his retirement in 2010. During that time, he had more than 30 bosses; that's how many selectmen came and went during his tenure. He used to keep a list in his desk of everyone who served on the board during his tenure.

Bob Lawton virtually invented the position of town administrator on Cape Cod, becoming the dean of administrators and a model for others to emulate. A quiet, calm leadership style is what separated him from others. Never the star of the show, he relished the role of working behind the scene to provide selectmen with the information they needed to make decisions for the town. He mastered budgets and knew how to craft a town meeting warrant that allowed voters to conduct the town's business in an orderly fashion.

Lawton told an interviewer that he was proud of the fact that Yarmouth closed its landfill and repurposed the site into a park, which won national recognition, during his tenure. And, in typically modest fashion, he said he was pleased that because good people had been hired for various town departments, he felt more comfortable leaving the job since the town was in good hands.

Noted for his youthful, neat-as-a-pin appearance, at his retirement party, Lawton's friends all showed up wearing wigs imitating his hairstyle.

An Air Force veteran, Lawton said he would spend more time flying his Cessna during his retirement years, although by 2013, he was back at work serving as interim town administrator in nearby Harwich. (Courtesy of the *Register*.)

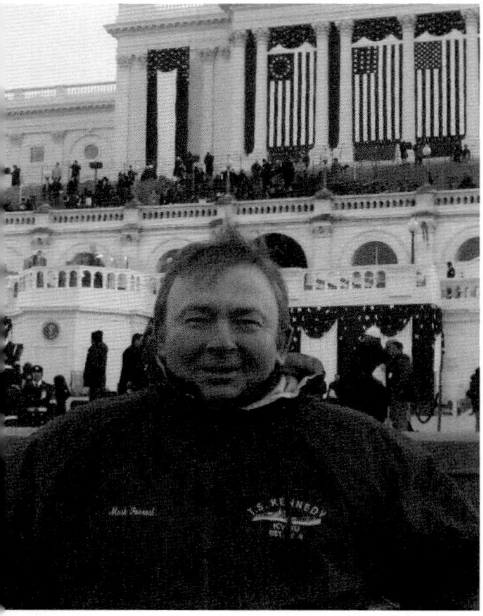

Mark Forest

As a top aide to two congressmen, Mark Forest knows how government works.

Forest was on the staff of the late congressman Gerry Studds, where he was instrumental in establishing the Stellwagen Bank National Marine Sanctuary. He also helped write the legislation that designated the Waquoit Bay National Estuarine Research Reserve in Falmouth and the Mashpee Wildlife Refuge.

After Studds's retirement, Forest went to work for Studds's successor, Congressman William Delahunt, where he continued his work on economic and environmental issues, securing $750 million for the cleanup of groundwater at the Massachusetts Military Reservation.

Continuing to work with Delahunt after the congressman's retirement, today Forest advises clients on how to deal with Congress, federal agencies, and local governments. He also teaches courses in American government and grant writing at Cape Cod Community College and Suffolk University. (Courtesy of Mark Forest.)

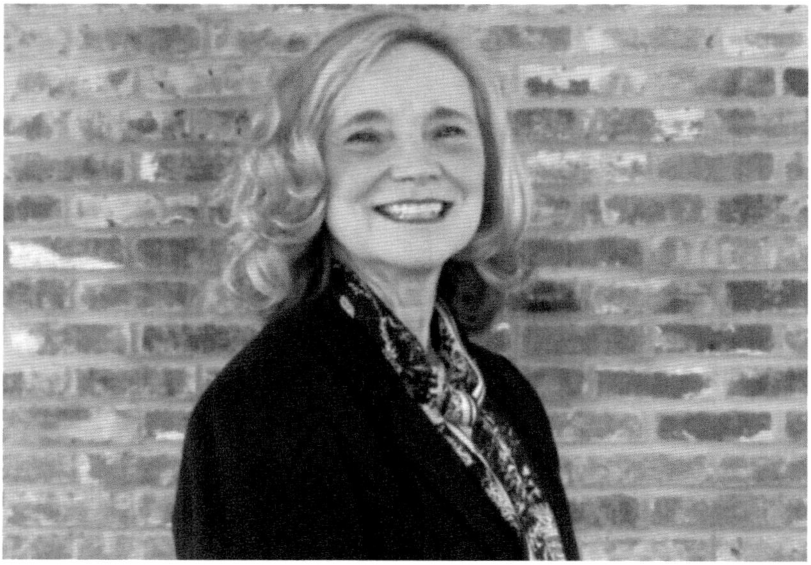

Suzanne McAuliffe

A longtime public servant in Yarmouth, Suzanne McAuliffe can trace her family history to Yarmouth's earliest days.

McAuliffe served 16 years on the Dennis-Yarmouth Regional School Committee and, in 2003, was elected to the Yarmouth Board of Selectmen, where she served nine years until 2012.

With training as a nurse, she also taught nursing before dedicating herself to public service and, with her husband Dr. Lawrence McAuliffe, raising their daughters in Yarmouth Port.

McAuliffe was born in Peru, as her family traveled due to her father's work, and lived in several states. Her Cape Cod ancestors were Baxters and Thachers, and McAuliffe says she was pleased when she and her husband decided to move to Yarmouth Port and ended up buying a house a quarter mile from the home of her great-grandmother. (Courtesy of Suzanne McAuliffe.)

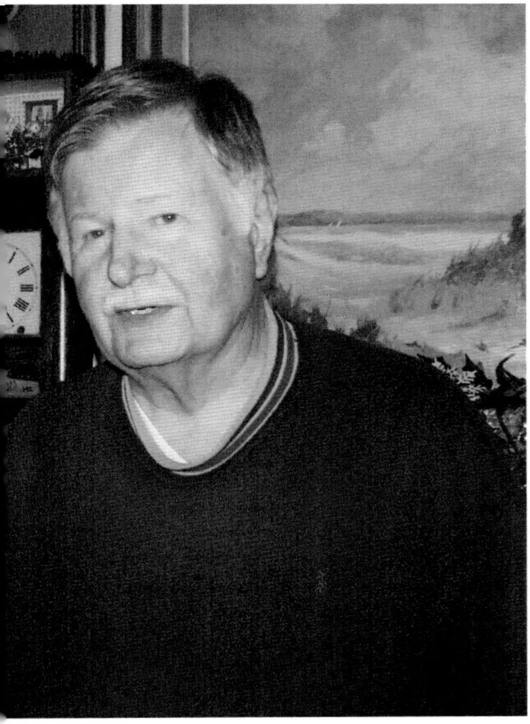

Walter Chapin

Walter Chapin's faith became the basis for community activism that ultimately saved one of Yarmouth's landmarks from neglect.

A member of the little-known Swedenborgian denomination, Chapin moved to South Yarmouth in the early 1980s and joined the Yarmouth Port Swedenborgian church, the Church of the New Jerusalem. The congregation, once flourishing and a major force in Yarmouth, could no longer afford to maintain its historic building, which was going to ruin.

In the late 1990s, Chapin began to organize an effort to get the church into the hands of a private nonprofit organization. The first step was to convince Swedenborgian church leaders to relinquish ownership of the building. With that accomplished, the Yarmouth New Church Foundation went to work raising funds to rehabilitate the historic church and revitalize it for future generations to use.

Today, as a meeting place and music venue and with its historic Tracker organ intact, the church is once again a functioning part of Yarmouth's north side community. (Photograph by author.)

John Simpkins (1862–1898)

John Simpkins's light burned early and bright but not for long.

Born into a prominent family with long ties to Yarmouth and educated in Yarmouth schools before attending prep school at St. Mark's in Southborough, Massachusetts, Simpkins graduated from Harvard in 1885. Just five years later he was elected to the Massachusetts Senate, where he served for two years. In 1892–1893 he served as president of the Republican Club of Massachusetts, making contacts that helped him win election to Congress from the 13th Massachusetts District, which included Cape Cod, in 1894 and again in 1896. In his mid-30s he seemed on a track for a long political career when he died of heart failure in March 1898.

The *New York Times* noted Simpkins's passing, saying he "was known to his colleagues as a man faithful to the interests of his constituents, although rarely taking part in debate." The *Times* obituary closed with the words: "He was a man of great wealth."

After Simpkins's death, his vast book collection was donated to the Yarmouth schools, and his name would become synonymous with education in Yarmouth. In 1930, a new school on Old Main Street was named for Simpkins. The school was in service until 2006. In 2013, it was converted to housing for senior citizens, and the building still bears Simpkins's name. (Courtesy of the Collection of the US House of Representatives.)

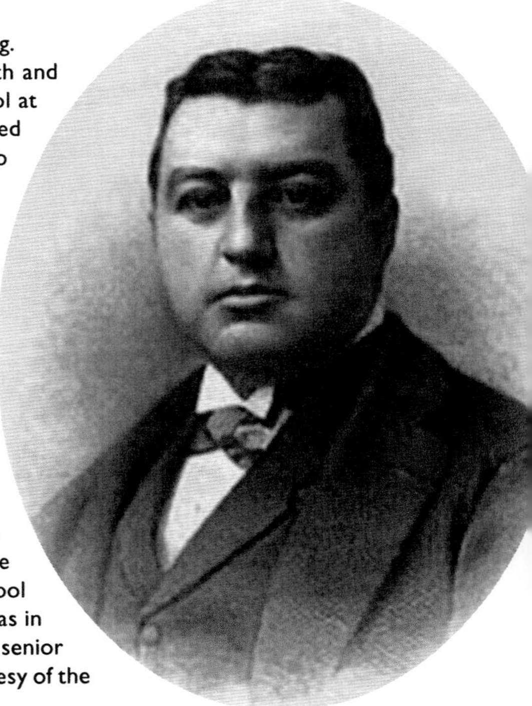

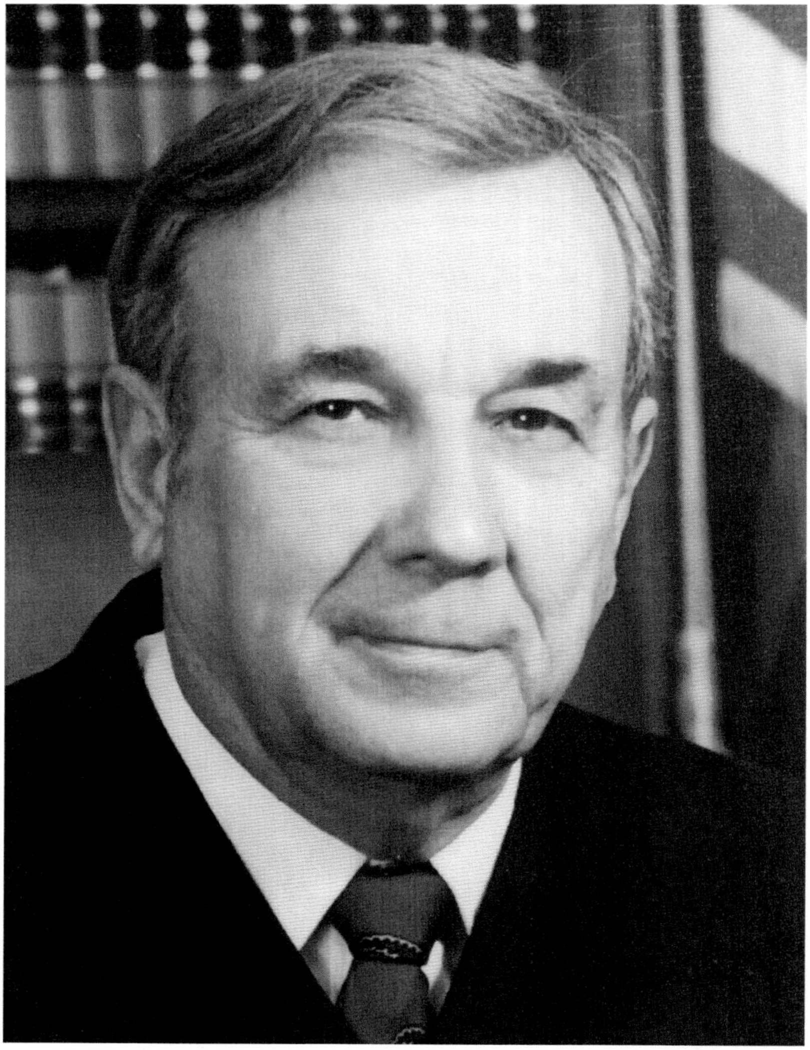

Richard O. Staff (1923–2013)

Judge, lawyer, and friend to the less fortunate, Richard O. Staff was a native of New Hampshire who came to Cape Cod to practice law.

Staff graduated from Boston University Law School in 1959 and was hired by a law firm in Hyannis on Cape Cod. Staff and his wife, Gail, adopted the Bass River section of South Yarmouth as their home and raised 10 children there. The proximity to the ocean allowed Staff to indulge his passion for sailing, and he was involved in neighborhood issues through the South Yarmouth Association.

While a practicing attorney, he was instrumental in the founding of Legal Services of Cape Cod, which provided assistance to those unable to pay for private attorneys. He was also legal counsel for the town of Mashpee.

Staff ran unsuccessfully for Barnstable County commissioner in the 1970s as a Democrat, in what was then a heavily Republican area, and in 1977, he was appointed a district court judge where he served until his retirement in 1993. After retirement, Staff practiced law and provided mediation services to help settle cases out of court and served on the board of Big Brothers Big Sisters of Cape Cod and the Islands. (Courtesy of the Staff family.)

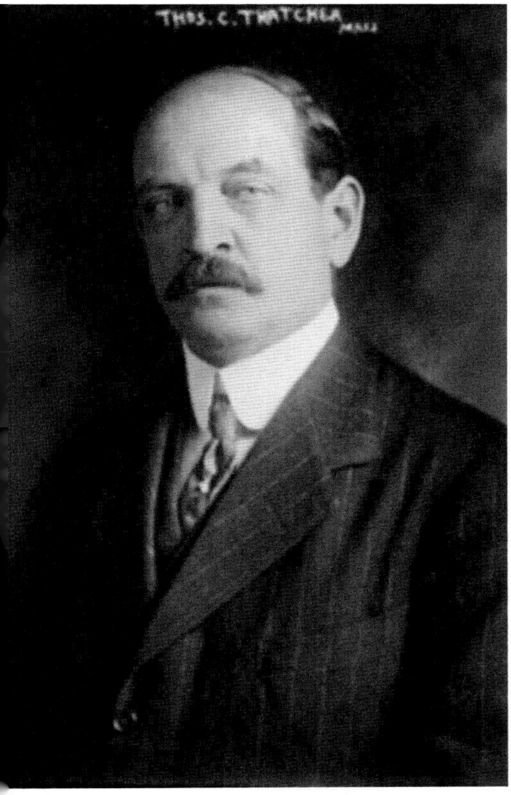

Thomas Chandler Thacher (1858–1945)

Thomas Chandler Thacher spent a brief time in Congress, but many years in the business world.

Born in Yarmouth Port, he attended local schools and then the Adams Academy in Quincy, Massachusetts, before he enrolled in Harvard University. Upon his graduation from Harvard in 1882, he entered the business world, based in Boston and dealing primarily in wool.

Thacher's base of business operations may have been in Boston, but he did not neglect his Cape Cod roots. He served as the president of the Barnstable County Agricultural Society and chaired the Yarmouth Planning Board. As a descendant of the first English settlers of Cape Cod, Thacher never lost touch with his family history. He served on the Cape Cod Pilgrim Monument Association and, in 1920, was the chairman of the Provincetown Tercentenary Committee, which organized the celebration of the town's founding.

In 1912, Thacher was elected to Congress, a rare Democrat to be elected from Cape Cod in those days. However, his time in Congress was short; he was defeated in his bid for reelection in 1914.

Following his service in Congress, Thacher returned to the business world and also dedicated himself to writing about business-related issues. (Courtesy of Lawrence Perera.)

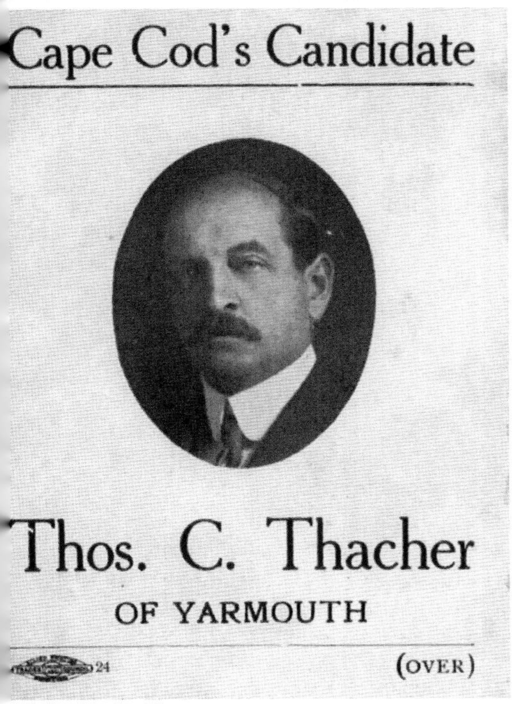

Thacher Political Advertisement

Thomas C. Thacher's political advertising in 1912 stressed his Cape Cod roots. He was the rare Democrat to be elected from Cape Cod in those days. (Courtesy of Lawrence Perera.)

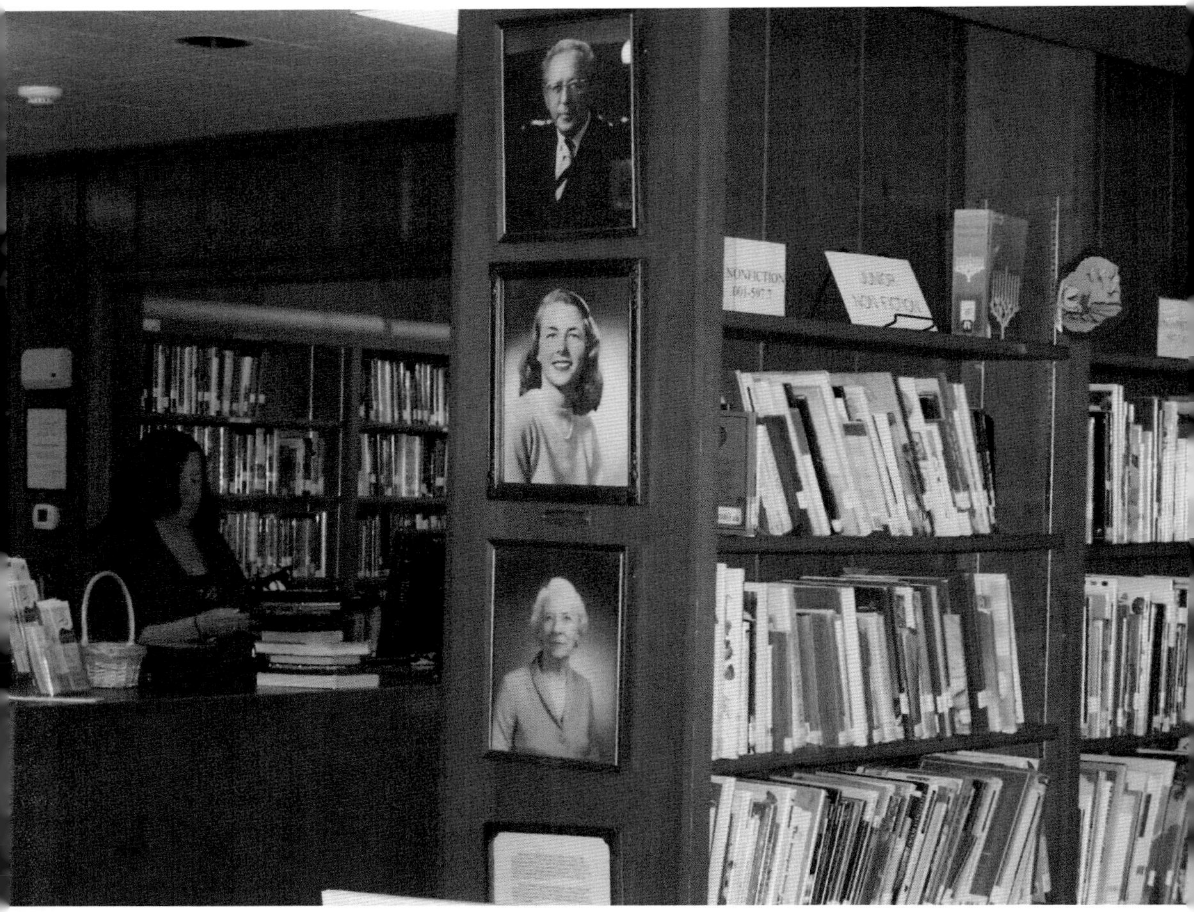

Castonguay Family

Although the Castonguay name is not heard much in West Yarmouth these days, the family had a long-lasting impact on that village.

As Yarmouth's town counsel and member of various town boards, A. Harold Castonguay served the town for many years. Born in Enfield, Connecticut, Castonguay graduated from Boston University Law School in 1935 and came to Cape Cod to practice law. Harold married Frances Williams, who had graduated from the Hyannis Normal School and was a teacher in West Barnstable.

Following the death of their daughter Ann in 1947 at age 17, the Castonguays donated in her memory funds for the construction of the West Yarmouth Library. They also created a scholarship fund that continues to help local students pay for their college education.

The Castonguays also donated to the Yarmouth schools in Ann's name a collection of carved birds, which adorned the South Yarmouth Elementary School for many years. With that school closed, the valuable collection was without a home, and in 2013, the Dennis-Yarmouth Regional School Committee voted to sell it; however, there was considerable community sentiment against that idea.

Harold Castonguay was instrumental in the refurbishing of the Baxter Mill on Route 28 in West Yarmouth in 1960; it reopened for public viewing just before Christmas in 1961 to much fanfare. His book *Two Men on a Mill* describes the effort he and George Kelley put into restoring the mill, which dates to around 1700. The mill was the first building in Yarmouth to be listed in the National Register of Historic Places.

The Castonguays are remembered at the West Yarmouth Library where their portraits hang near the entrance. (Photograph by author.)

Dana Whittemore

During Dana Whittemore's years as fire chief in Yarmouth, the department grew from one that relied on call firefighters to one that employed professional firefighters and emergency medical technicians. The changes were driven by an expanding need in a town that still had a relatively small year-round population, but hosted hundreds of thousands of visitors each summer.

Whittemore succeeded Oliver Studley as fire chief in 1952 after Studley's untimely death at a fire. Whittemore had been a call firefighter and did not pursue the chief's job, but when many of his fellow call firefighters publicly endorsed him, the selectmen offered it to him.

At the time Whittemore became chief, the Yarmouth Fire Department had no ambulance. Rescue calls were handled by the police department, which used a station wagon with minimal lifesaving equipment to transport ill or injured people to Cape Cod Hospital in Hyannis. Whittemore convinced selectmen to start a rescue service within the fire department. This was the first move toward what is today a sophisticated rescue operation, employing highly skilled paramedics using advanced lifesaving techniques and equipment.

Yarmouth has not forgotten Whittemore's work to establish a rescue service. From time to time, the department gives the Chief Whittemore Lifesaving Award to fire department personnel who provide exceptional lifesaving service.

Under Whittemore's leadership, the Yarmouth Fire Department also upgraded its fire engines, buying two pumper trucks.

Whittemore has nothing but good things to say about his years as chief, which ended with his retirement in 1975.

"The people were exceptionally nice to me. It was a happy situation."

In this photograph, Chief Whittemore and his wife attend a ceremony for the Chief Whittemore Lifesaving Award in 2010. (Courtesy of Dana Whittemore.)

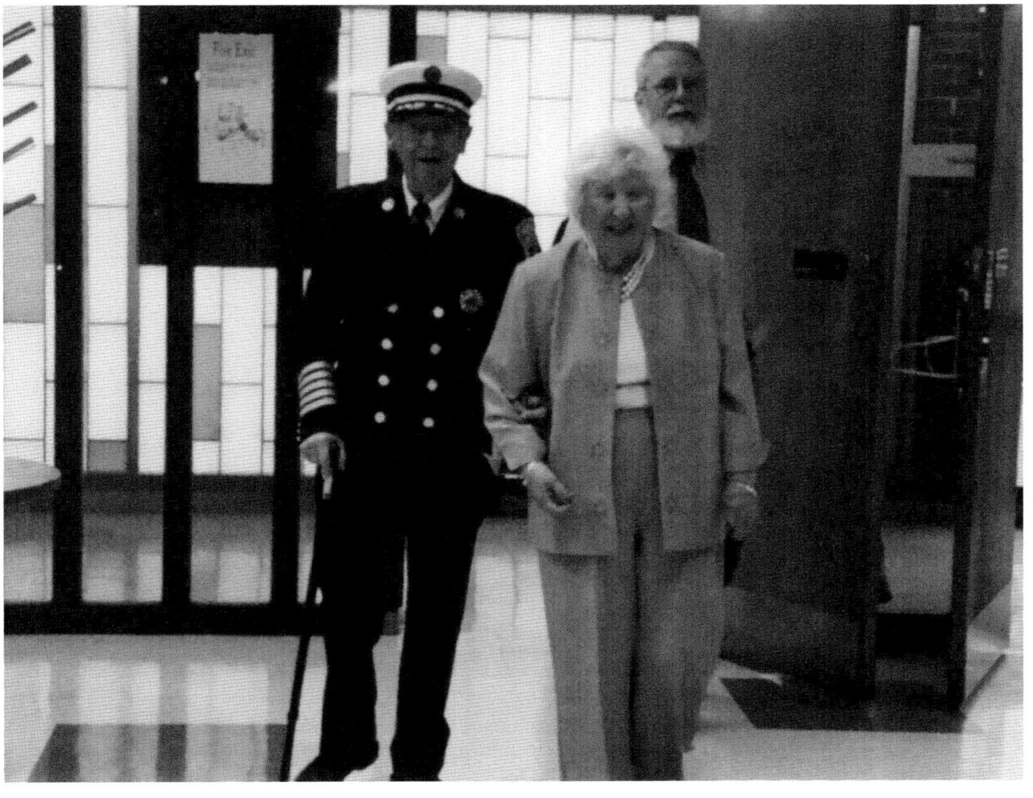

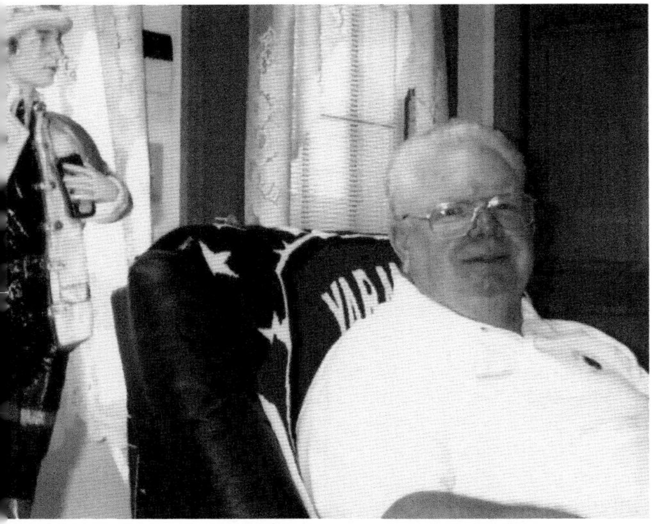

William Greene

Deputy fire chief Bill Greene served Yarmouth from 1969 to 2003, rising through the ranks. He came to Cape Cod as a special police officer, patrolling the beaches in Dennis while still a college student. Serving as an auxiliary firefighter in his native Arlington, Massachusetts, Greene joined the Yarmouth Fire Department and embarked on a career that would make him part of a fast-growing department.

In Yarmouth, Greene has also been prominent in the Masons, and in retirement, with his wife, Chris, he has been active in the Eastern Star, serving statewide and beyond. (Courtesy of Yarmouth Fire Department.)

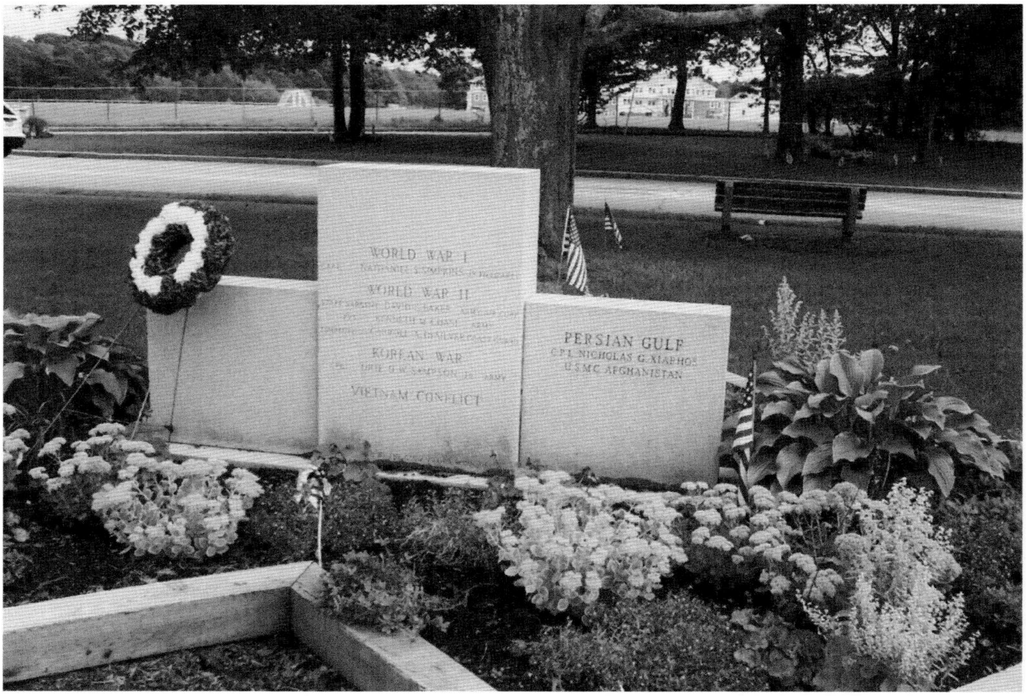

The Ultimate Sacrifice

Yarmouth has lost six native sons in wars. They are memorialized with a monument in front of Yarmouth Town Hall.

In World War I, Capt. Nathaniel S. Simpkins Jr. died while serving in the Army Field Artillery.

In World War II, Army Staff Sgt. David E. Baker and Pvt. Kenneth M. Chase and Coast Guard Fireman 2nd Class Carroll A. DeSilver were killed in action.

In the Korean War, Army Cpl. Orie D. Sampson Jr. was killed in action.

In recent times, US Marine Cpl. Nicholas G. Xiarhos was killed in action while serving in Afghanistan. (Photograph by author.)

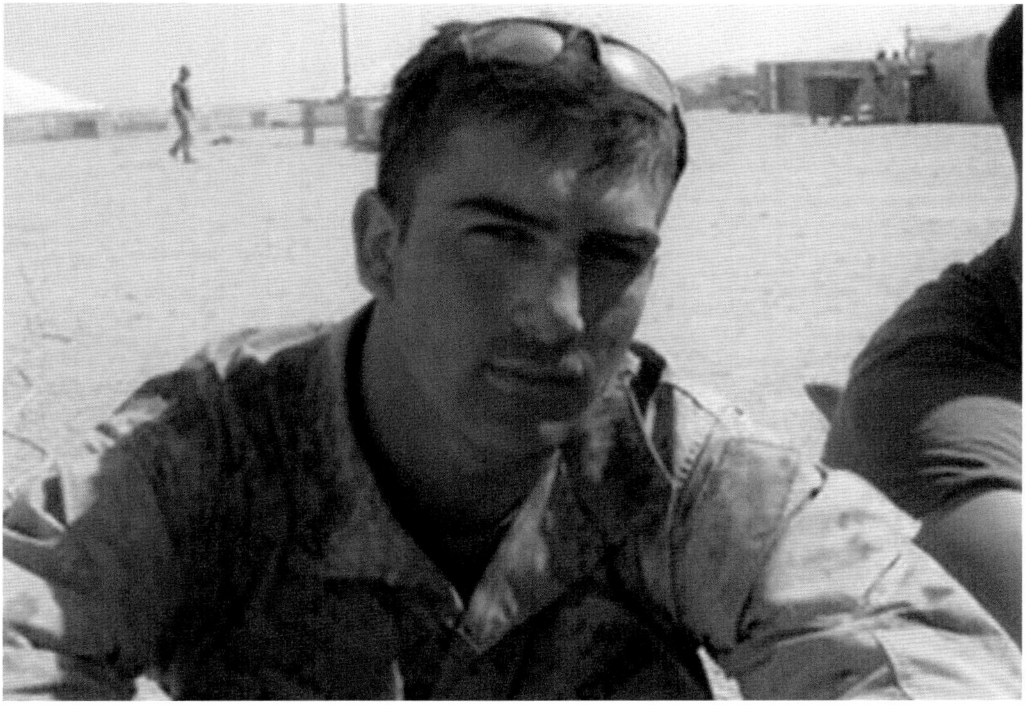

Nicholas Xiarhos

While serving with the Marines in Afghanistan in 2009, Cpl. Nicholas G. Xiarhos was killed by an improvised explosive.

His death touched off an outpouring of emotion seldom seen in Yarmouth. At a public wake held at Dennis-Yarmouth Regional High School, from which Xiarhos graduated in 2006, thousands of mourners paid their respects.

Later, an overpass spanning Route 6 in Yarmouth, a spot Nick passed most days when he lived in town, was named for him.

Nick Xiarhos was remembered as a young man who was generous, outgoing, and dedicated to his family and friends. Today, road races and other charitable events are held in his name to raise funds for various veterans' support organizations. (Courtesy of the Xiarhos family.)

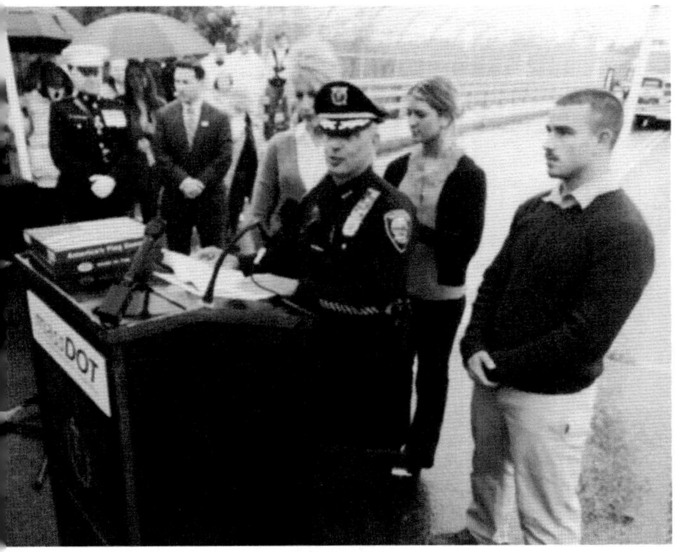

The Xiarhos Family

Following the loss of Nicholas Xiarhos in Afghanistan in 2009, the Xiarhos family became involved in efforts to honor not only Nicholas but also everyone who served. In this picture, the Xiarhos family, with Yarmouth deputy police chief Steven Xiarhos at the podium, gathered for the ceremonies naming an overpass of Route 6 for Nicholas. (Courtesy of the *Register*.)

Aubrey "Bud" Groskopf

Bud Groskopf has a flair for the dramatic.

Trained as a lawyer, Groskopf spent his career as a broadcasting executive and, in 1985, helped to revive the Republic Pictures brand. The movie studio, home to classic B movies with stars including John Wayne, Gene Autry, and Roy Rogers, had been defunct since the 1960s; in the 1980s, its products were again in circulation and became involved in home video and produced some new programming.

Retiring to Yarmouth, Groskopf became involved in the South Yarmouth Library Association and ran for selectman, winning a seat in 2005. While in office, he would often appear in parades wearing an Uncle Sam–style red-white-and-blue top hat, and he sometimes espoused positions that turned out to be unpopular, including a plan to convert the former Simpkins School to a library.

Groskopf won a second term as a selectman in 2008, but his bid for a third term crashed when, as a stunt, he pulled out a fake handgun during a candidate forum to try to make the point that the town was being held hostage by those who wanted it to commit to a costly wastewater treatment system. The incident made national news and images of Groskopf holding the prop gun were widely circulated. This bit of theater, perhaps a remnant from his days at Republic Pictures, turned out to be his political undoing, although he remains active in town affairs. Here, he counts votes at Yarmouth Town Meeting. (Courtesy of the *Register.*)

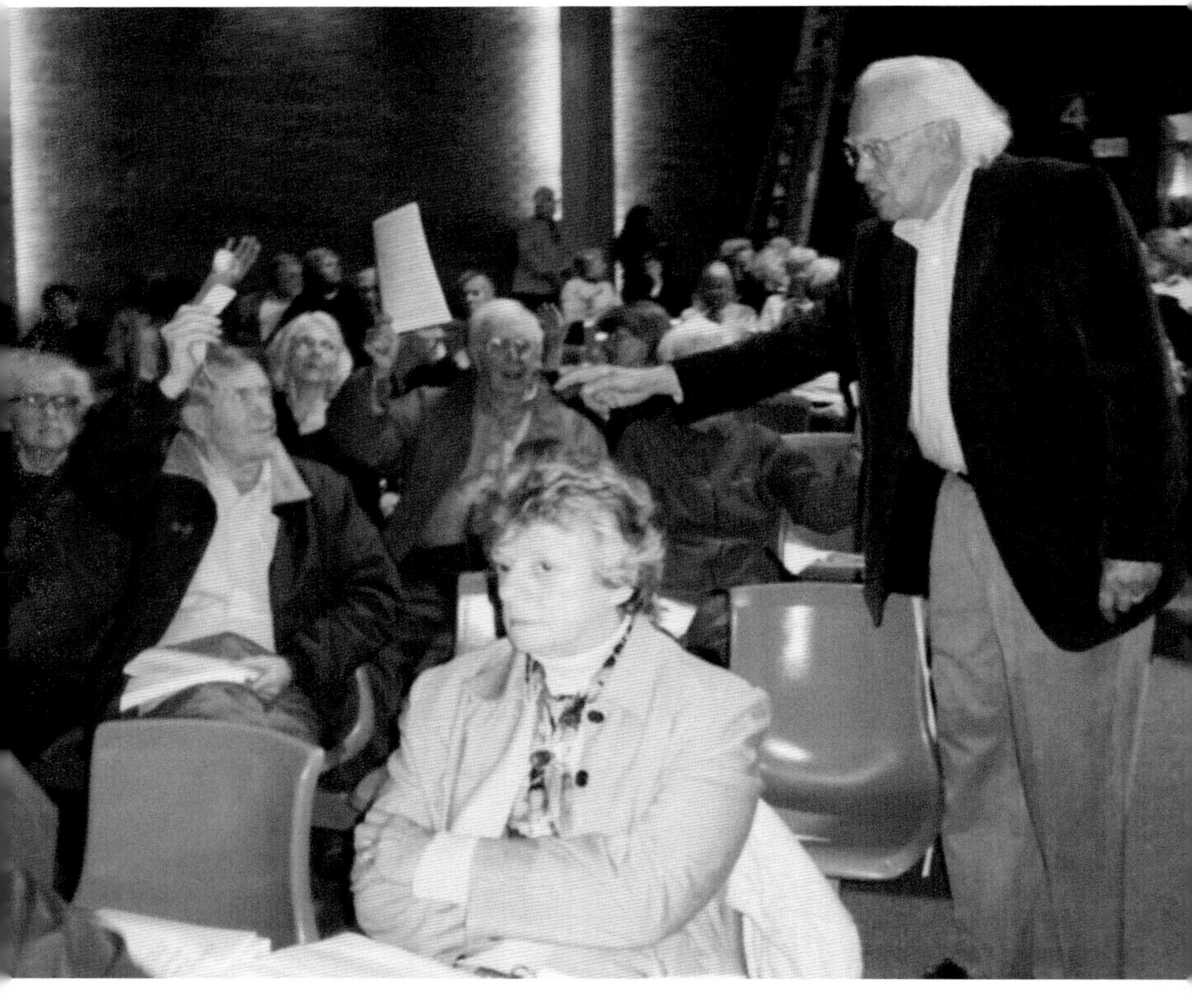

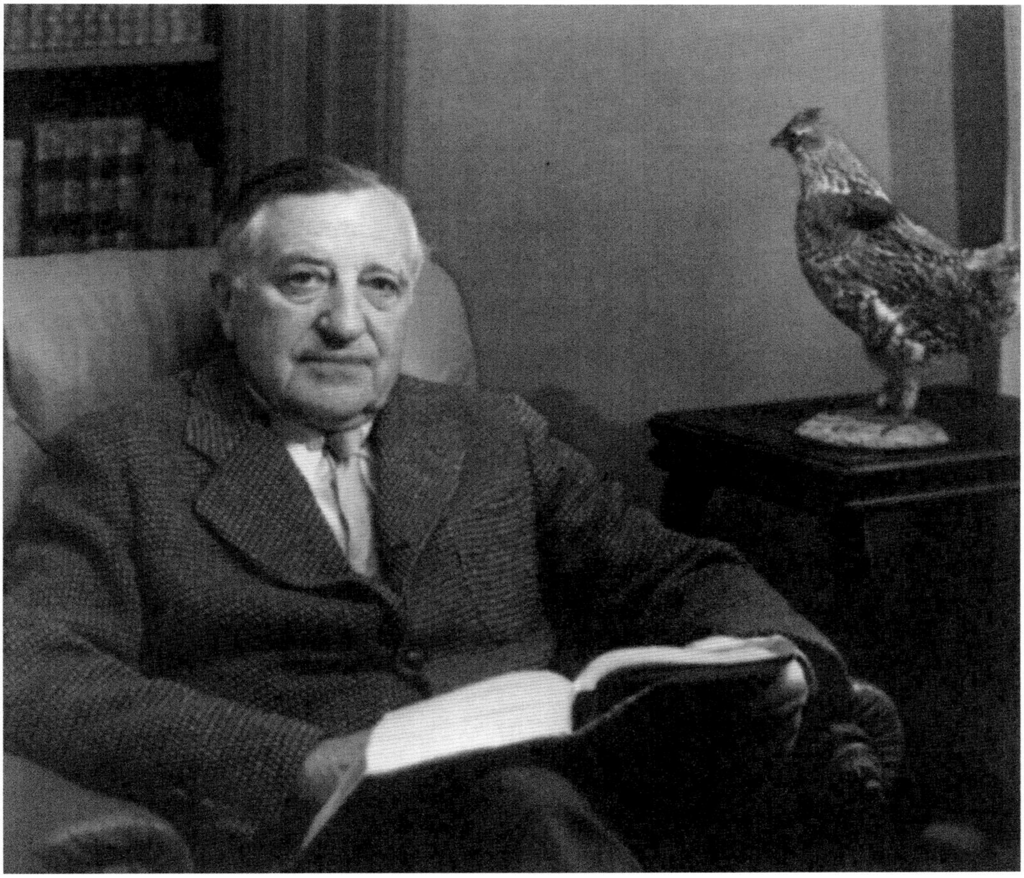

Guido R. Perera (1902–1999)
Guido Perera is perhaps the key figure in the preservation of open spaces in Yarmouth.

The son of Gino Perera, who had immigrated to the United States from Italy to pursue his career as a musician and artist, and Caroline Thacher Perera, Guido pursued law as a career. He became a partner with the firm of Hutchins & Wheeler, was commissioned as a captain in the Army's Judge Advocate General Corps, and was later assigned to the Army Air Corps in Washington, DC, where he worked on the reorganization of the Air Corps as air power began to play a larger role in World War II, according to his son Lawrence Perera's book *The Homestead Saga*.

Married to Faith Phillips, in later years, he concentrated on organizing the Perera/Thacher family's real estate holdings, overseeing donations of large tracts to the town of Yarmouth for conservation purposes; served on the planning board, where he helped to write zoning laws; helped to organize the Old King's Highway Historic District; and was a founder of the Historical Society of Old Yarmouth, which he viewed as a means of keeping the town's and his family's history alive.

In 1954, Guido Perera donated the Capt. Bangs Hallet House to the Historical Society of Old Yarmouth. The house on Strawberry Lane dates to the 1830s and was originally in the Thacher family. It was then owned by Capt. Bangs Hallet and later by the Knowles family before coming back into the Thacher and Perera family. Today, the house is not only the Historical Society of Old Yarmouth's headquarters but also a living history museum. (Courtesy of Lawrence Perera.)

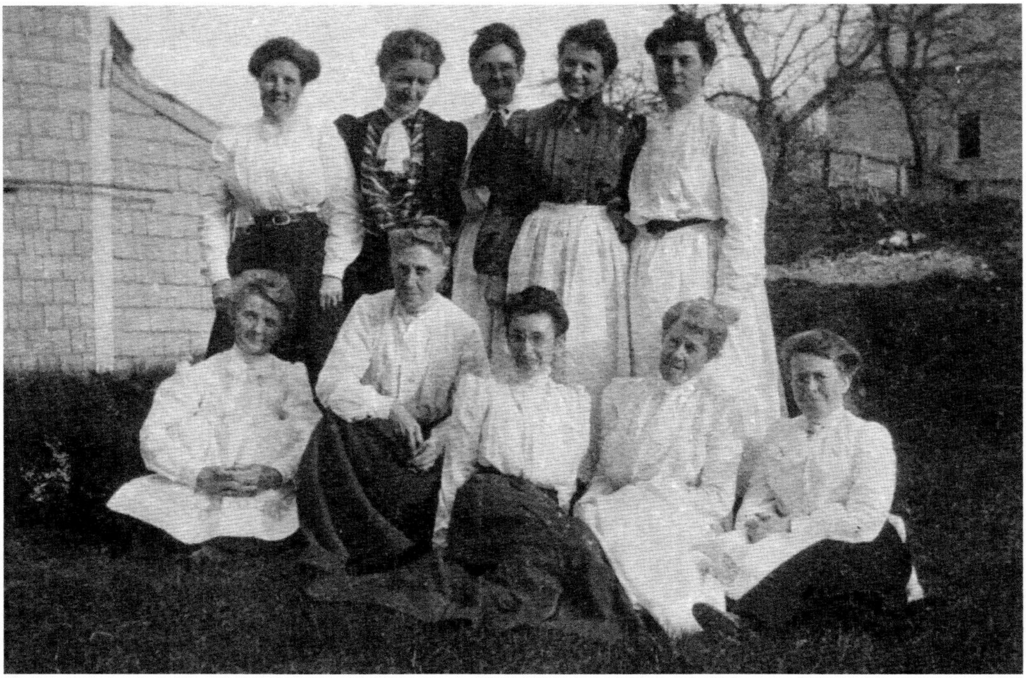

The Friday Club

For more than 100 years, the Friday Club has been of service to the town of Yarmouth.

Formed in 1901 by Mrs. John Walker, the wife of the pastor of the First Congregational Church of Yarmouth Port, the club was to be a "charitable organization for the women of Yarmouth as a community."

The club derives its name from the fact that the women met every Friday to sew. According to a history of the club, "There was no welfare then, so the members made layettes for expectant mothers of the poorer families, made outfits for children, and helped older, needy people with fuel, food and shoes."

The club raised funds through dances and other entertainments, usually held in Lyceum Hall in Yarmouth Port. The club purchased its house on Route 6A in Yarmouth Port in 1911 from Emma Gorham and, by 1928, had modernized it with electricity and indoor plumbing. In 1989, the house was listed in the National Register of Historic Places. In 2001, the club observed its 100th anniversary by placing a time capsule on the clubhouse grounds.

As times changed, the specific work of the Friday Club also changed, but its mission has not varied; the club still supports the community through scholarships and other projects. (Courtesy of the Friday Club.)

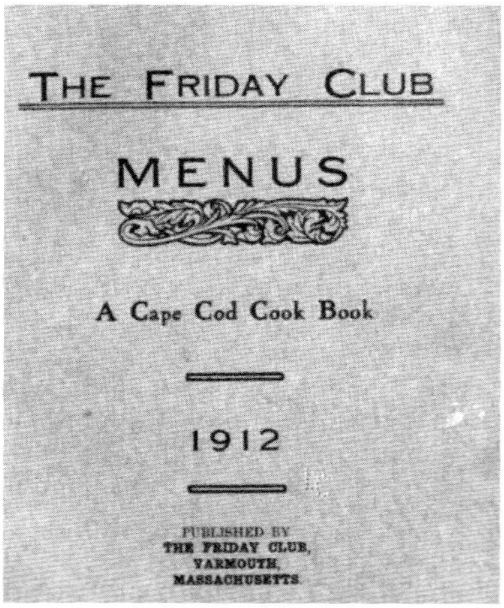

Friday Club Cookbook

In 1912, the Friday Club published a cookbook of recipes from club members. It was dedicated, "To the friends of the club whose loyalty has ever been an inspiration." (Courtesy of the Friday Club.)

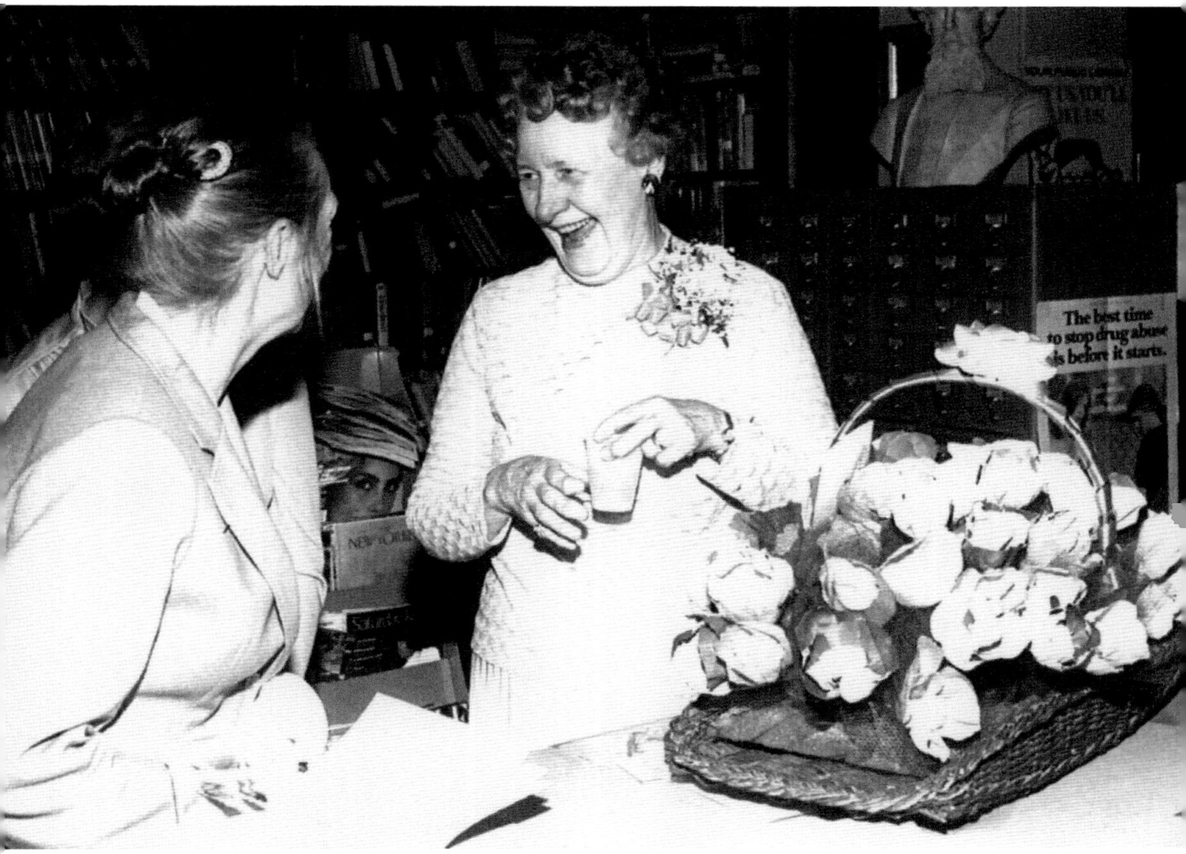

Martha U. White (1907–2000)
A Yarmouth Port native, Martha Usher White would go on to become the longest-serving librarian in the history of the library in Yarmouth Port, serving in that capacity from 1936 to 1990.

A Yarmouth Port native, as a girl, White visited the library often. However, in a videotaped interview after her retirement, she said she felt intimidated by the fact that many of the village's prominent people would often be on hand, seemingly keeping a critical eye on her.

In 1936, the library's trustees lured her away from a job with a local insurance company with a salary of $375 per year plus an apartment in the library. This was an attractive offer to a young woman with a husband and small daughter.

When White was hired, her predecessor, Lydia Matthews, was still on the job. The library trustees did not want to hurt Matthews's feelings, so they told her White was hired as her assistant. In 1937, a formal announcement was made that Martha White had been appointed librarian.

White and her family lived in the apartment at the library until 1983; she was the last of the librarians to do so.

Over the decades, White worked with many benefactors who supported the library. She was instrumental in helping the library to grow with the addition of a children's room. During her tenure, the Yarmouth Port Library became part of the town-wide Yarmouth library system. After her time at the library, the library reverted to independent status when the town decided to no longer fund it.

The reference room at the library is now named in her honor and her portrait hangs behind the circulation desk. This 1981 picture was taken at the celebration of Martha White's 45 years as librarian. (Courtesy of the Yarmouth Port Library.)

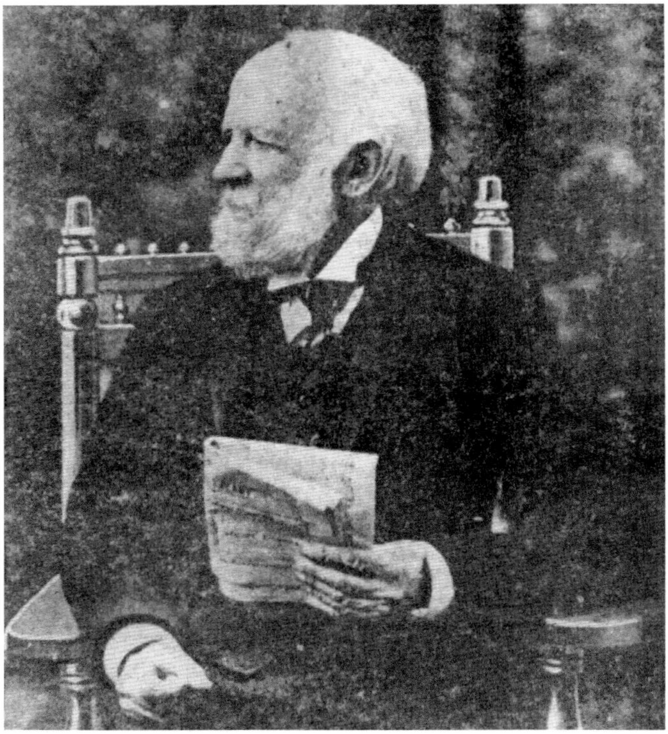

Charles Francis Swift (1825–1903)
Charles Francis Swift did as much as anyone to record the early history of Yarmouth through his *History of Old Yarmouth*, published in 1884. This book, though flawed, is among the first glimpses into what Yarmouth and its people were like in the earliest days following its settlement by the English.

Swift was born in Falmouth, about 20 miles from Yarmouth, and came to Yarmouth at age 15.

He pursued his interest in newspapers by becoming an apprentice at the *Yarmouth Register*, still in its infancy and still owned by its founder Nathaniel S. Simpkins. In a few years, Swift purchased half interest in the newspaper, and in 1849, he became the sole owner, operating the paper with the help of his children until his death in 1903.

Swift's interest was not solely in newspapers, however. In his mind, chronicling the events of the day and making events happen seemed to be closely linked. Swift served on many civic committees, was elected treasurer of Barnstable County, served as a state representative, was briefly register of probate for Barnstable County, was collector of customs for the port of Barnstable, and organized the Yarmouth Library Association, which exists today.

In the 1975 edition of Swift's history of Yarmouth, edited by Charles A. Holbrook Jr., the preface cites Swift's unpublished autobiography in which he said of himself: "It is not egotism for me to say that I did as much as any other person to shape the public policy for the county from 1860 to 1890."

While Charles Francis Swift did in fact shape the history of Yarmouth and Barnstable County, he also was a tireless booster of those things he loved.

The 1975 preface to Swift's book goes on to note that, for Swift, "there was only one church—the Swedenborgian—with a lofty bow to the founder of the Congregational Society. There was only one library of importance—the Yarmouth Library Association, of which he was a founder. The other two sturdy library associations, in South Yarmouth and West Yarmouth, are dismissed with a single patronizing sentence. There was only one important section of the town—Yarmouth Port. South Yarmouth and West Yarmouth, despite their flourishing commerce and participation in the growth of the town, are given scant notice." (Courtesy of the *Register*.)

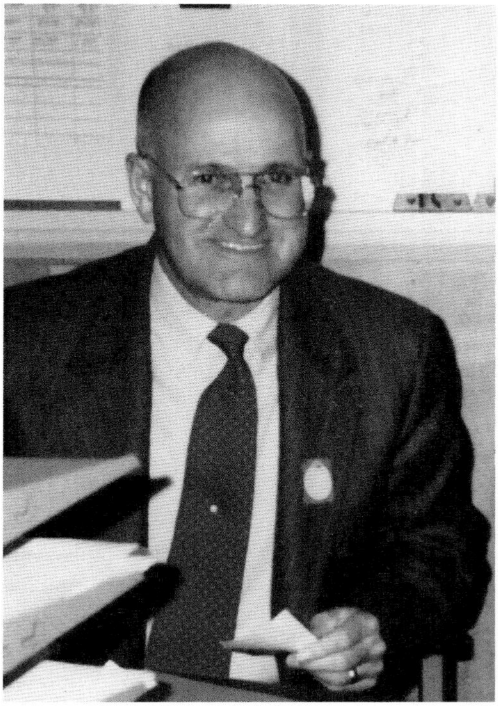

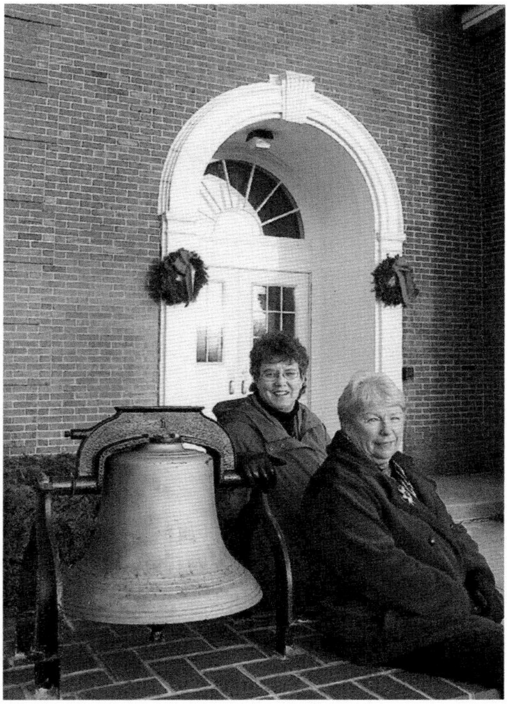

Laurence C. MacArthur (1935–1995)
As an educator in Yarmouth, Laurence MacArthur will always be remembered.

After service in the Navy, MacArthur began his teaching career in his hometown of Brockton, Massachusetts. He came to Cape Cod in 1968 to teach at the Ezra Baker School in Dennis and was named assistant principal in 1973. In 1982, he moved across the Bass River to the South Yarmouth Elementary School, where he was named principal. He served there until his untimely death in 1995.

MacArthur was known as a caring, involved principal who had a goal for his school that was unfulfilled in his lifetime but ultimately came to fruition.

MacArthur dreamed of one day finding a bell for the South Yarmouth Elementary School, which, for reasons unknown, had a belfry but no bell. After MacArthur's death, Jeanne Carrick became principal and continued the search for a suitable bell for the school, now named for MacArthur. As it turned out, there was one in the fire station in West Yarmouth. The school's belfry could not support the large brass bell, but Carrick made sure it was installed on a brick base in front of the school by the time she retired in 2003.

In 2013, the school closed due to declining enrolment. However, plans are in the works for Bridgewater State University, the school from which MacArthur received his bachelor's and master's degrees, to open a satellite campus in the building.

The bell has been moved to the Station Avenue Elementary School where MacArthur's wife, Pat, teaches. Above on the right, In 2003, Patricia MacArthur, left, and Principal Jeanne Carrick were on hand as the bell Laurence MacArthur had sought was installed at the school named for the late principal. (Left, courtesy of Patricia MacArthur; right, courtesy of the *Register.*)

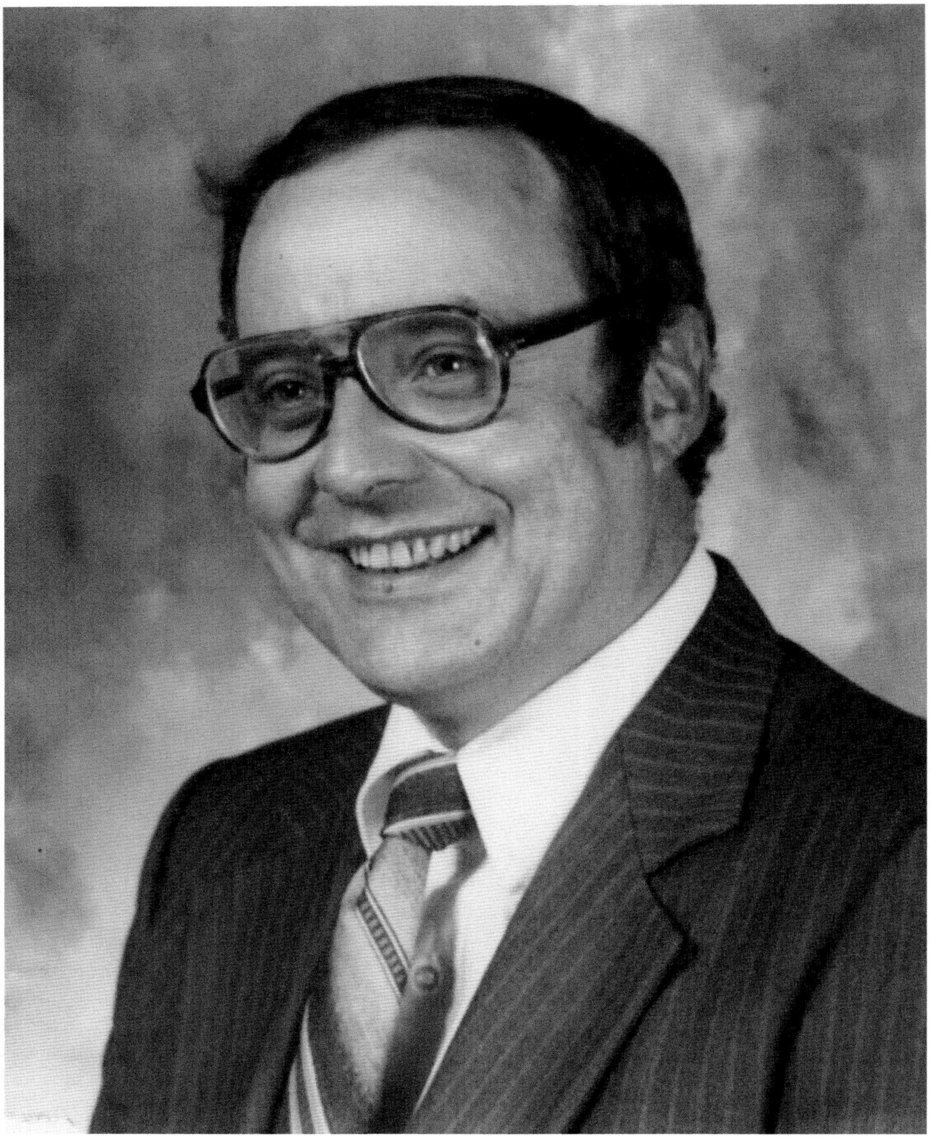

Michael McCaffrey (1941–2009)
Michael McCaffrey's devotion to education led him to the Dennis-Yarmouth Regional School District, where he was superintendent of schools from 1983 to 2001.

Born and raised in New Hampshire, McCaffrey began his career as a teacher in Groton, Vermont, while earning his master's and doctorate degrees. He became superintendent of schools in Rockport, Massachusetts, in 1978, and in 1983, he was named superintendent of the Dennis-Yarmouth School District.

During his 18 years as superintendent, the regional district underwent enormous changes as the towns of Yarmouth and Dennis experienced population growth. He guided the district at a time when spending was restricted by the passage of Proposition 2½ in Massachusetts. Even after his retirement due to health concerns, McCaffrey remained a strong supporter of public education in the Dennis-Yarmouth School District and an advocate for the Education Foundation for Dennis and Yarmouth, which supports education through private donations. (Courtesy of the McCaffrey family.)

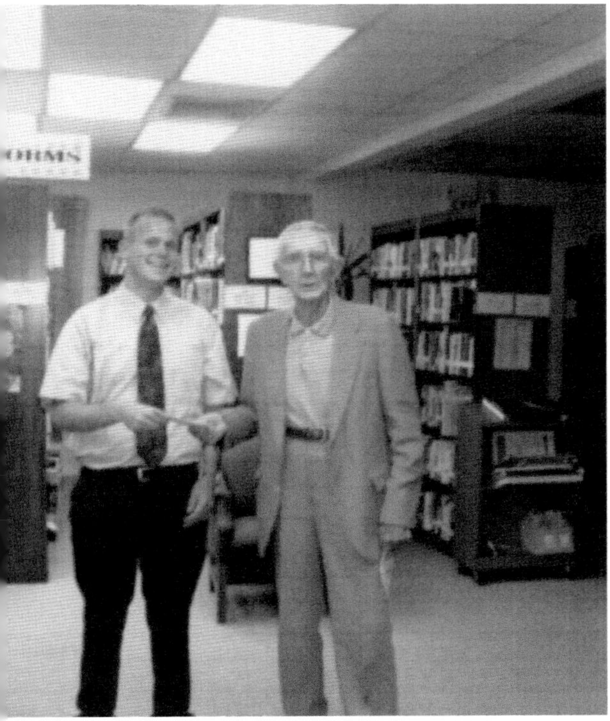

Sven Edward Siemen (1915–2008)
Sven Siemen's philanthropy will make the town a better place for generations to come.

Siemen honored his wife, Cecelia, a painter and art teacher who died in 1999, by creating a scholarship in the visual arts in her name awarded through the South Yarmouth Library Association. Each year, a selection committee chooses a promising artist to benefit from Siemen's generosity.

When Sven Siemen died in 2008, his will stipulated that additional funds be given to the South Yarmouth Library, ensuring that not only the scholarship program but also other community programs at the library will be funded well into the future.

In this photograph, Siemen presents a scholarship award to Abraham Storer in 2004. (Courtesy of the South Yarmouth Library Association.)

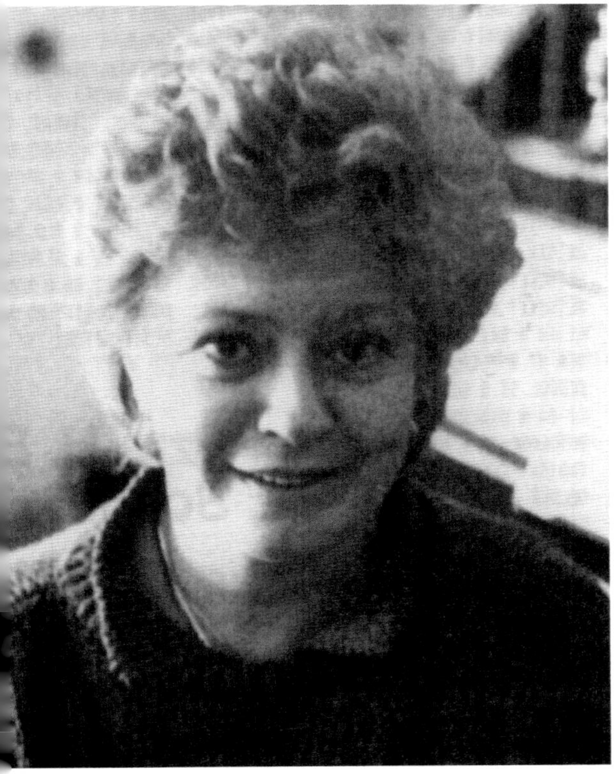

Jan Butler
Every October, Yarmouth is home to the Seaside Festival, a three-day event featuring a parade, carnival, road race, and many other attractions. And the town has Jan Butler to thank for it.

Butler is always more interested in giving the festival committee's volunteers the credit, but she was the one who got the event started. These days, thousands of visitors come to Yarmouth every Columbus Day weekend to enjoy one final weekend by the sea before the autumn chill sets in. (Courtesy of the *Register.*)

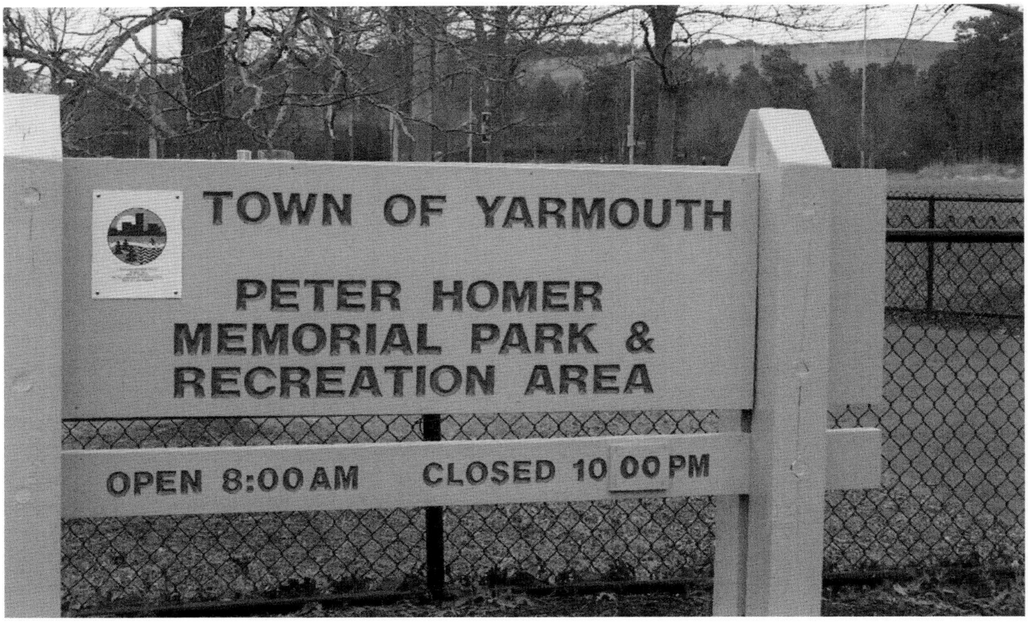

Peter Homer (1938–2003)
Peter G. Homer was a lifelong Yarmouth resident affectionately known as the town's "head garbologist," for his management of the town's landfill and later its trash transfer station.

Homer graduated from Yarmouth High School in 1956, and married his high school sweetheart, Linda. Starting in 1960, he worked in a variety of roles in town government until 1974, when he became head of the town's sanitation department. Earning another nickname, as "the dump seagull wrangler," Homer oversaw the closure of the landfill and the site's eventual conversion to a park, which won national recognition for its innovative reuse of town land.

In 2009, Homer was honored when the park he helped create was named in his honor. (Photograph by author.)

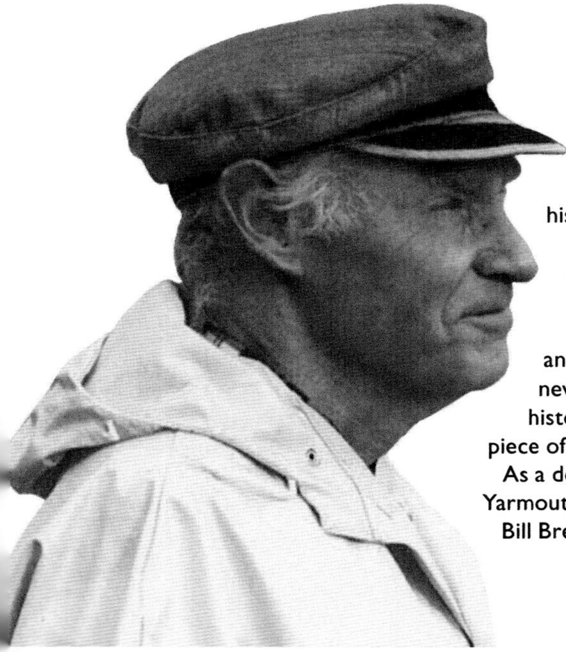

Haynes Mahoney (1920–2014)
Haynes Mahoney's career as a foreign service officer took him around the globe and, ultimately, to Yarmouth Port, where he became a scholar of local history and an author of significance.

After a stint as a reporter in Washington, DC, and service with the Army in World War II, Mahoney served in Thailand, Japan, West Berlin, and Malaysia.

Upon his retirement to Cape Cod with his wife, Kay, and their family, Mahoney, an avid and skillful sailor, began a new chapter in his life as an expert on Cape Cod's maritime history. His book *Yarmouth's Proud Packets* remains a vital piece of local scholarship.

As a devoted member of the Historical Society of Old Yarmouth, he wrote well and often on local history. (Courtesy of Bill Breisky.)

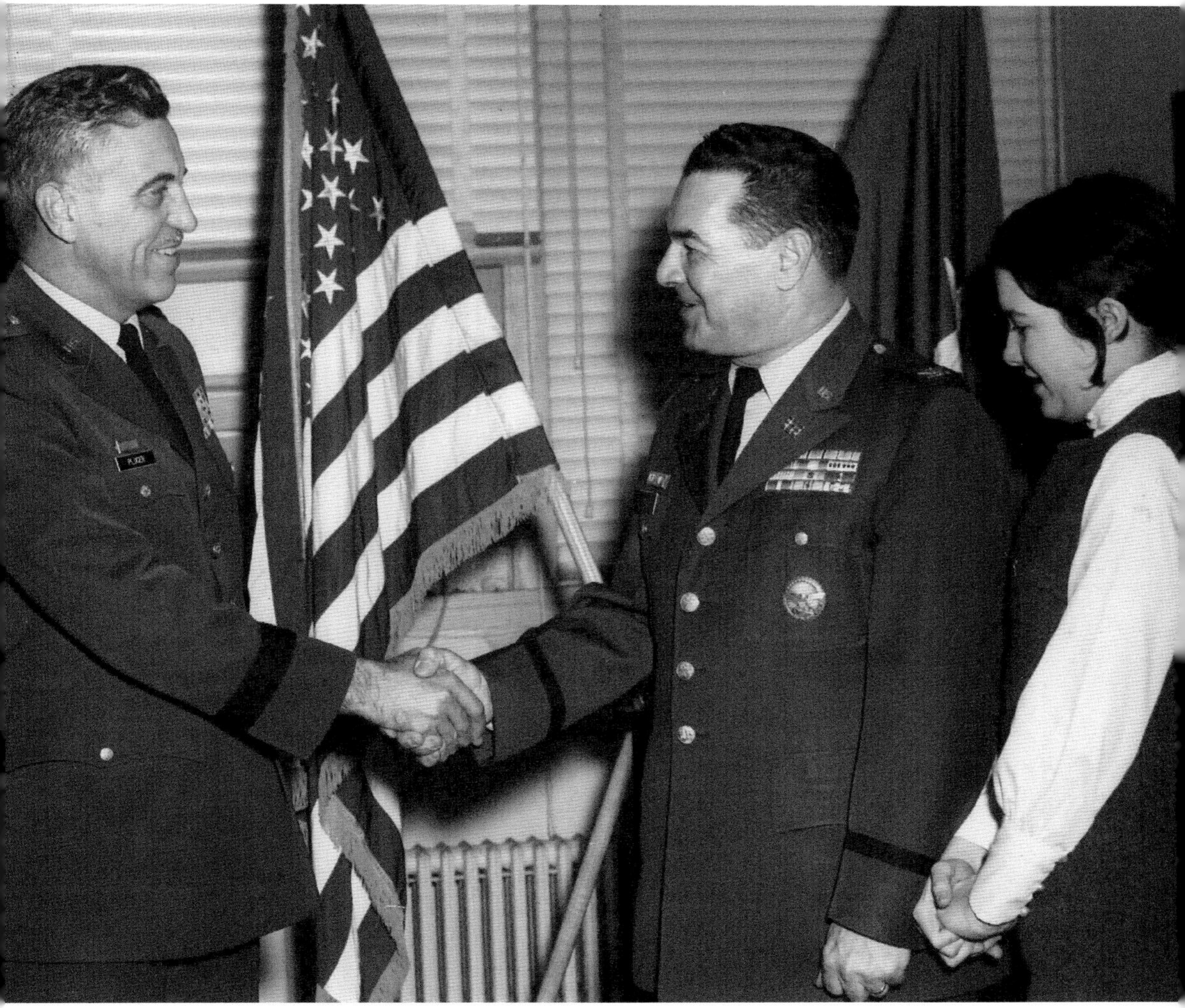

Col. Ralph Cipolla (1916–1993)

When Ralph Cipolla completed his career in the Army and retired to Yarmouth Port in 1972 with his wife, Doris, he planned to "buy a boat and go fishing." But things did not work out that way. In a few years, Cipolla found himself elected to the board of selectmen in a major upset of an incumbent at a time when Yarmouth was undergoing great change. Leading the effort to replace the full-time board of selectmen with a part-time board and a professional administrator, Cipolla often was at the center of controversy but stuck to his belief that the change was what the town needed. Serving as a selectman until 1983, Cipolla then devoted his time to various town boards, to the council on aging, and the chamber of commerce.

In 1987, more than 200 people turned out for a testimonial dinner to honor the man who, in a relatively short time in public life, had influenced Yarmouth greatly.

Here, Ralph Cipolla, second from right, is promoted to colonel in 1969 by Gen. Robert Ploger as his daughter Leslie Ann Cipolla looks on. (Courtesy of Doris Cipolla.)

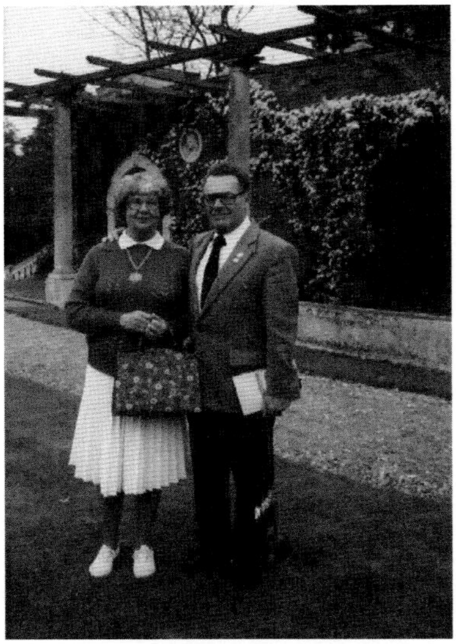

Doris and Ralph Cipolla

Not simply the wife of a popular and influential politician in Yarmouth, Doris Cipolla made an important place for herself in Yarmouth. Working with the Historical Society of Old Yarmouth, the Friday Club, and other organizations, she has been involved in projects large and small for many years.

In 1987, the Historical Society of Old Yarmouth honored her for a dozen years of service to the organization with a plaque bearing the inscription "kindness makes friends."

Doris Cipolla is also known for the tradition she began in 2005 at age 86 when she began gathering a group of friends for a dip into the ocean each New Year's Day.

"I like a challenge and I just thought it was fun and sometimes you need tradition," Cipolla said of her jaunts to the ocean. (Courtesy of Doris Cipolla.)

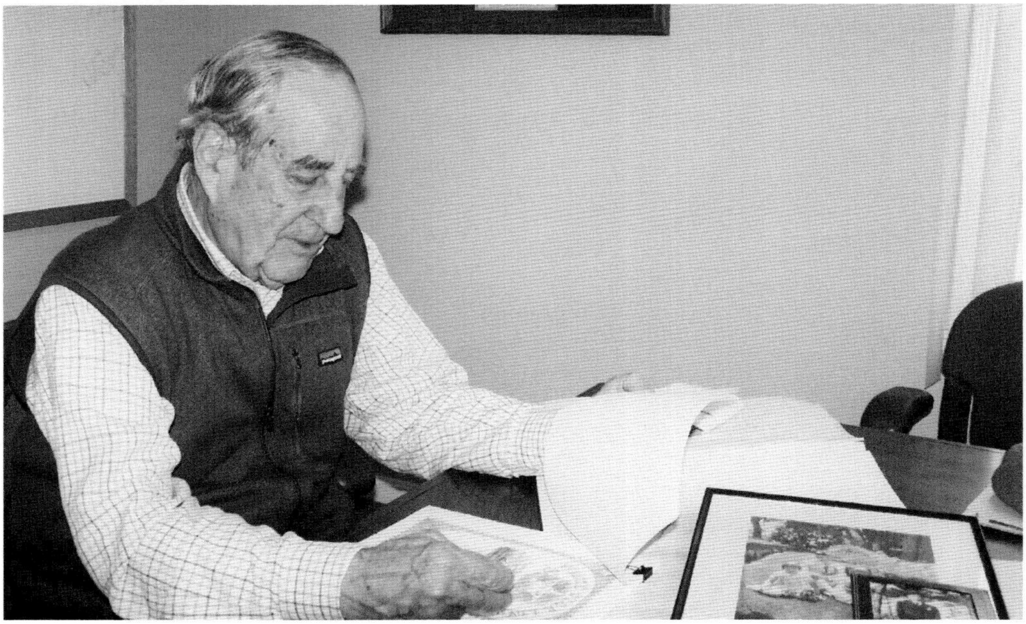

Lawrence Thacher Perera

Lawrence Thacher Perera can trace his heritage to the founding of Yarmouth. His ancestor Antony Thacher was among the first to receive land grants in what became Yarmouth.

His family tree includes not only one of the very first European settlers of Yarmouth but also some of the town's first business and political leaders and some of its most important preservationists.

Lawrence Perera is also the person most responsible for chronicling the history of the Thacher and Perera families. Perera's 2012 book *The Homestead Saga* tells not only the story of his illustrious family but also the story of the house in which he and his wife reside. It is a story centered on the Yarmouth Port Common but with roots and branches stretching to Boston, Italy, and elsewhere.

Perera, an attorney and former Probate Court judge, has also been involved in conserving much of his family's land in Yarmouth to protect it from development. (Photograph by author.)

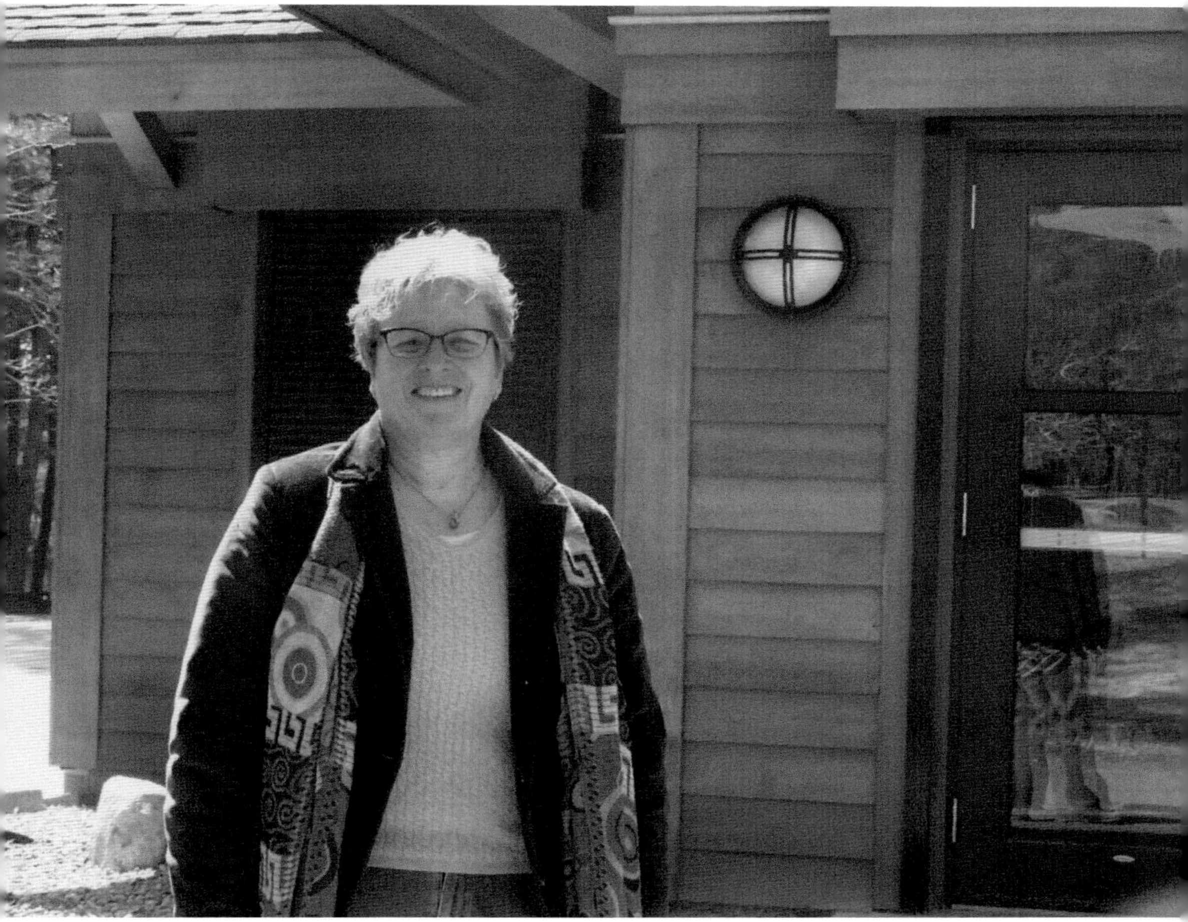

Patricia Armstrong

Patricia Armstrong is a tireless worker on behalf of the town of Yarmouth's recreation programs. Appointed in 1986 as the town's first full-time director of recreation, she served in that role until 1992, when she went to work for the YMCA of Cape Cod; was involved in private recreation-related business; and operated her own restaurant. In 1997, she returned to Yarmouth as recreation director and, since that time, has overseen the growth of the town's summer programs for residents and visitors and has redeveloped the popular Flax Pond Recreation Area.

Armstrong has been recognized by the Massachusetts Recreation and Park Association with its humanitarian award, has received the Rotary Club of Yarmouth Vocational Service Award, has served as the president of the New England Regional Council of Park and Recreation Directors, and has been president of the Yarmouth Rotary and Yarmouth Rotary Foundation.

"Even though I will always be considered a wash-ashore, I have put my heart and soul into making Yarmouth a better place to live, work and visit. The people I have had the privilege to work with and serve are some of the most interesting and generous people I have ever encountered," she said of her experience in Yarmouth. (Photograph by author.)

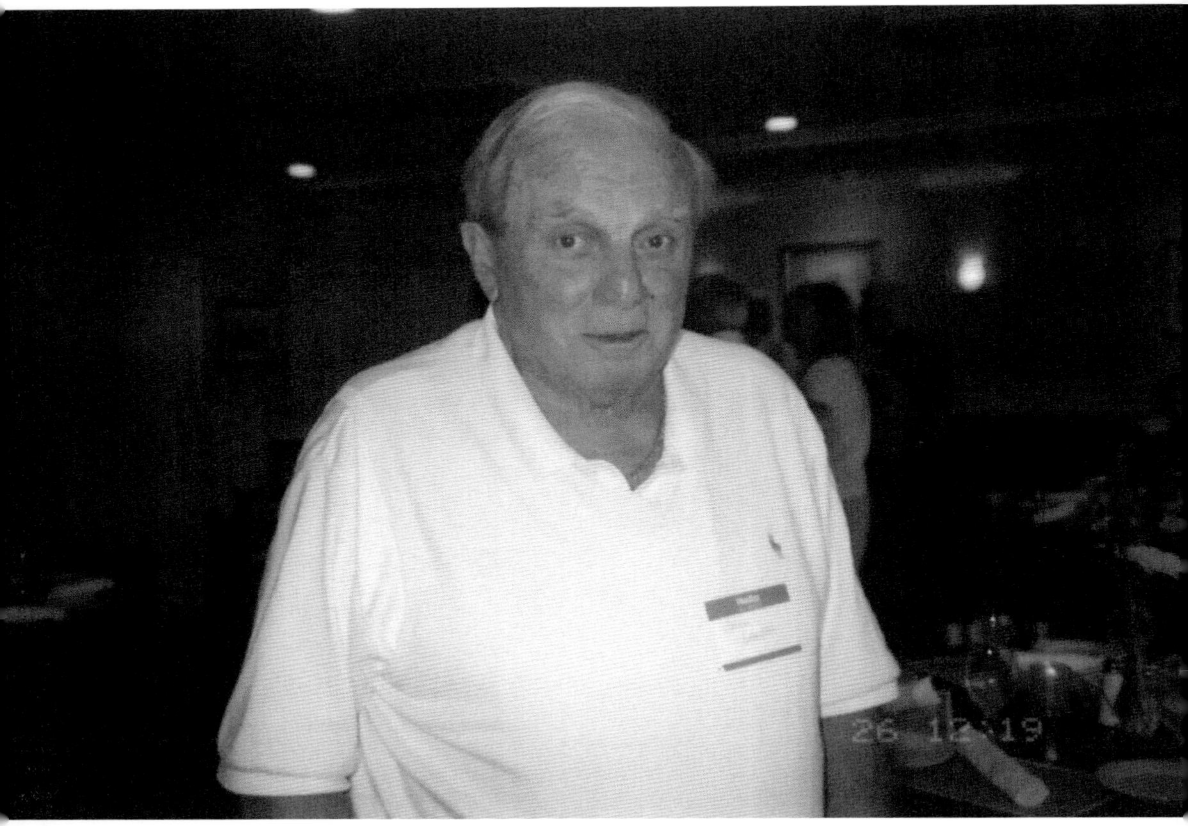

Charles Liberty

Charles "Chuck" Liberty devoted his life to education, athletics, and public service.

Before becoming an educator, Liberty was a standout athlete, starring on Yarmouth High School football, basketball, and baseball teams in the early 1950s. Attending the University of New Hampshire, he was a four-year baseball player and three-season football player. Returning to Yarmouth, he played for six seasons for the Yarmouth Indians in the Cape Cod Baseball League, which, at the time, was a town team allowed by league rules to have only three players brought in from elsewhere.

While serving in the Army from 1959 to 1963, Liberty played on the Fort Bliss team, which won the fourth Army championship. While stationed in Korea, he played on another top-notch Army team. After his active duty ended, Liberty remained in the Army Reserve. He became a teacher at the new Dennis-Yarmouth Regional High School while also serving as an assistant coach in three sports. Rising to principal, Liberty remained until 1977, when his career took him to Mashpee, where he was responsible for the building of a new middle school for that fast-growing town, something he described as, "like building a boat and seeing if it will float."

Liberty retired in 1993 but remains very busy as a volunteer for the Yarmouth-Dennis Red Sox, often greeting fans as they enter Red Wilson Field in Yarmouth. (Courtesy of Charles Liberty.)

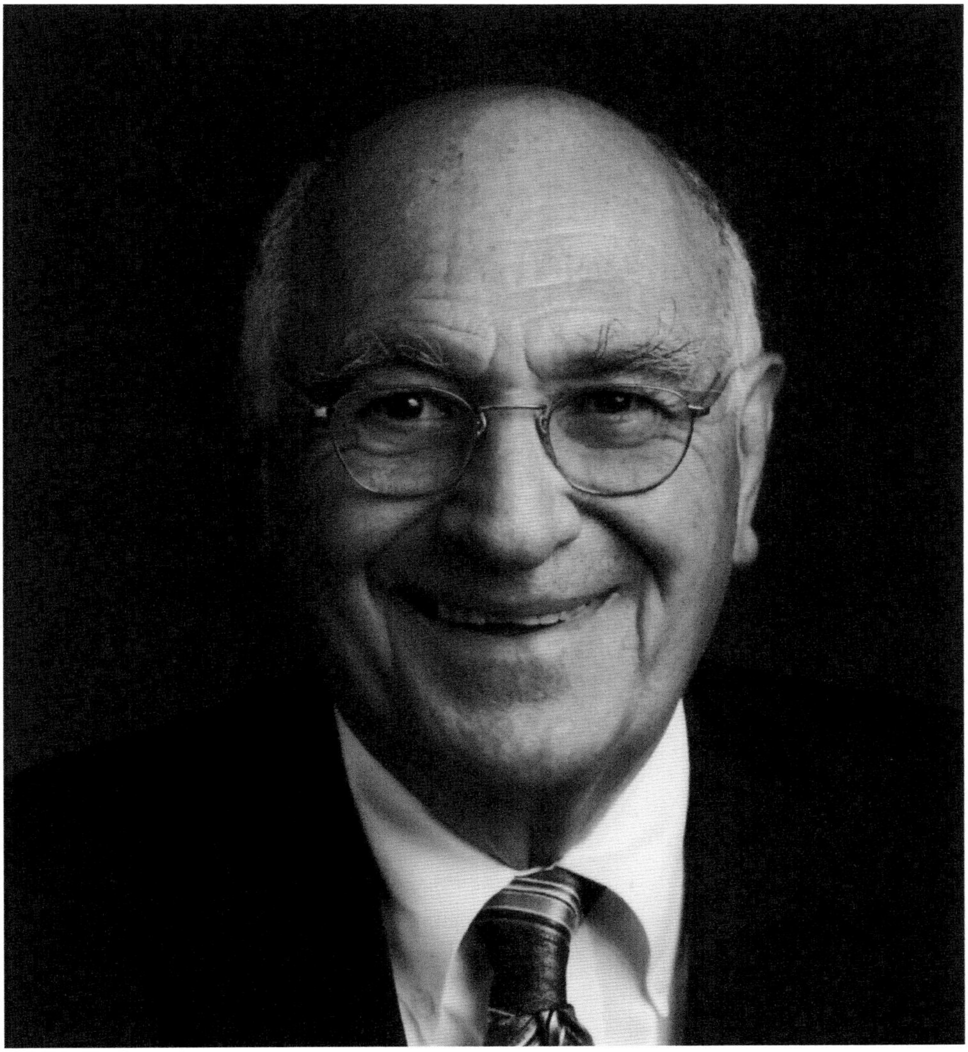

Thomas George
Thomas George is the longest-serving moderator in Yarmouth history, but it was not a position he sought.

George became moderator in 1973 when, in the midst of a town meeting, moderator James Quirk, frustrated with the way the meeting was going, abruptly resigned the position. Needing someone to run the proceedings, a vote was taken on the spot, and George was elected. He would go on to serve as moderator for 35 years.

Born and raised in Worcester, Massachusetts, George came to Yarmouth like so many others, in pursuit of a summer job. Working in restaurants for several summers in the 1960s, George met his future wife, Alice, and after service in the Army and completing law school, he settled on Cape Cod to practice law.

George became interested in Republican Party politics and was elected state representative in 1994 while remaining as Yarmouth town moderator. Serving in the Massachusetts legislature until 2003, George says he always attempted to be an advocate for his constituents while serving as their representative on Beacon Hill. (Courtesy of Thomas George.)

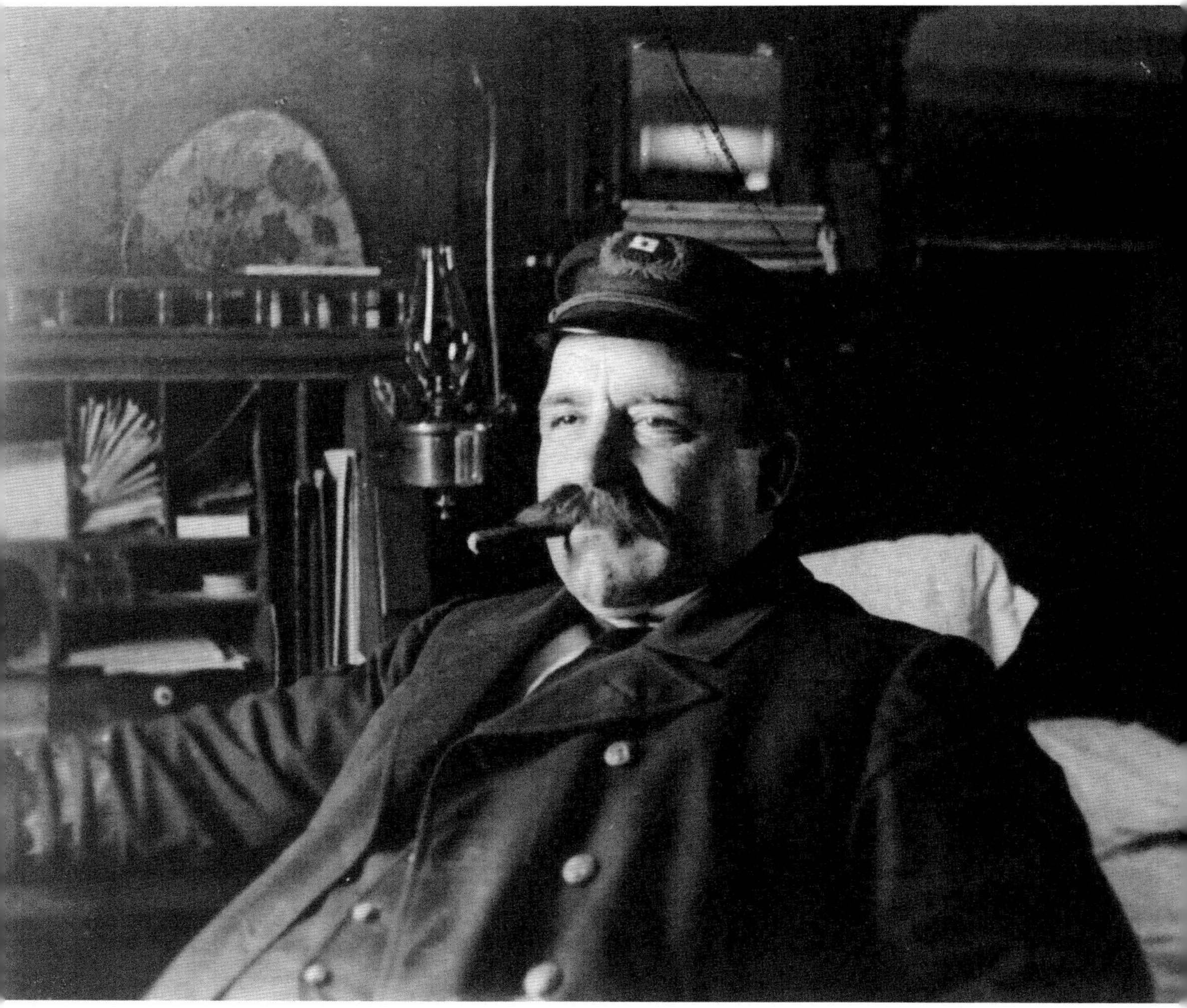

Capt. Joseph Lewis (1860–1917)
His 1917 obituary summed up the reputation of Capt. Joseph Lewis when it said he was "known to every seafaring man from Eastport to Tierra Del Fuego."

Lewis worked for many years as a wreckmaster for the Boston Towboat Company. His specialty was rescuing ships that had run aground, often helping ship owners to salvage their vessels and valuable cargo.

Lewis is known for devising an innovative way of transporting large cargoes at sea, converting out-of-date sailing ships into barges. Towing three barges at a time with a steam-powered vessel, he was able to move large amounts of coal and other bulk cargoes more efficiently. (Courtesy of the Historical Society of Old Yarmouth.)

CHAPTER FOUR

Doing the Job

With a modern-day business zone that runs parallel to the Atlantic Ocean, Yarmouth is blessed with opportunities.

Throughout the town's history, business in Yarmouth has involved the ocean and tourism. Early businesspeople made their money along the King's Highway on the north side. Today, the center of business has shifted south. Some very successful businesspeople have emerged from Yarmouth, some keeping their business close to home, others growing companies that spread far from Yarmouth and Cape Cod.

Gerry Manning is among the businesspeople who have put Yarmouth on the map. His popular restaurant featuring award-winning clam chowder is a regular stop for many visitors. The Davenport family has built homes and commercial buildings for generations and expanded its holdings into motels and other businesses. The Bilezekian family grew its Christmas Tree Shops empire from its Yarmouth home base, and in the early years of the 20th century, Charles Henry Davis engaged in business on a national scale while always returning to his home by the Bass River.

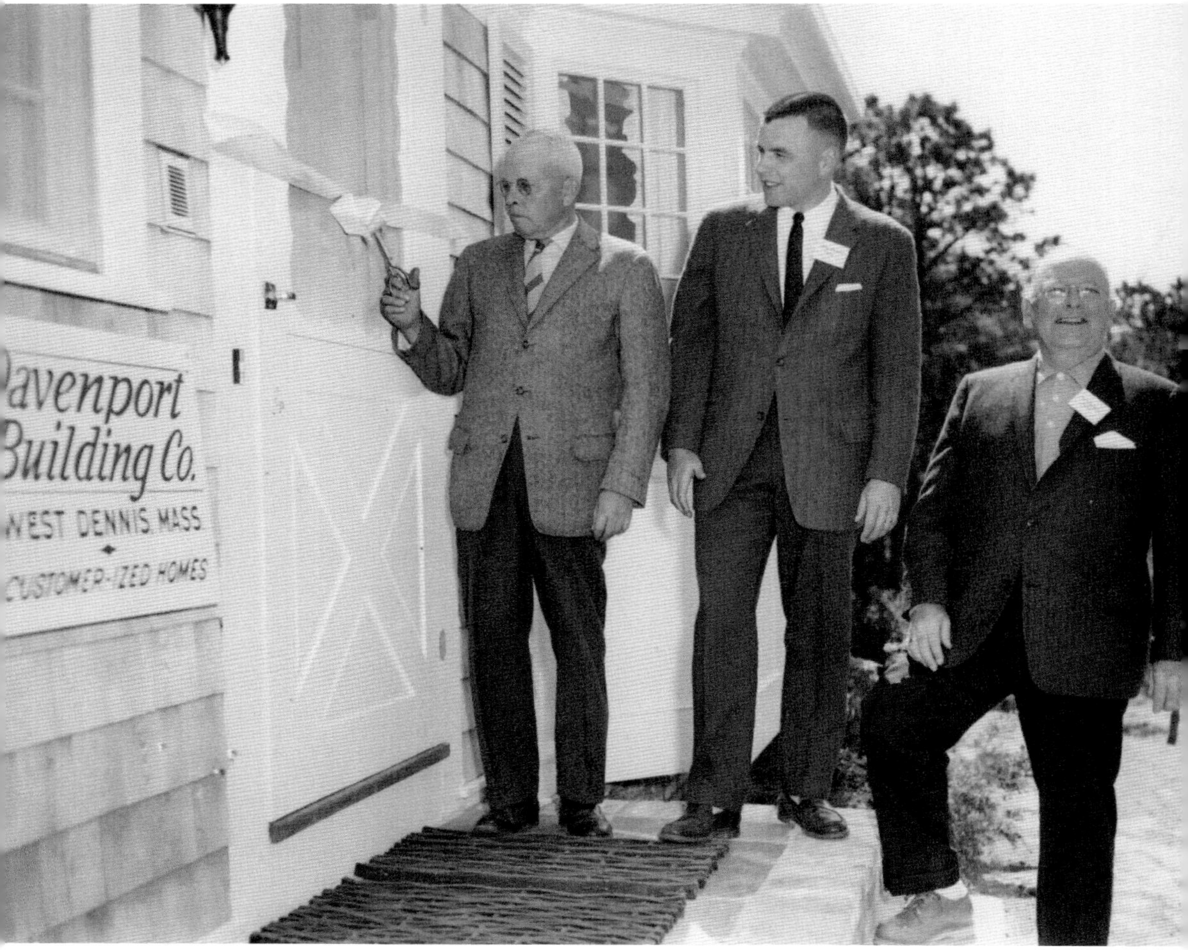

Davenport Family

Doing business in many locations, but always calling Yarmouth home, the Davenport family has been a mainstay in the business community since the 1950s.

It started in 1956 when John K. Davenport and his son Palmer built their first housing development, Wrinkle Point, just over the town line from Yarmouth in West Dennis. Following that success, additional projects followed, and in the more than half century since the first development, the company has expanded into more than a dozen ventures, including commercial and residential real estate and associated businesses, assisted living, construction, resort hotels in Yarmouth and New Hampshire, and a golf course in South Yarmouth.

The Davenport Companies is now a fourth-generation business and is still family owned, employing more than 1,300 people throughout New England. The Davenport Companies also support the community through sponsorship of the annual Seaside LeMans race, in which local businesses enter teams to compete on a race track while raising money for Cape Cod charities.

In this picture, John Davenport, right, and Palmer Davenport look on as a customer cuts the ribbon on a new home in the Davenport Company's first development at Wrinkle Point. (Courtesy of the Davenport Companies.)

DeWitt Davenport
Today, DeWitt Davenport is the president of the Davenport Companies. His son Christian has also joined the company, making it a four-generation family-owned business. (Courtesy of the Davenport Companies.)

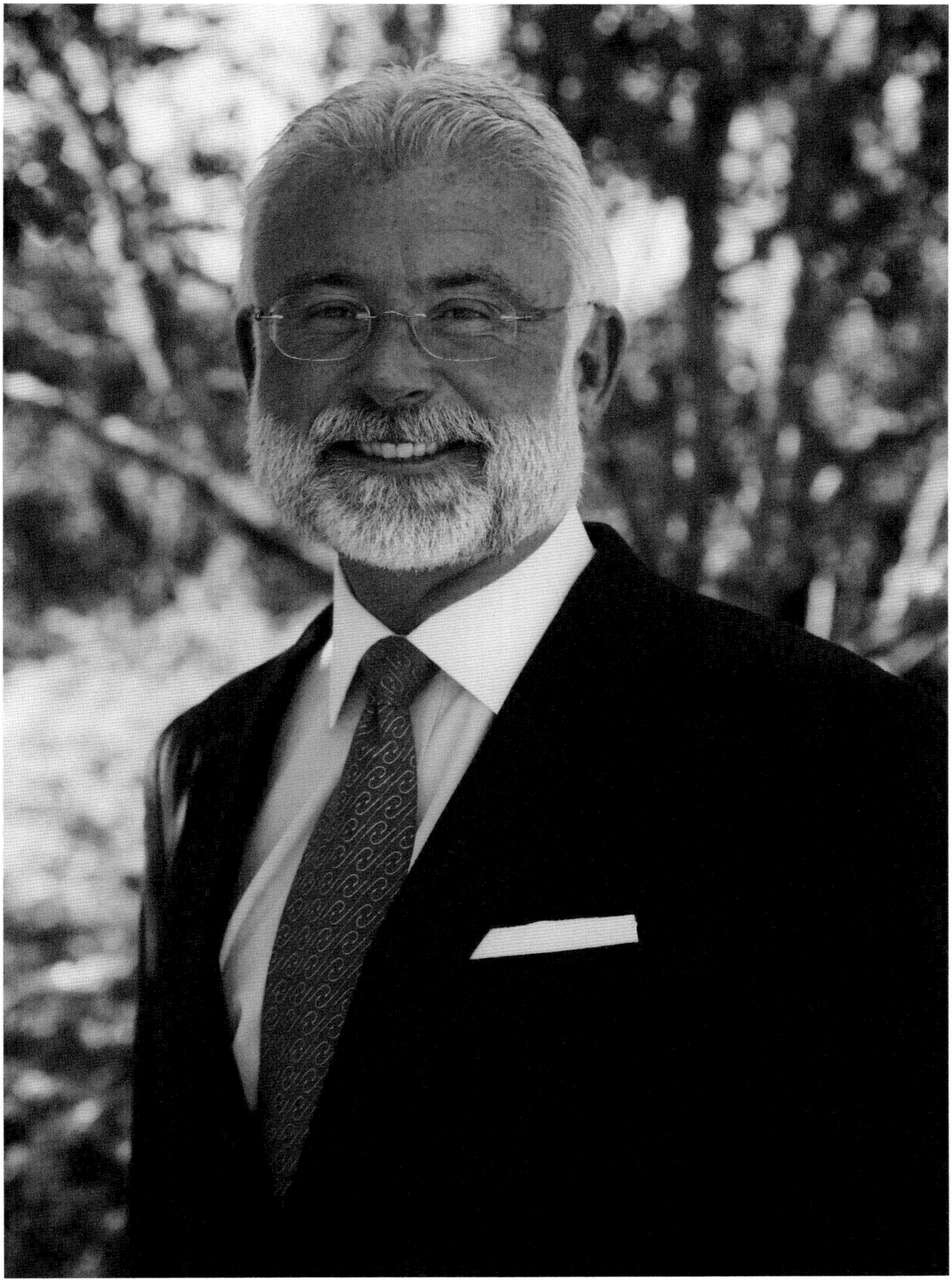

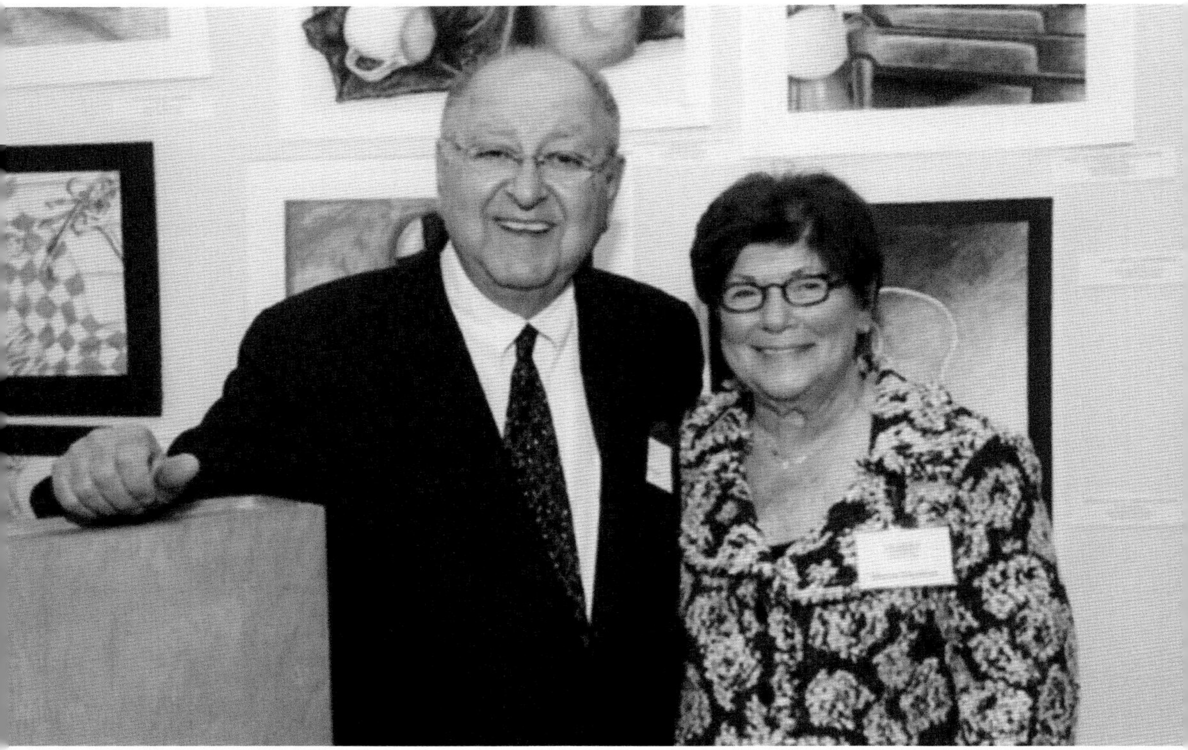

Doreen and Chuck Bilezekian

An American success story if there ever was one, Doreen and Chuck Bilezekian started a small business and ended up with a retail giant called the Christmas Tree Shops.

It was in 1970 that the Bilezekians came up with the idea of opening a store at the corner of Route 6A and Willow Street in Yarmouth Port. The store was actually a group of three small shops, hence the plural in the store's name. The upstairs of the building was also the family's home for several years as the chain began to grow. The Bilezekians quickly hit on a formula of selling inexpensive, fun items for home decorating, the kitchen, and garden. By the 1980s, the chain expanded around Cape Cod and soon well beyond the Cape.

As part of their strategy, the Bilezekians often opened stores in distinctive settings; one store has a thatched roof and another looks like a Victorian house. In 2003, the Bilezekians sold the chain to Bed, Bath & Beyond but remained involved at the executive level. In 2007, Christmas Tree Shops moved its headquarters from the former Cape Cod Coliseum building in South Yarmouth to Middleborough, Massachusetts.

As a coda to their phenomenal success story, the family returned to its roots when in 2011 the Bilezekians' son Greg opened a store called Just Picked on the site of the original Christmas Tree Shops at the corner of Route 6A and Willow Street in Yarmouth Port. (Courtesy of Heritage Museums & Gardens.)

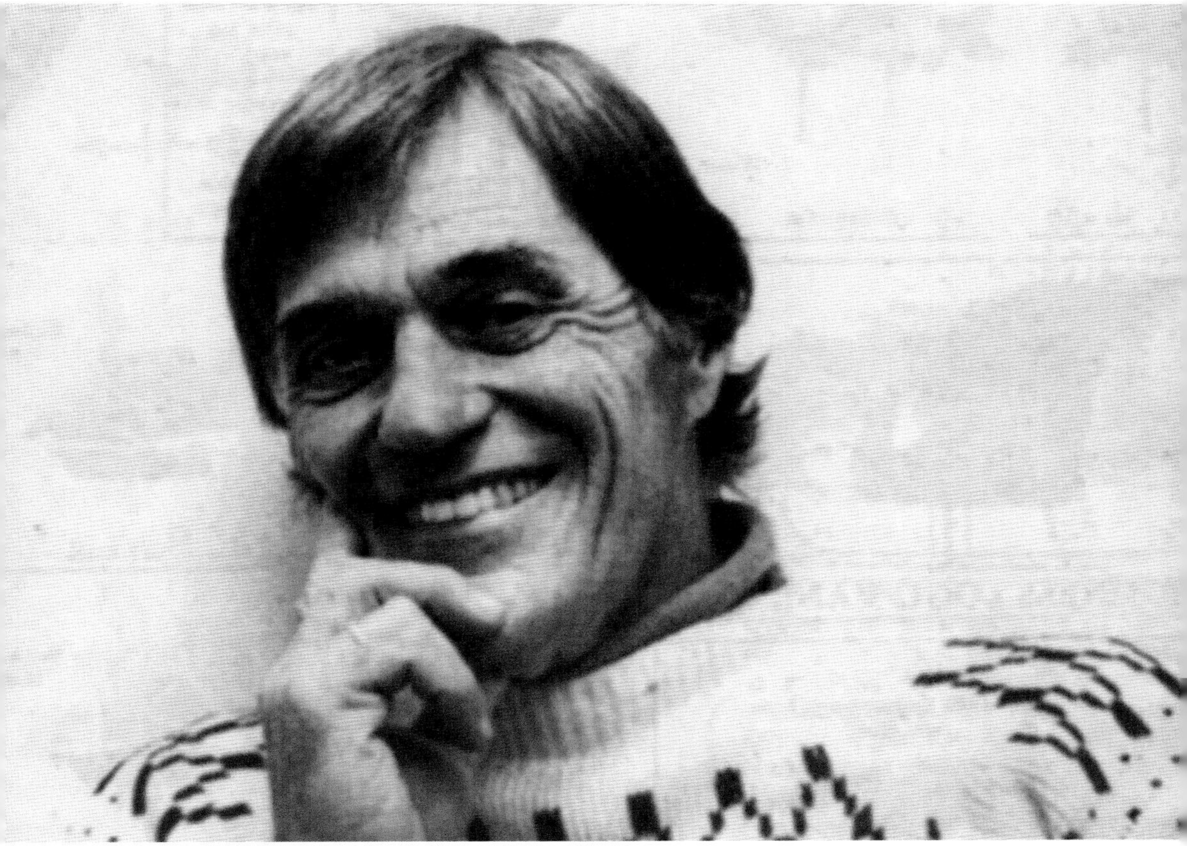

Horatio Rogers Jr. (1928–2003)
Horatio Rogers Jr., known as Ray, rescued the *Yarmouth Register* newspaper in 1956 when it was on the brink of extinction.

Rogers was the epitome of the small-town editor/publisher; he was feisty, practical, and devoted to his newspaper. Operating the paper until 1975, he guided its growth and was "an exceptional journalist, lyrical writer and insightful commentator," in the words of his successor Dana Hornig.

In a reminiscence published in 1986, Rogers said he worked for two years for a newspaper in Ashtabulah, Ohio, "in a position best described as indentured slave" before scouting out newspaper jobs on Cape Cod.

Visiting the *Register*'s offices, then on Railroad Avenue in Yarmouth Port, Rogers watched the paper coming off the printing press. "The quality of the printing was exquisite, the content somewhat bland," he wrote. The owner of the paper, Charles F. Swift, didn't offer Rogers a job but offered to sell the paper to him. Rogers agreed to work for no pay for a while to see if he wanted to buy it. "Then I bought it. Price, one dollar."

Under Rogers's stewardship, the *Register* acquired a new printing press, relocated to more modern offices, and purchased its first computer, affectionately named Igor. "Every now and then it would write its own stories and we would have to call the manufacturer to discipline it," Rogers wrote.

The *Register* became a thriving local institution under Rogers's ownership. In 1975, he passed the *Register* on to Barry Paster and Dana Hornig. (Courtesy of the *Register*.)

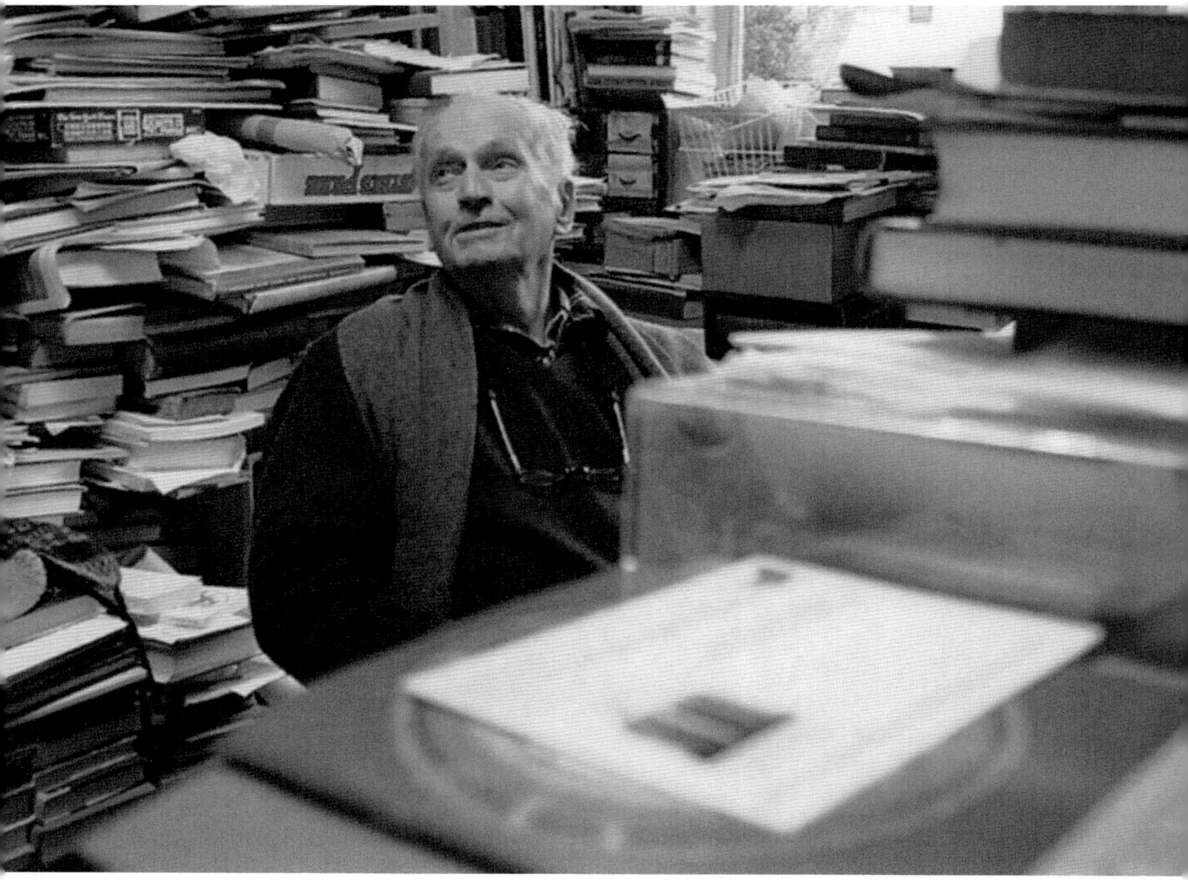

Ben Muse (1927–2012)

Known as the proprietor of Parnassus Book Service, the iconic bookstore at the bend of Route 6A in Yarmouth Port, Ben Muse was devoted to his wife, Ruth (MacEachern), and their eight children, his books, and his community.

One of the three "Grumpy Old Men of Yarmouth Port" along with artist Edward Gorey and restaurateur Jack Braginton-Smith, Muse was often inscrutable in his business dealings—he sometimes seemed to want to hold on to books more than sell them—and was a knowledgeable bibliophile, a local historian, and longtime volunteer at local libraries in need of assistance.

Born in Paris, he lived in South America and Virginia as a child and came to Cape Cod almost by chance when he and his wife bought a house while on a weekend visit to the Cape to visit Ruth's parents.

Parnassus Book Service started out small but grew to become one of the more prominent used book shops in New England. For all his years of devotion to the book trade, Muse said Parnassus was "just a book shop by the side of the road." (Courtesy of the *Register*.)

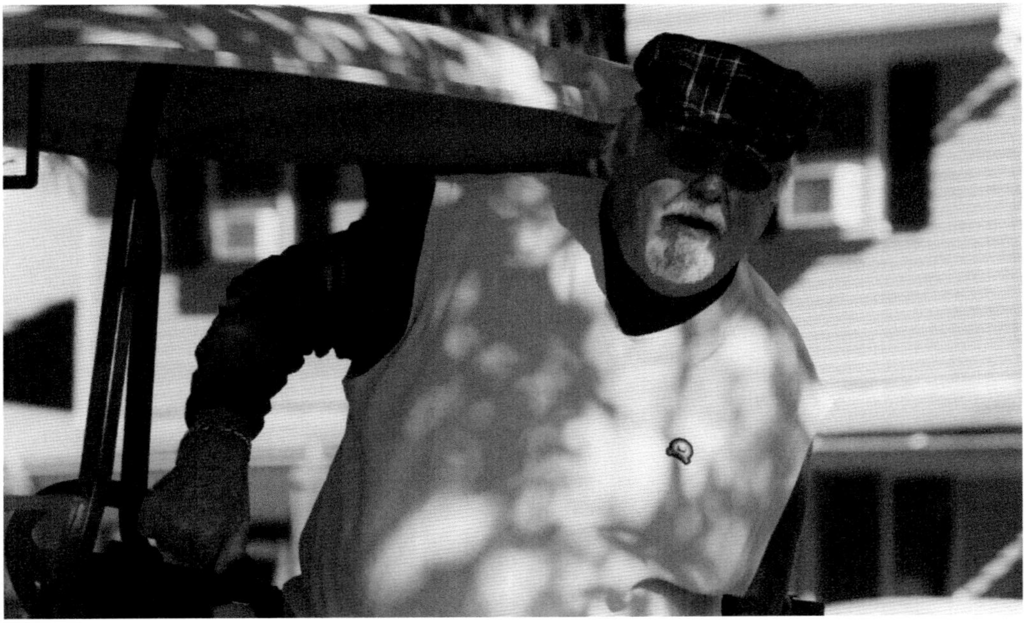

Tom Martin
If golf is Yarmouth's top business in the 21st century, then Tom Martin is among the people who made that happen.

Through his company Tee Ball Golf, founded in 1989, Martin markets golf on Cape Cod, and in particular in Yarmouth, to people around the world. Today, his business has evolved into one in which he works with local hotels to develop packages built around golf. He also started the annual Hickory Heritage Media Golf Classic as a way of promoting golf and Cape Cod.

Martin grew up in Yarmouth and graduated from Dennis-Yarmouth Regional High School in 1961, a member of the first class to have completed four years in the then-new school. (Courtesy of Tom Martin.)

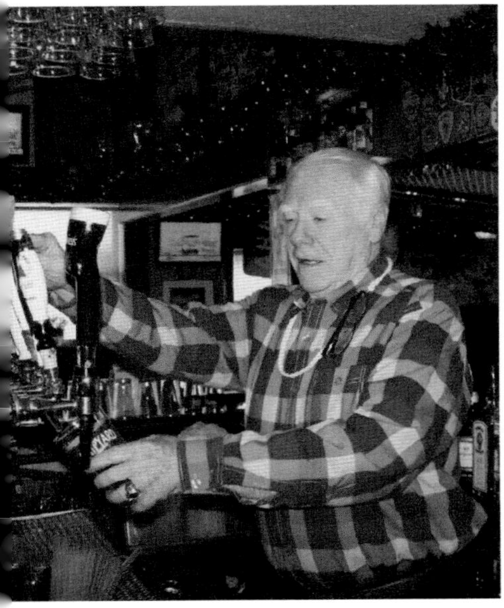

Gerry Manning
Gerry Manning is perhaps responsible for drawing more hungry people to Yarmouth than any other restaurateur. Manning's extremely popular restaurant Captain Parker's Pub is situated alongside Parker's River in West Yarmouth, but people flock there for more than the spectacular view. For many, it is the award-winning clam chowder that keeps them coming back.

Captain Parker's chowder, developed over more than 30 years, has won the title of top chowder on Cape Cod eight times, the Boston Chowder Festival title six times, and the Newport Chowder Festival title three times.

Manning, who was a schoolteacher in Boston, landed in Yarmouth almost by accident. When a friend told him about a beautiful location for a restaurant that was available, Manning decided to indulge his lifelong interest in the restaurant business and try his hand as a pub owner. Today, Captain Parker's is an essential stop on Cape Cod for visitors and locals alike. (Photograph by author.)

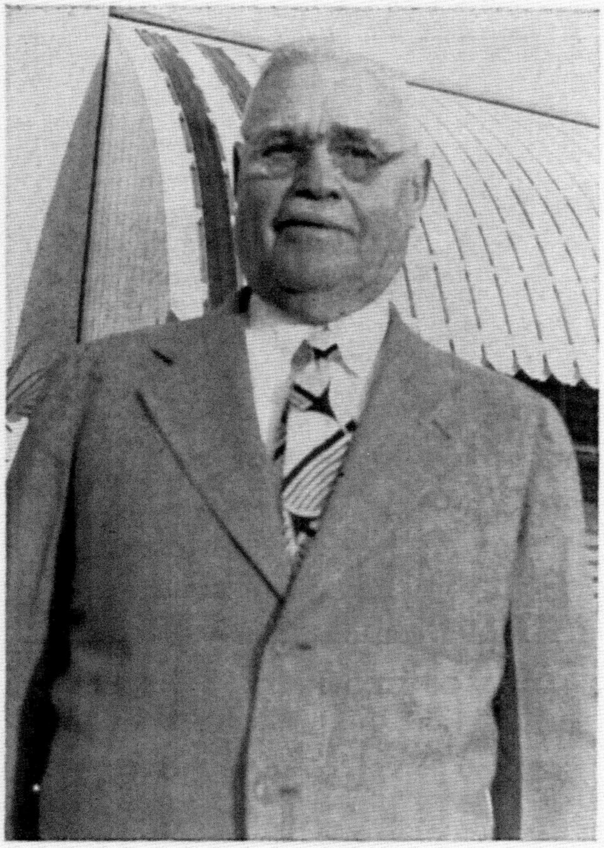

1901 - 1950

FIFTY years ago Mr. P. T. Morin came to the Englewood Beach development, and its new hotel, for his first season. He was associated with a partner for only two years, and in 1903 he leased it alone. In 1912 he bought it from the Englewood Beach Associates and with his family continued what was to be fifty years of service to vacationers on Cape Cod.

Page 1

P.T. Morin

For nearly 60 years, generations of one family operated one of West Yarmouth's vacation destination places, the Hotel Englewood.

At the turn of the 20th century, French chef Philias T. Morin, known almost exclusively as "P.T.," came to work at the Englewood. In 1903, he leased the place as the sole operator. In 1912, he became its owner and began making improvements, adding a new kitchen, installing electric lights, and building cottages adjacent to the 25-room hotel. A 1930 expansion added 14 guest rooms, a large first-floor lounge, and an additional porch to allow guest to better enjoy the sea air.

The Hotel Englewood attracted an upscale clientele in the days when travel to Cape Cod was still a difficult task involving train travel to Hyannis and local transport to the beach. Stays were lengthy, usually two weeks at least, and guests enjoyed seven-course meals at breakfast, lunch, and dinner.

The house regulations cautioned that "guests are requested to see that their children do not make any unnecessary noise at all times; especially do not let them run in the halls in the morning or afternoon." (Courtesy of Anne Morin McNamara.)

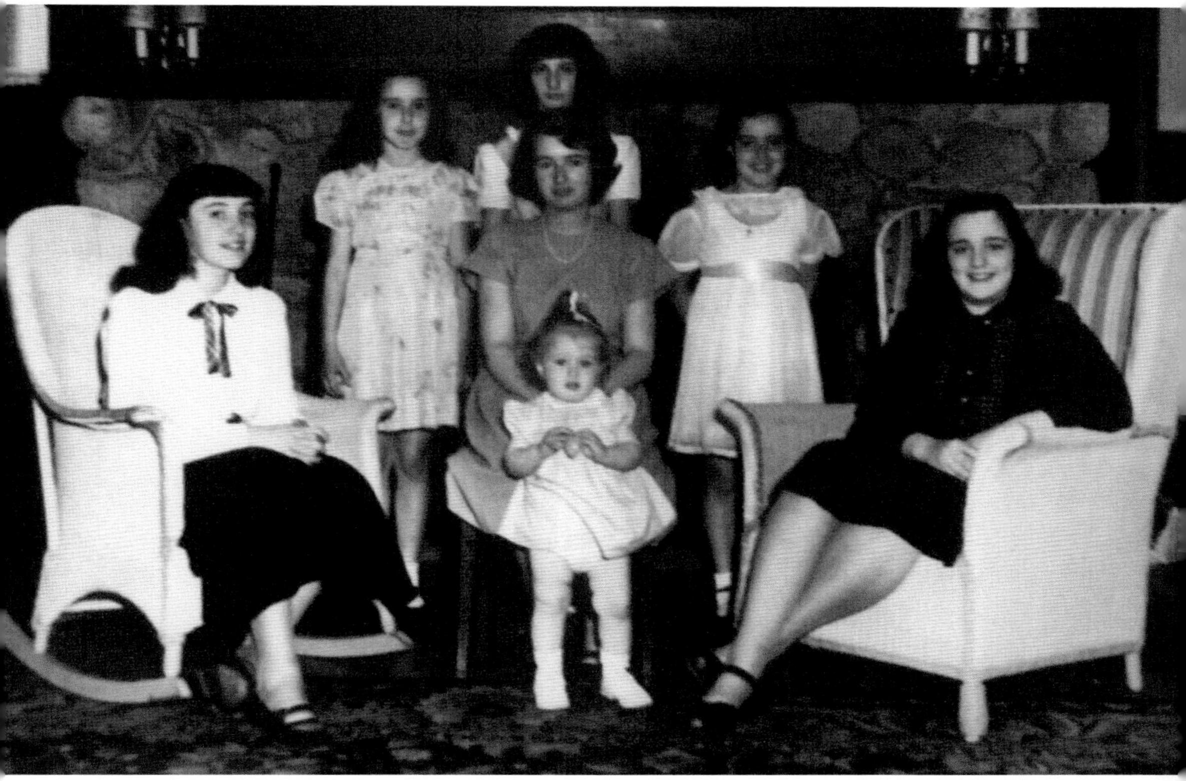

Morin Family

Members of the Morin family lived nearby and were active in the Hotel Englewood's operation. In 1945, P.T. Morin turned over operation of the hotel to his three children, sons Francis and Hobart Morin and daughter Pauline Cassen.

Pictured in the Englewood's lobby in the 1950s are, from left to right, (sitting) Anne, Helene with young Beth, and Mary; (standing) Agnes, Kay, and Peggy.

When the highway came to Cape Cod, guests began arriving by car, tourism changed, and stays began to be shorter. A new generation of summer visitors wanted a more fast-paced vacation than what the old seaside hotels like the Englewood offered.

The Morin family sold the hotel in 1960, ending an era. In January 1962, the old hotel was destroyed in a fire that newspaper accounts say was battled by more than 100 firefighters from nine communities. New summer accommodations were built on the Englewood site, with none of the grandeur of the old hotel. (Courtesy of Anne Morin McNamara.)

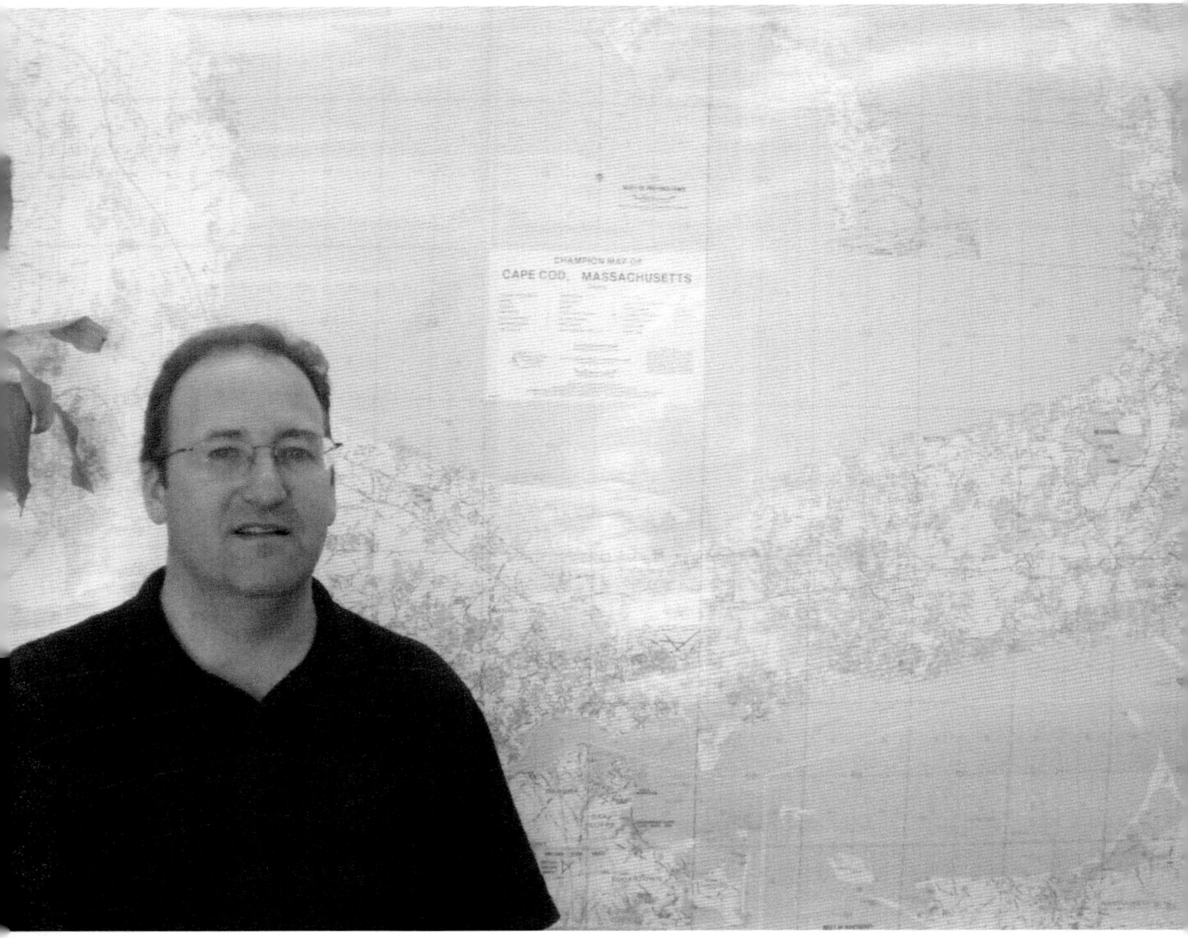

Robert Dubois

Bob Dubois did not set out to make Yarmouth his home for nearly a quarter of a century—things just worked out that way.

Dubois, an upstate New York native, came to Yarmouth in 1990, joining the chamber of commerce as its executive director for what he thought would be a three- or four-year commitment. He never dreamed he would remain until 2013.

What he encountered in his early years on the job was a chamber of commerce not always in sync with the town's political leaders or its residents. "We went on a many, many year education program," he told an interviewer about the chamber's work to convince leaders to take advantage of Yarmouth's reputation as a summer destination.

When he arrived, having a functioning 800 number was a key to success for the chamber. As he left, one of his last major projects was to redesign the Yarmouth Area Chamber of Commerce website to help the town's businesses compete in the 21st century. (Courtesy of the *Register.*)

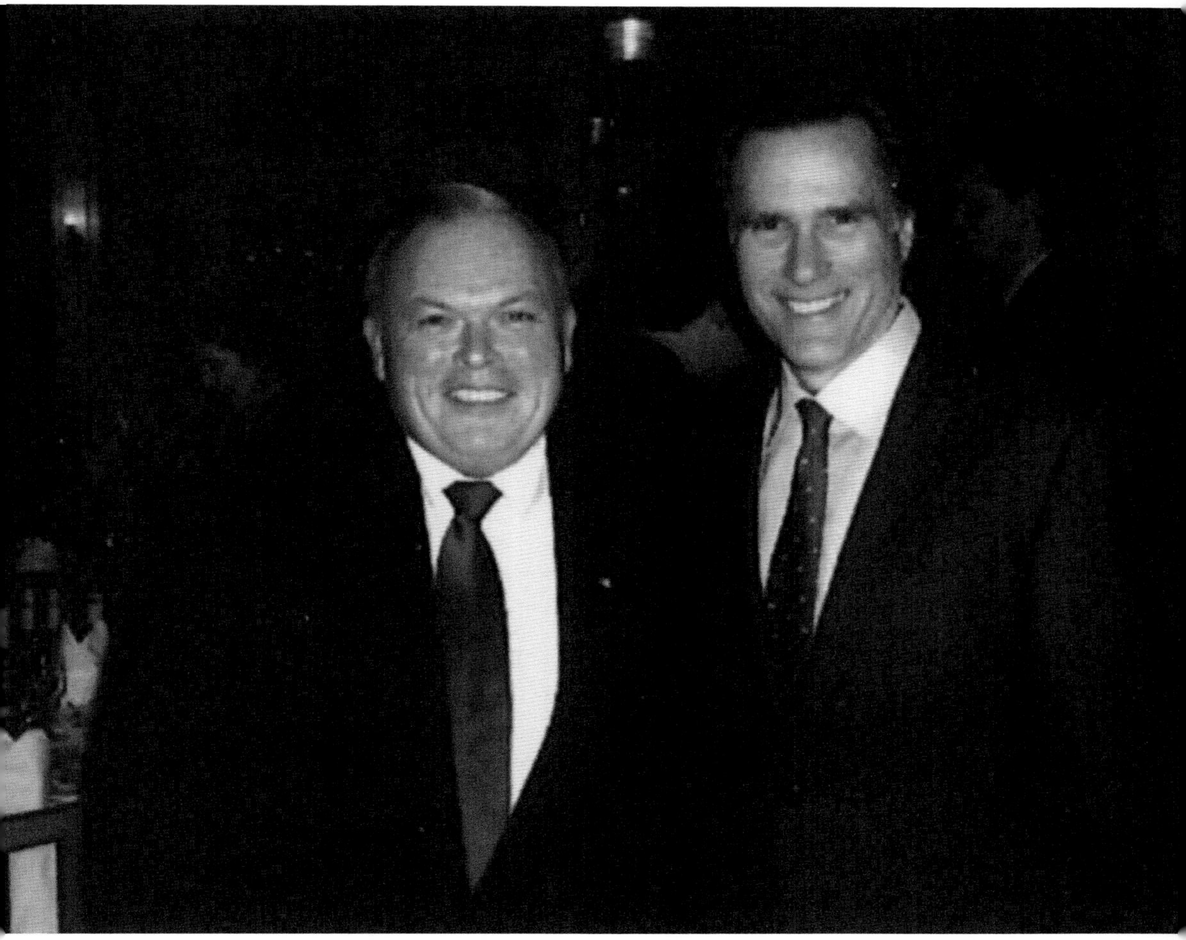

Dick Neitz

Shown here with former Massachusetts governor and presidential candidate Mitt Romney, Dick Neitz has owned and operated a successful real estate office in South Yarmouth since 1971.

In addition to his business, Neitz also finds time to serve his community. His list of accomplishments includes a term as president of the Cape Cod and Islands Association of Realtors, service as an associate member of the Yarmouth Zoning Board of Appeals, a term on the Cape Cod Economic Development Council, an appointment to the Massachusetts Board of Registration of Real Estate Brokers and Salesmen, and a term as president of the Cape Cod Chamber of Commerce. Neitz also serves on the board of the John F. Kennedy Hyannis Museum. His political interests were evident when he twice ran as a Republican candidate for state representative and in his service as the federal political coordinator for the National Association of Realtors. (Courtesy of the *Register*.)

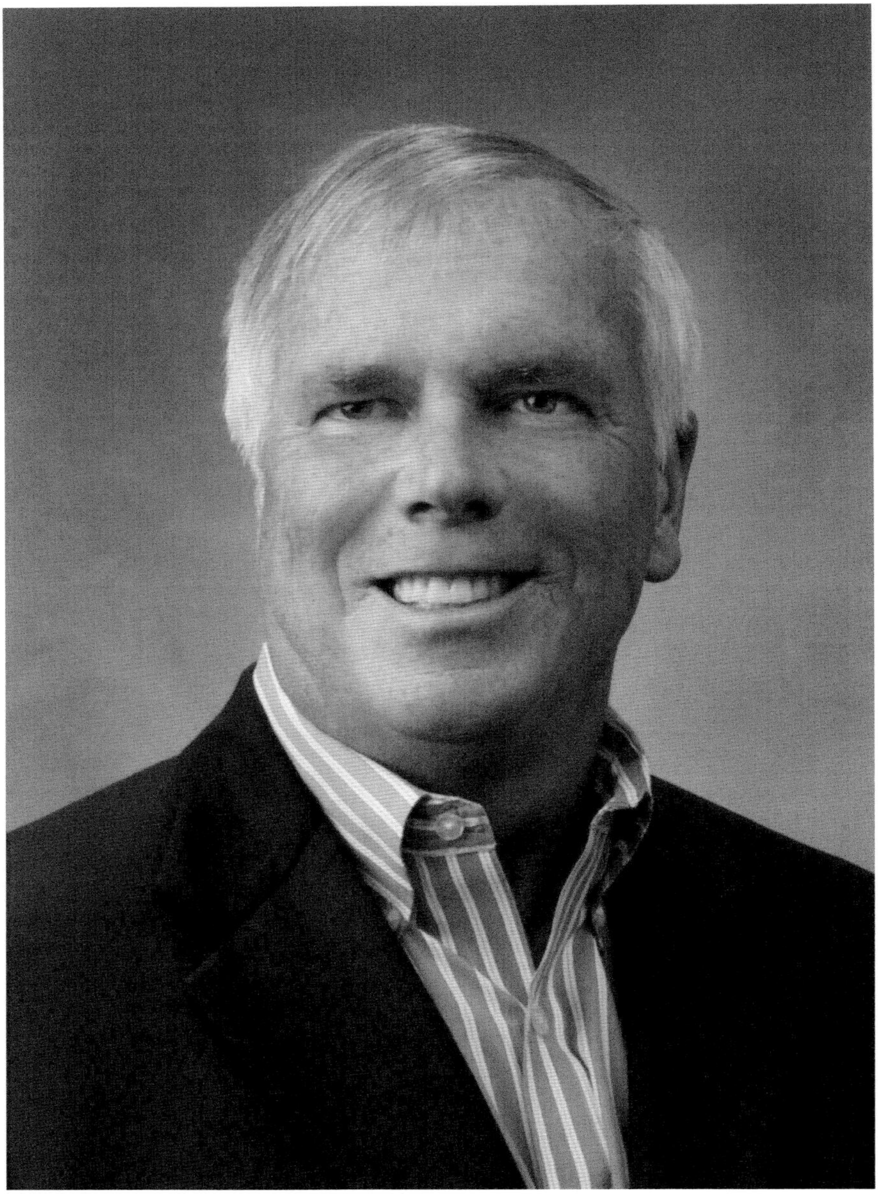

Dick Martin

Dick Martin combines a sharp business sense with a concern for his town and its natural environment.

Over nearly 40 years, Martin has operated one of the more successful real estate offices on Cape Cod. He has sold more than 4,000 properties and become a highly respected member of his profession, named Realtor of the Year in 1999 by the Cape Cod and Islands Association of Realtors.

In his municipal activities, Martin is equally successful. He has served as chairman of the Yarmouth Planning Board and has served on the land and beach acquisition committees, the Commercial Design Review Committee, the Route 28 Task Force and on the Yarmouth Land Bank. Martin has also been a trustee of the Yarmouth Conservation Trust and received the Paul E. Tsongas Environmental Recognition Award in 2000. (Courtesy of Dick Martin.)

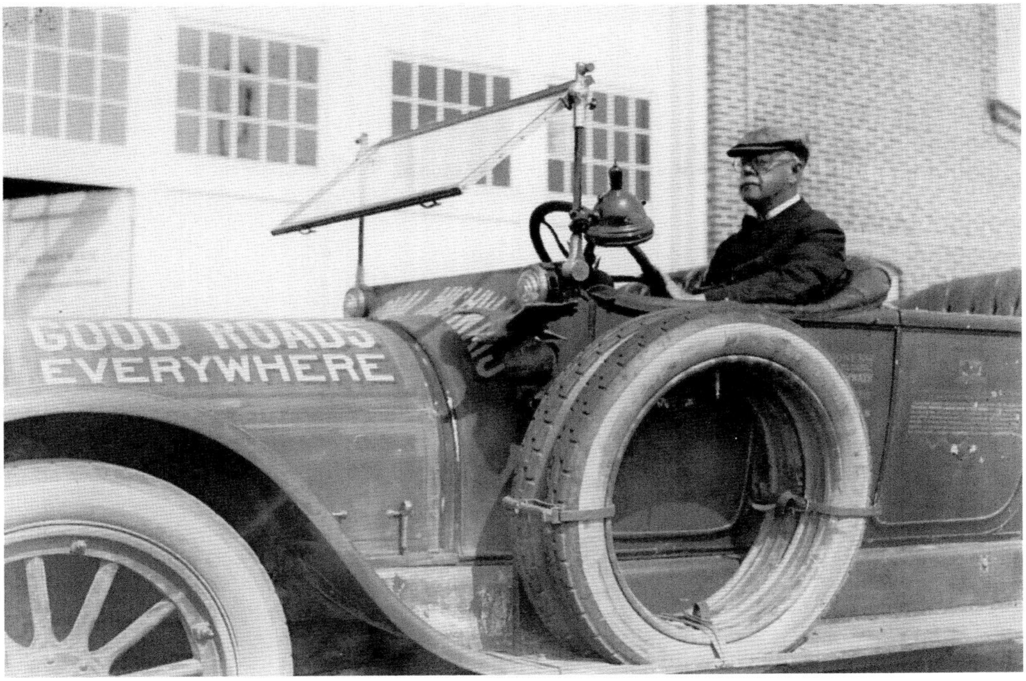

Charles Henry Davis (1865–1951)
Philanthropist, businessman, yachtsman, Quaker, and most of all, visionary are all titles that can be applied to Charles Henry Davis.

Davis was raised in a Quaker family in Philadelphia, and by the time he was a young man, he had adopted South Yarmouth as his home. A man of means, he inherited the American Road Machine Company, had extensive mining interests, and built the first high-speed tram linking Washington, DC, and Mount Vernon, Virginia.

His passion was boats, first sailing craft and later powerboats, which he raced in the waters off Yarmouth. He founded the Bass River Yacht Club primarily as a facility to house his own vessels.

Davis was a visionary when it came to the role the automobile would play in American life. A cofounder of the National Highways Association, which advocated for the construction of interstate highways, he also designed what is believed to be the nation's first traffic circle and had it built near his home in the Bass River area of Yarmouth, then known as the Lower Village.

Davis's home just opposite the Bass River was, and still is, known as the House of the Seven Chimneys. In 1972, Ted Frothingham, a neighbor of Davis, described the house: "The home itself was at one time a single unit made up of three old Cape houses and a barn that were artistically connected together to form the whole. Later, when the six daughters were born, a sleeping porch and runway were added to make the house complete a square with a courtyard in the center. The huge barn doors gave onto this square which was at once a garden and a courtyard." The house had 217 windows and 17 doors.

"There was no electricity in the whole establishment. Lighting was by hundreds of oil lamps and as many candle lanterns," Frothingham wrote. "Seven Chimneys had at least twice that number of open fire places, each one unique in its mantel, hearth, and surrounding architecture."

The House of the Seven Chimneys has since been divided into separate parts, some moved off the original site. Today, Charles Henry Davis is remembered in Yarmouth mainly as one of the many colorful characters who called the town home and for the traffic circle still in use near his grand Cape Cod house. (Courtesy of the Federal Highway Administration.)

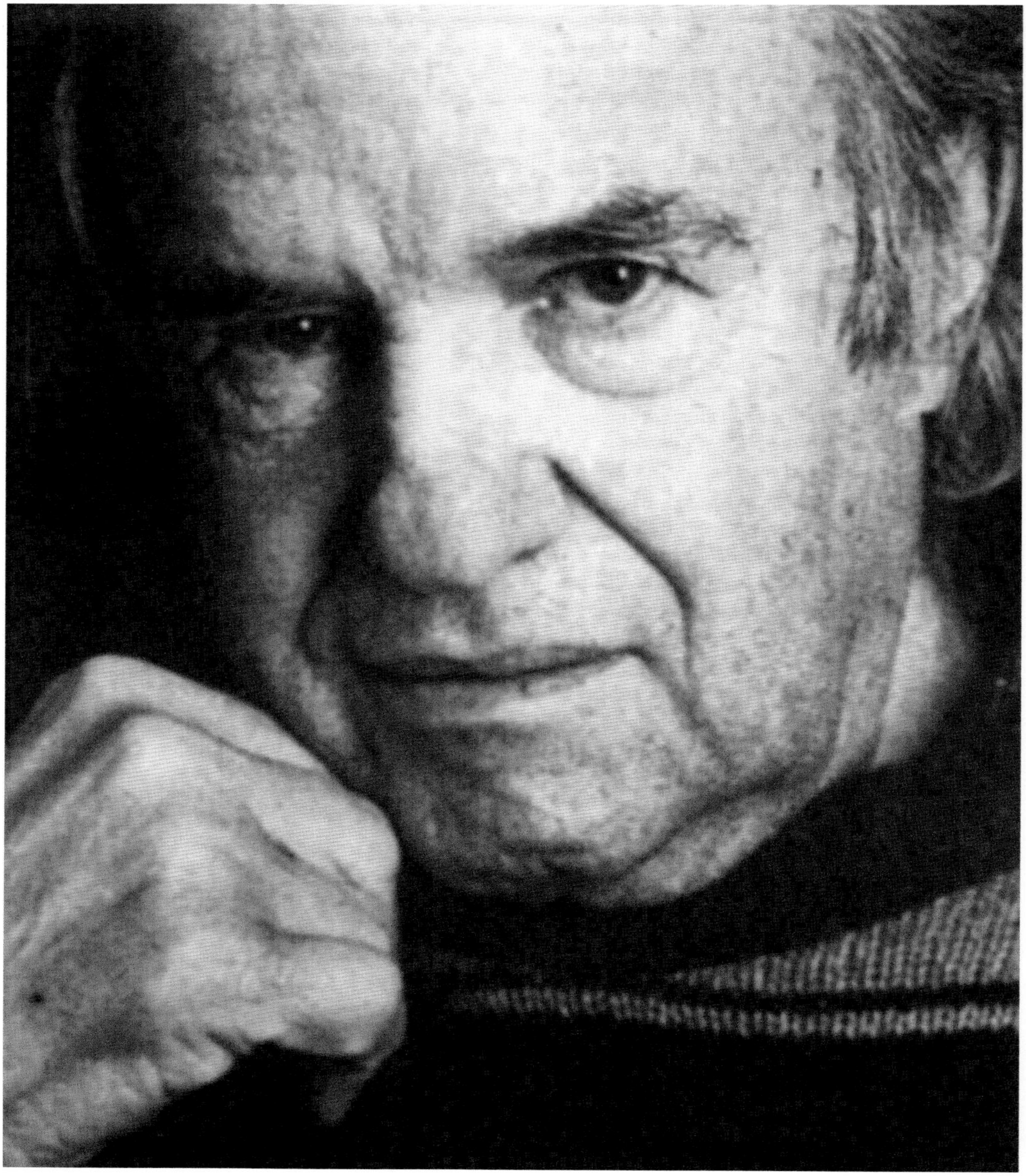

Charles Swift (1920–1991)

Charlie Swift operated the *Register* newspaper from the 1940s to the mid-1950s at a time when the paper had limited circulation and a small advertising base. The grandson of Charles F. Swift, who took over ownership of the paper in 1849, and the son of Charles Warner Swift, Charles Swift was trained as a printer, not a journalist, and he never had ambitions to be a journalist. However, when he inherited the paper he saw the need to keep it operating as a community resource, finally turning it over to Ray Rogers Jr. in 1956. (Courtesy of the *Register*.)

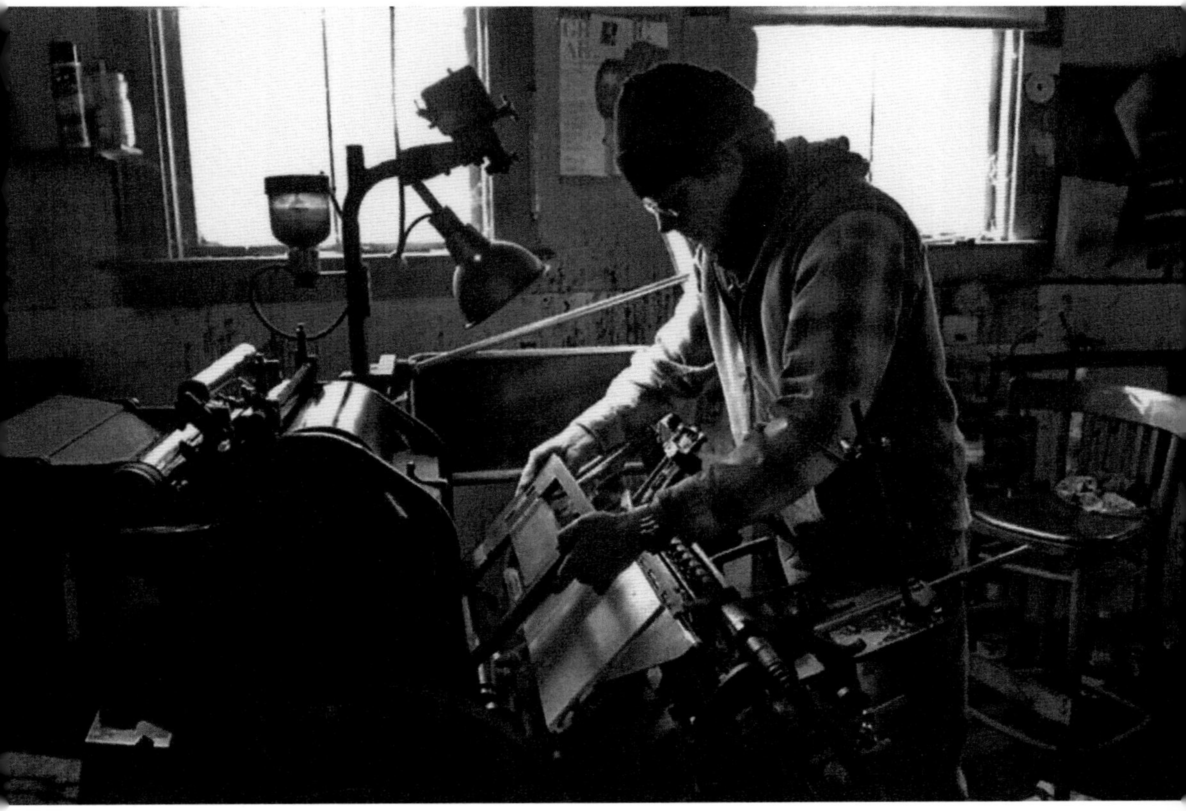

David Swift
A printer of the old school, David Swift maintained a small print shop on Railroad Avenue in Yarmouth Port long after other old-fashioned printers had disappeared.

He is a stepson of the second Charles F. Swift, who was in turn descended from the original owner of the *Register* newspaper by the same name. The print shop was for many years where the *Register* was printed but was separated from the newspaper in 1956. Four generations of Swifts, however, operated the print shop, with David Swift keeping the tradition alive until around 2012, working on a Heidelberg letterpress machine purchased in 1953. (Courtesy of the *Register*.)

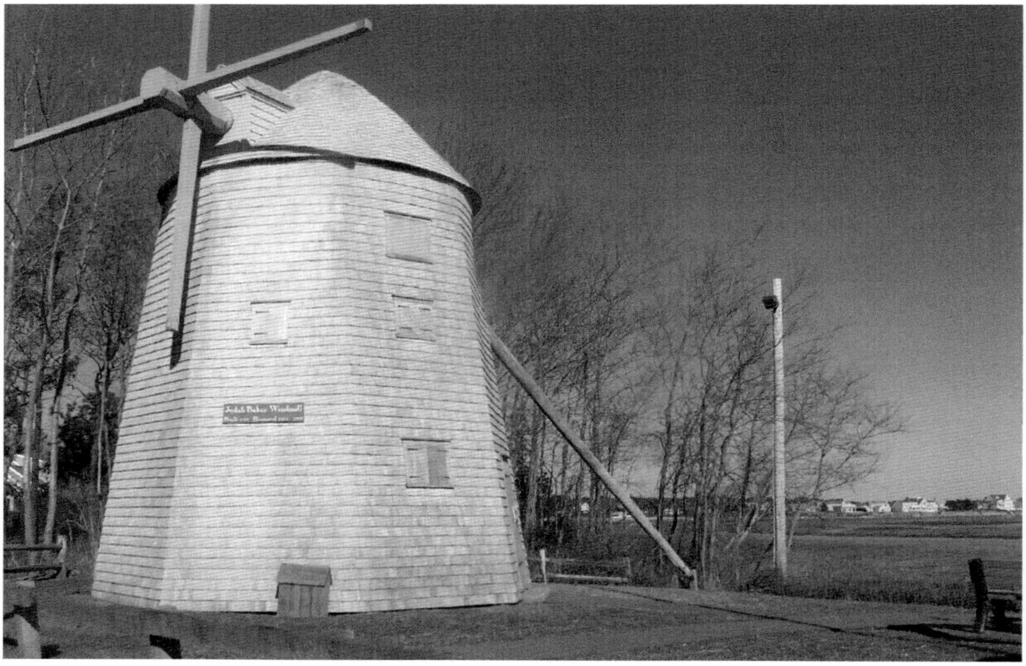

Judah Baker (1771–1830)

There is no known image of Judah Baker, and his milling business is long gone, but the mill he built remains as a symbol of Yankee ingenuity and perseverance.

Baker built his mill in 1791 in Dennis. Upon his death, his son sold it to Capt. Freeman Crowell, who moved it to another location in Dennis, where it operated until 1866, when Capt. Braddock Matthews bought it and moved it to the Lower Village of Yarmouth, now known as Bass River. The mill would eventually be owned once again by a Baker, as Seth Baker bought it in 1875 and operated it until his death in 1891. Two years later, the Baker family sold the mill to William Stone, although the mill had ceased to function. The mill sat relatively neglected and was heavily damaged in a storm in 1916. The civic-minded Charles Henry Davis became the mill's unofficial guardian during the years it belonged to a member of his extended family, and Davis engineered its move a short distance to its present location on the banks of the Bass River. In 1953, the town of Yarmouth took ownership of the mill and the small park surrounding it from the Davis family, creating a neighborhood beach. (Photograph by author.)

Judah Baker's Mill

Judah Baker's mill was renovated in 1974, and as shown in this photograph in 1999, it was given a major overhaul by Andrew Shrake. Its inner workings remain intact, and the mill hosts visitors during the summer season as new generations learn how grain was milled and business was done in Yarmouth's earlier days. (Photograph by author.)

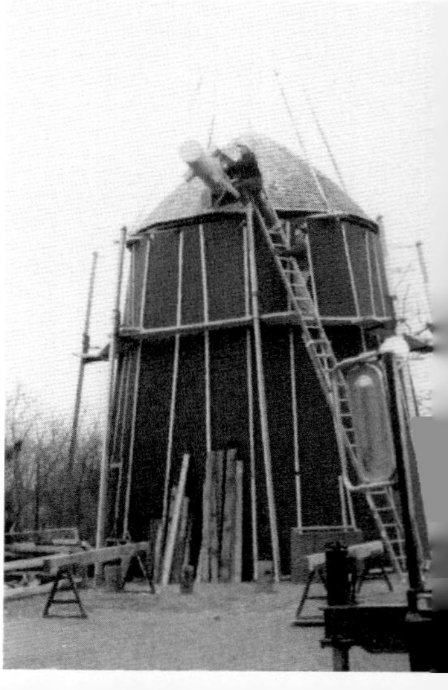

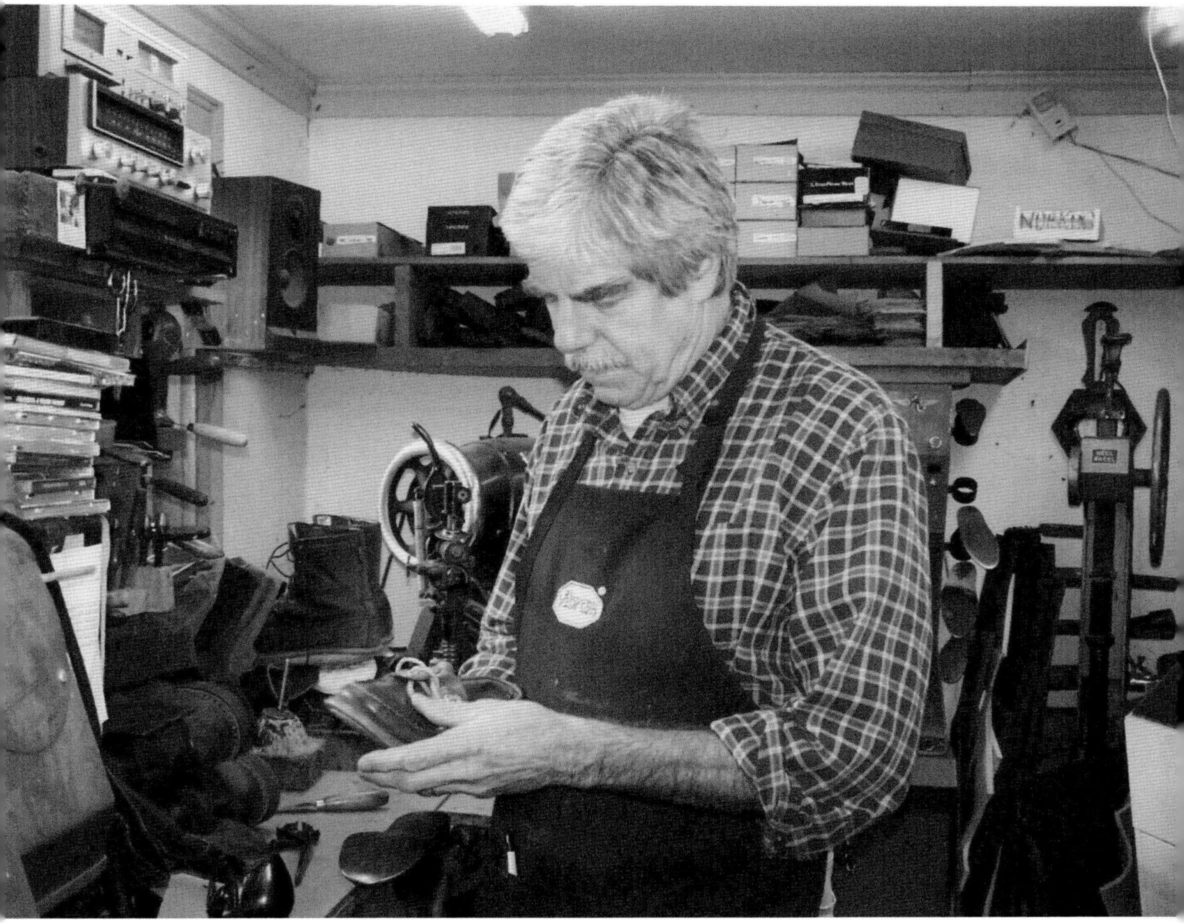

Bob Hagopian
One of the last of the old-time craftsmen, Bob Hagopian, with his wife, Cathy, has operated Bass River Shoe Repair on Old Main Street for more than 30 years. Thousands of families have taken their shoes, belts, catcher's mitts, and other leather items to him for repair over the years.

The shop is in the building dating to 1860 adjacent to the Simpkins School and known as Blind Reuben's Store, so called because Ruben Baker ran his general store there.

Hagopian learned his trade with an uncle in Northern California and opened his first shop in West Yarmouth in 1977 before moving to the Old Main Street storefront.

A talented musician as well as a gifted cobbler, Hagopian performs on bass and guitar in various local groups. (Photograph by author.)

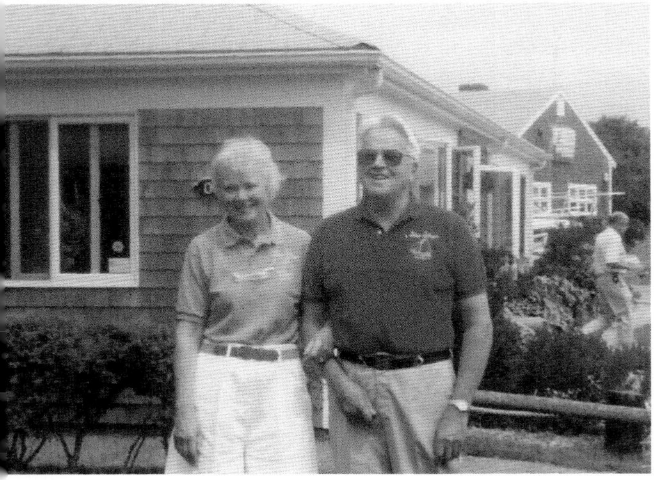

Ruth and Allan Priddy

Ruth and Allan Priddy took over ownership of the Ship Shops on the Bass River in 1957 from Ted Frothingham, and over the years, they expanded and redeveloped it into a contemporary boatyard and a mainstay for mariners along the Bass River. Adding a retail store to the existing boatyard and marine repair business, the Priddys kept Ship Shops current with the changing times.

Allan, who was a well-known competitive sailor, died in 1998, and Ruth passed away in 2011. Their daughter Alyson and her husband, Marty Taubert, continue to operate the business. (Courtesy of Alyson Taubert.)

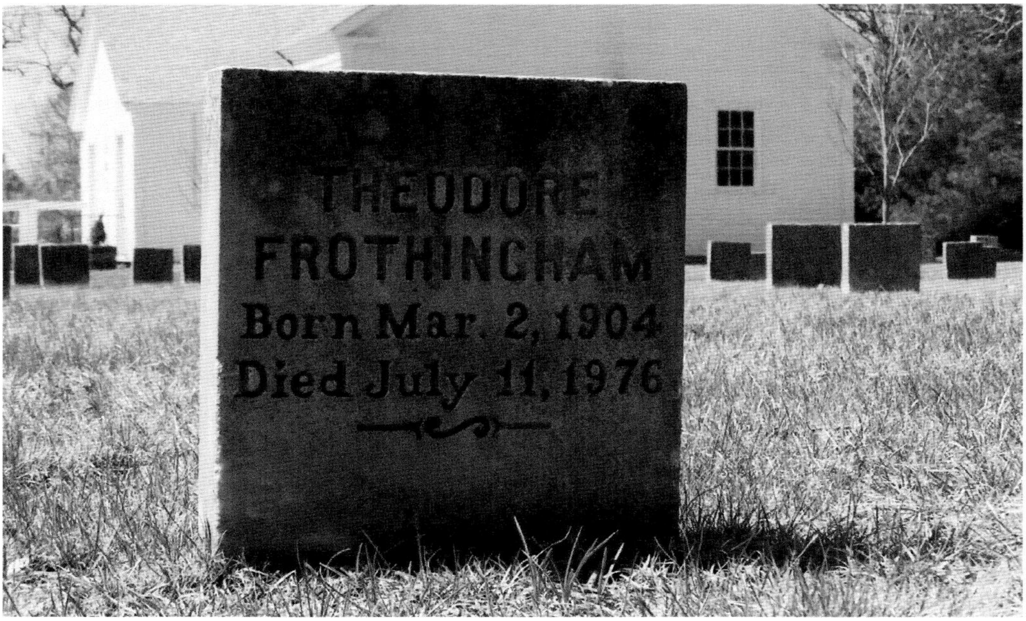

Ted Frothingham (1904–1976)

Ted Frothingham owned and operated the Ship Shops on the Bass River for about 30 years, and was also responsible for chronicling the history of Bass River village through a series of articles in the *Register*.

Brooklyn-born, Frothingham had no interest in city life. Vacationing on Cape Cod and working for steamship companies as a young man, he became a top-notch sailor and builder of boats.

Frothingham met Charles Henry Davis, and as he wrote, "We worked out a scheme that I would come to the Cape for a summer and make his riverfront boathouse into a store, and sell off the marine hardware and supplies left over from his yachting days. I could run a marine operation on his Bass River shore."

His Ship Shops employed many young people, "for as much as a dollar a day," Frothingham wrote. He redeveloped the property and created a home for himself along the river. Ultimately, he was not a successful businessman, and in 1957, Frothingham sold Ship Shops to Allan Priddy. Throughout the remainder of his life, he was a prolific writer whose many articles and books serve as an archive of local history. His gravesite is near his beloved Bass River in the Quaker Cemetery. (Photograph by author.)

CHAPTER FIVE

Giving Character to a Community

Every town has a group of people whose importance defies category. They may serve in public office, or be successful in business, athletics, education, communications, or any other endeavor. But, mainly they are known for contributions to the community that go beyond the usual. They are, in a word, irreplaceable.

Yarmouth has been blessed throughout its history with a group of people of great compassion, humor, and community spirit. They have given countless hours of their time to private organizations, schools, town government, church life, historic preservation, and the arts. In the process, they make Yarmouth an attractive place for their fellow citizens and the many thousands of people who visit each year. Their contributions are immediate and also long lasting.

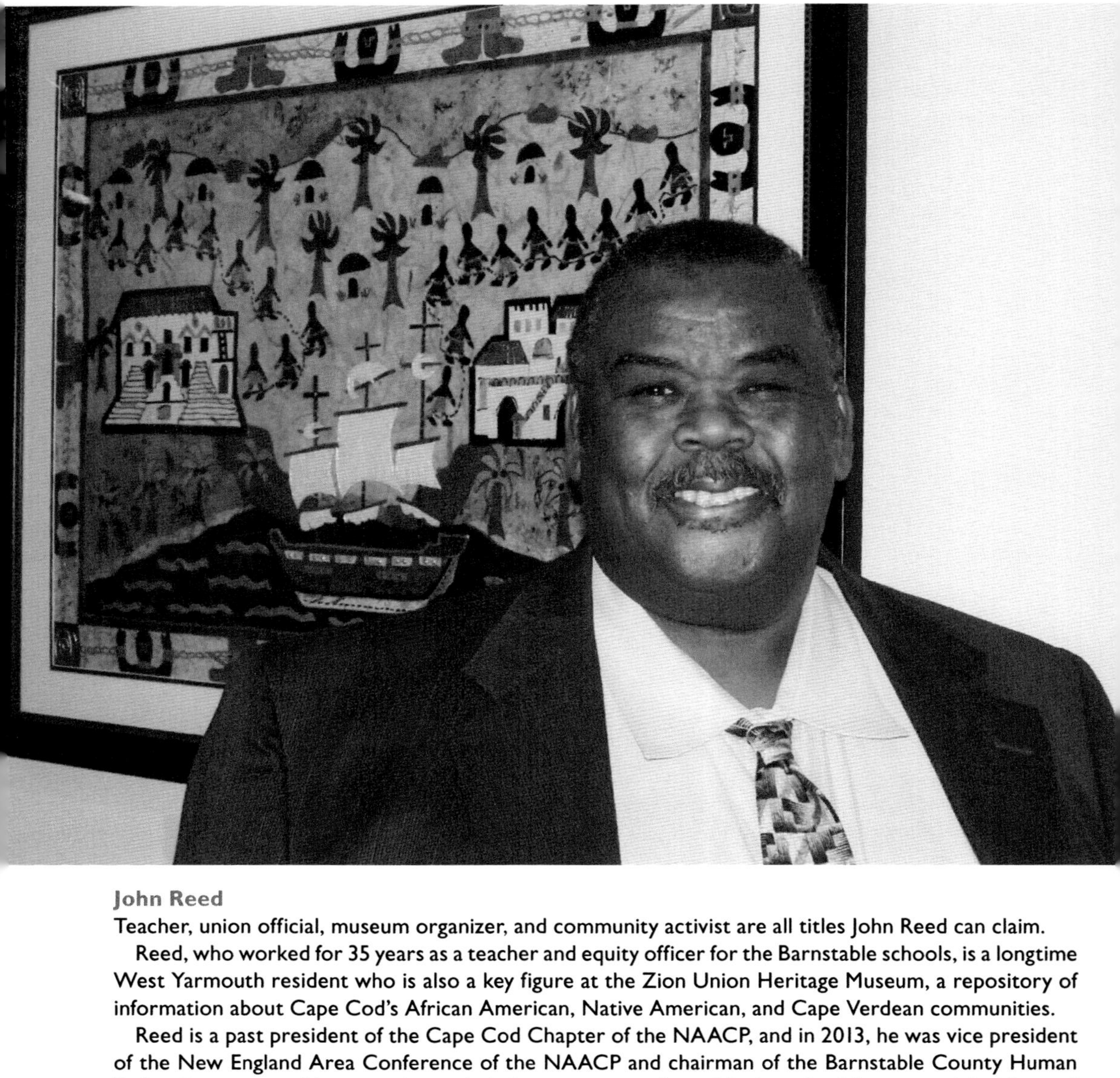

John Reed

Teacher, union official, museum organizer, and community activist are all titles John Reed can claim.

Reed, who worked for 35 years as a teacher and equity officer for the Barnstable schools, is a longtime West Yarmouth resident who is also a key figure at the Zion Union Heritage Museum, a repository of information about Cape Cod's African American, Native American, and Cape Verdean communities.

Reed is a past president of the Cape Cod Chapter of the NAACP, and in 2013, he was vice president of the New England Area Conference of the NAACP and chairman of the Barnstable County Human Rights Commission. His career has included stints as a member of the boards of directors of the National Education Association and the Massachusetts Teachers Association. (Photograph by author.)

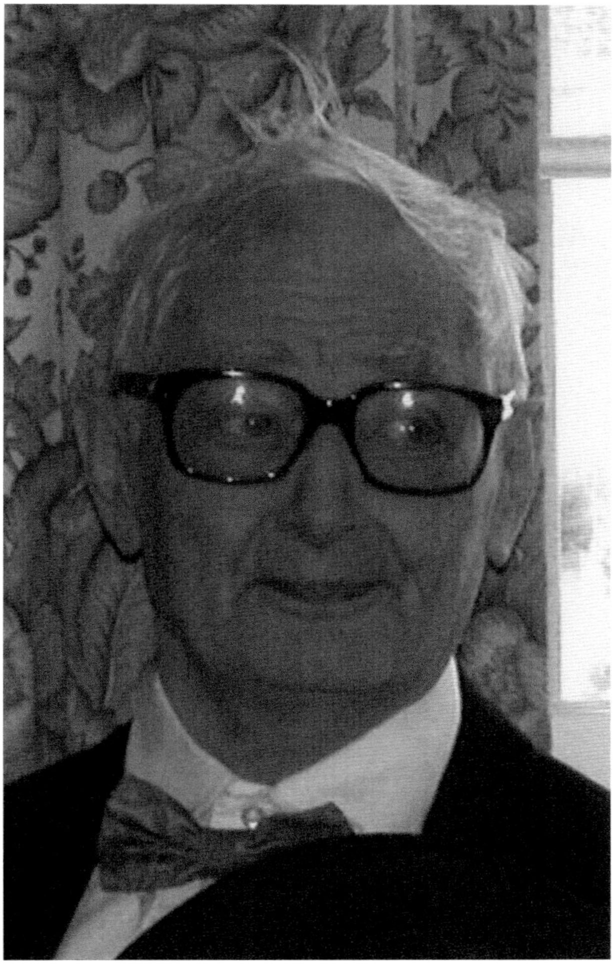

Jack Braginton-Smith (1925–2005)
One of Yarmouth Port's three Grumpy Old Men, along with antiquarian bookseller Ben Muse and artist Edward Gorey, Jack Braginton-Smith ran restaurants and told great tales.

Braginton-Smith bought the Sandy Pond Club in a secluded part of West Yarmouth in 1953 and ran it until 1971. The Sandy Pond Club became a popular local hangout for townies and visitors. Boating, music, and a bar in a secluded setting were the attractions.

"It had an air of casual camaraderie," he told a reporter in 1999. "We had a lot of people who displayed their individuality in different ways."

Braginton-Smith's next business venture was the one he is best remembered for—Jack's Outback restaurant, hidden off Route 6A in Yarmouth Port. Jack's Outback's most-famous regular was Edward Gorey, whose art adorned the walls, but the star was Braginton-Smith, whose wisecracks to customers became part of the scene. "You call that a tip?" was a frequently heard remark to departing diners.

Braginton-Smith and Muse engaged in pie-eating contests at Jack's Outback, but no winner was ever declared.

A famous grouch, Braginton-Smith nevertheless found time to engage in community projects. He wrote extensively on local history and memorably performed in a benefit stage production of *Love Letters* with the actress Betsy Palmer in 2003.

"He was a sweet man and I adored him," Palmer said in 2009. (Courtesy of the *Register*.)

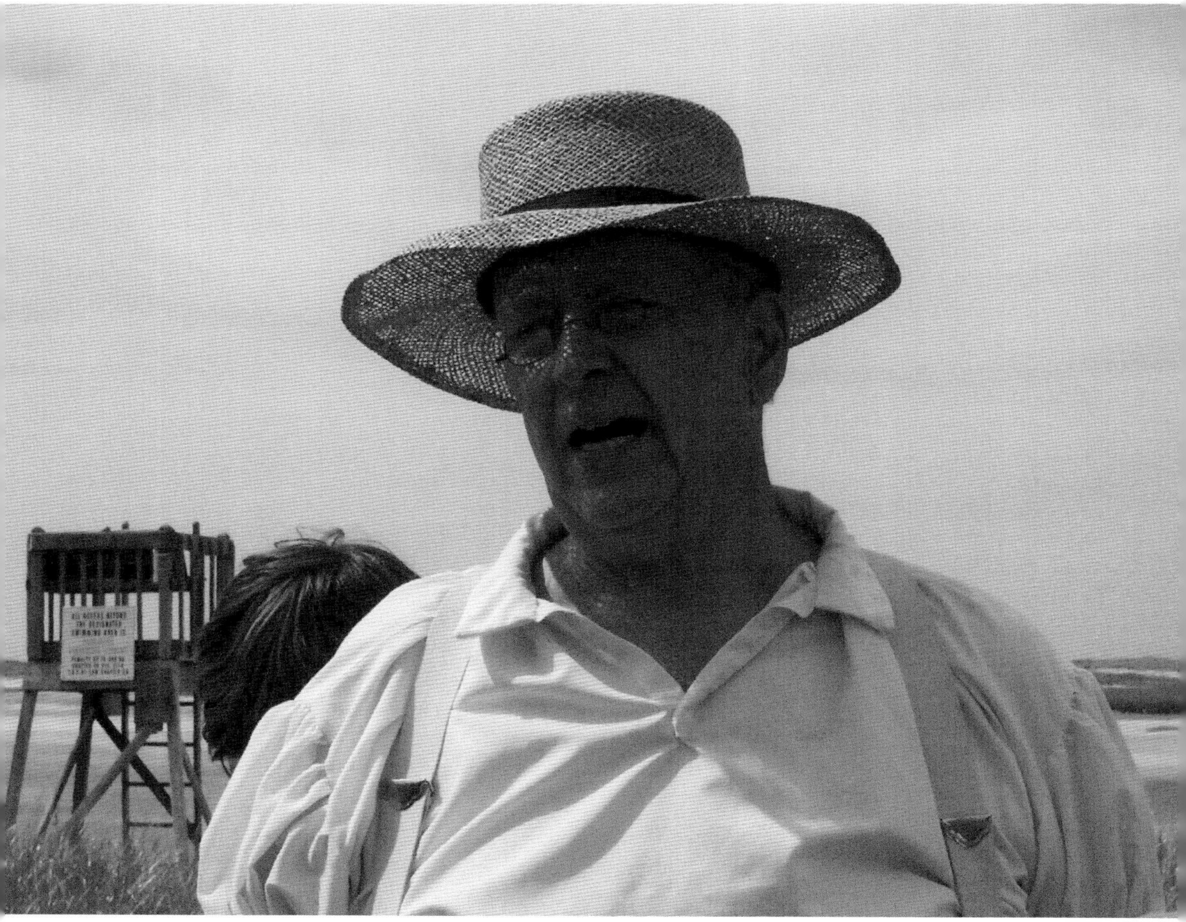

Duncan Oliver

Duncan Oliver is a mainstay in Yarmouth historical circles, working tirelessly to keep the town's history alive.

Oliver retired as principal of Oliver Ames High School in Easton, Massachusetts, where he was the president of the Easton Historical Society and helped write books on local history. After moving to Yarmouth Port in 2000, Oliver continued his work on local history, becoming active in the Historical Society of Old Yarmouth and serving at various times as the Historical Society of Old Yarmouth's president and publications committee chairman. As in this photograph, he often portrays figures from Yarmouth history. Here, he portrays shipbuilder William Bray. He has also written two books (with Jack Braginton-Smith) about Cape Cod and more than 70 articles for newspapers and magazines.

Still an educator, Oliver has taught classes on Cape Cod history for Dennis-Yarmouth Adult Education. (Courtesy of Duncan Oliver.)

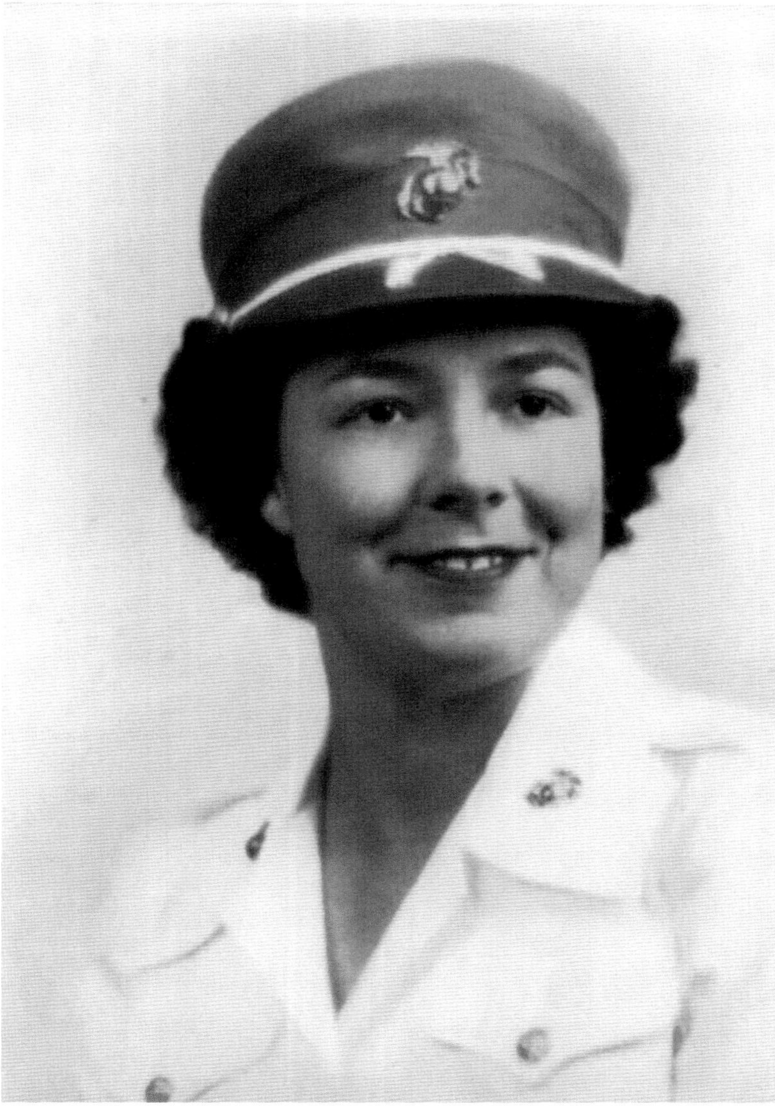

Dorene Coombs

When Dorene Coombs was 25, World War II was raging, and she felt the need to do her part to help.

She enlisted in the Marine Corps prepared to serve in whatever capacity she could. As it turned out, she spent the war working as a hairdresser at Camp Lejeune, North Carolina. "I never thought I was going to be a hairdresser in the Marine Corps, but there was a need for that service because all the female Marines had to have their hair cut short so it didn't reach their collars," Coombs told a reporter on Veterans Day 2012 when she was 94.

Coombs married her husband, Lee, also a Marine, and they moved to Cape Cod where he could pursue his work as a commercial fisherman. Dorene operated her own beauty shop and, in retirement, remained active in Yarmouth knitting groups and senior organizations. She maintained her old-fashioned ideas, never wearing pants, never smoking, and never drinking.

As the oldest, and only female, Marine to attend the annual Marine anniversary party on Cape Cod, Coombs keeps alive her commitment to the Marine Corps. (Courtesy of Dorene Coombs.)

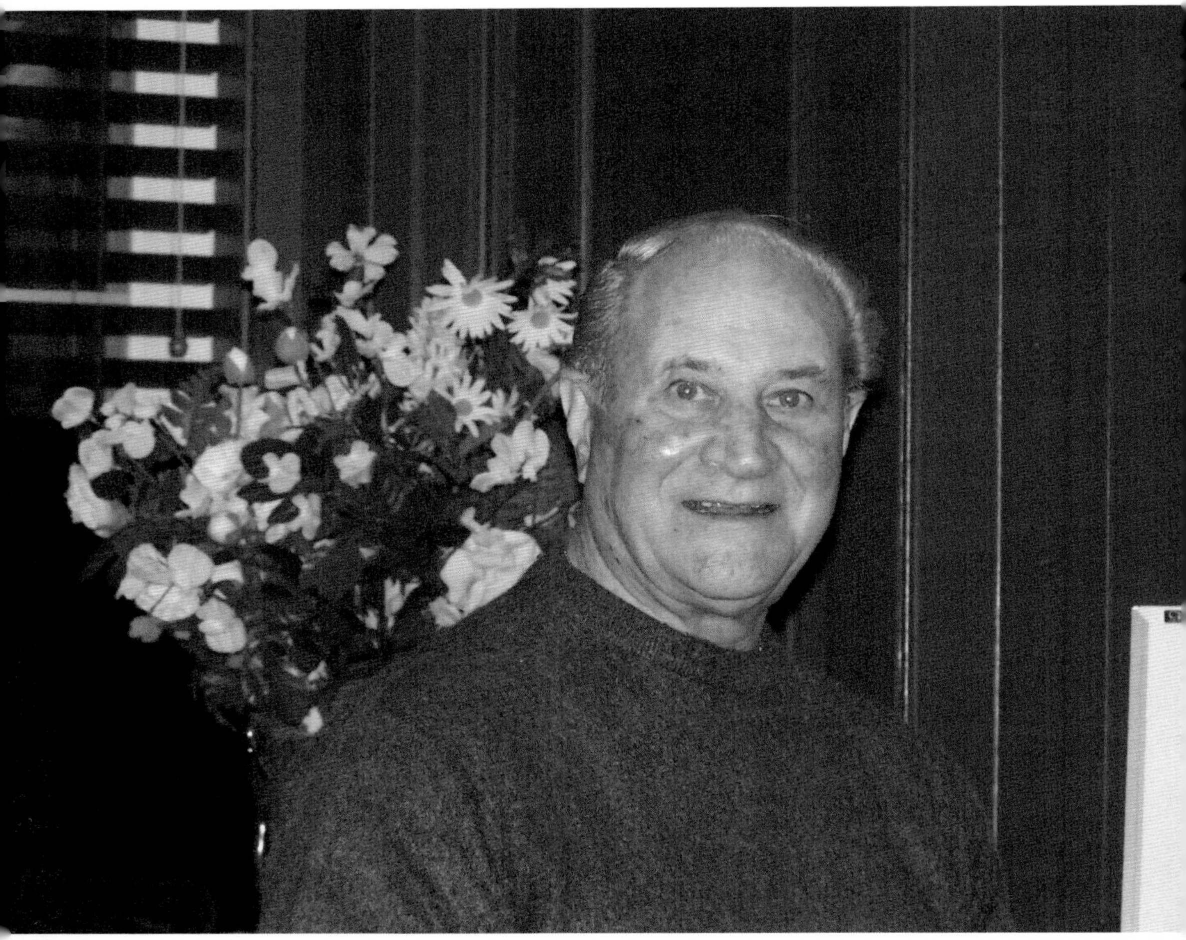

Guido Farina

Guido Farina saw World War II in a way most people can only imagine. As a boy growing up in the town of Montecassino, Italy, Farina watched as Allied and Axis forces clashed for control of the strategic mountain town. First one side, then the other controlled the town before the Allies finally won out.

Later immigrating to the United States, Farina became a teacher of languages in the Newton, Massachusetts, public schools, where he taught for many years.

In retirement, with his wife, Elfriede, Farina came to South Yarmouth, where he began a new career as a writer. His first book, *Montecassino: The People's Real Battle*, told his story through the eyes of a young boy. He followed it with additional books and became a teacher of popular Italian language courses in Yarmouth, where he shares his language skills and his insights on Italian life and culture. (Photograph by author.)

Bainbridge Crist (1916–2003)

Bainbridge Crist's interests were in journalism, business, history, and his community.

The son of the composer Lucien Bainbridge Crist, the younger Crist was educated in Yarmouth schools and at Harvard University. He worked as a reporter for the *Washington Evening Star*, considered the paper of record in Washington. During World War II, he went to work for the US Office of Price Administration, created by Pres. Franklin Roosevelt's administration to control prices on most goods and to ration scarce commodities.

Following the war, Crist worked in public relations in Washington, and later returned to live in South Yarmouth, where he was a member of the Bass River Yacht Club and involved with the Historical Society of Old Yarmouth. Crist amassed an impressive library of books about history and politics.

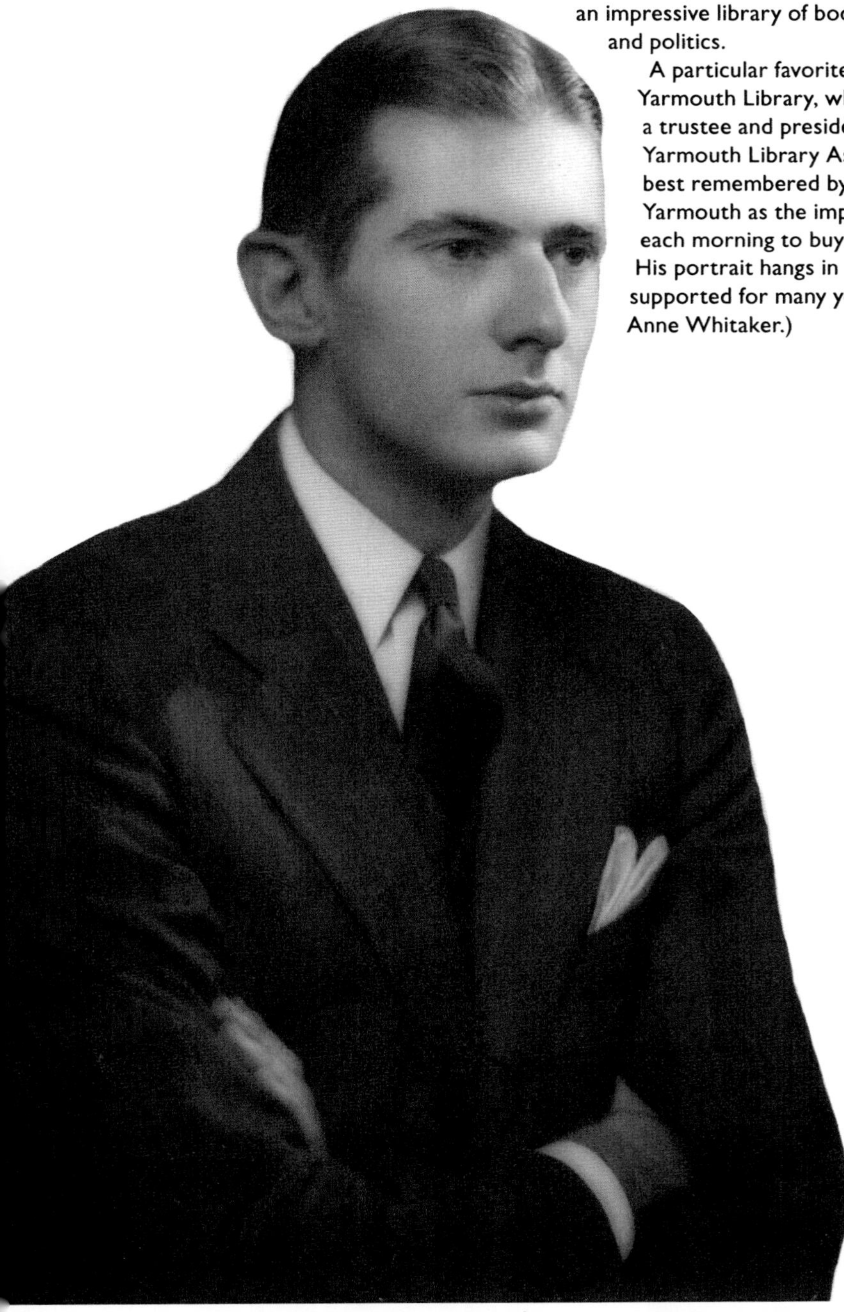

A particular favorite of his was the South Yarmouth Library, where he served as a trustee and president of the South Yarmouth Library Association. He is best remembered by many in South Yarmouth as the imposing figure walking each morning to buy his daily newspapers. His portrait hangs in the library he supported for many years. (Courtesy of Anne Whitaker.)

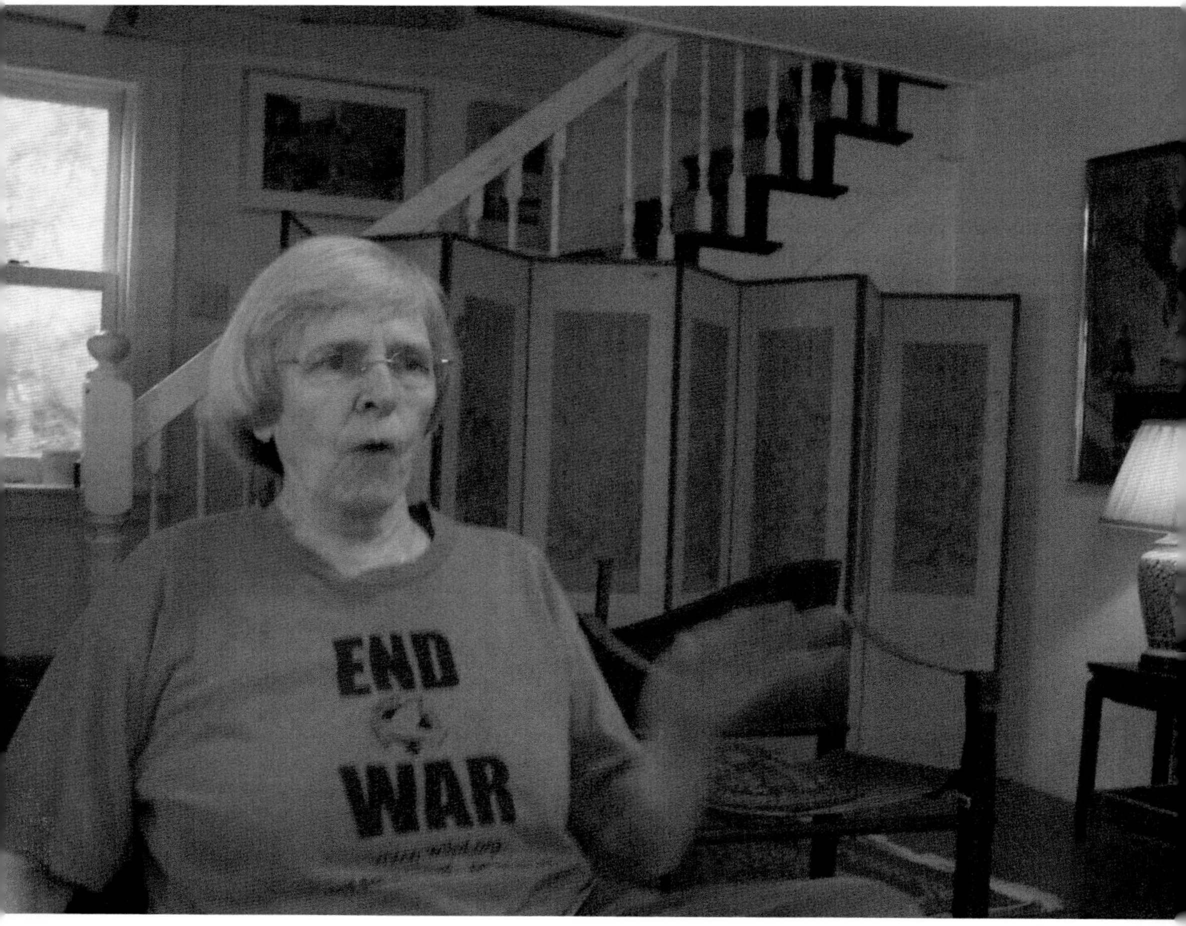

Mary Zepernick

Political activist Mary Zepernick is admittedly a product of the times in which she came of age.

A schoolteacher in Washington, DC, and later in Harlem in New York, Zepernick became involved in the anti–Vietnam War movement of the 1960s and the women's rights movement that sprang up at the same time.

After moving to Yarmouth, Mary Zepernick, often with her husband, Fred (who died in 1991), took on many causes, from US involvement in Central America in the 1980s to social justice issues at home. A longtime member of the Women's International League for Peace and Freedom (WILPF), Zepernick worked with Margaret Mosely to start a Cape Cod chapter of the organization. She became a national board member of WILPF and rose to US president of the organization, serving four years in that office.

A newspaper columnist and an organizer of conferences on women's issues including an event titled The Roots of Violence, Zepernick has in recent years turned her attention to the effort to overturn the US Supreme Court's Citizens United ruling saying corporations are persons.

In 2013, Zepernick was selected as Yarmouth's representative to the Barnstable County Human Rights Commission. (Photograph by author.)

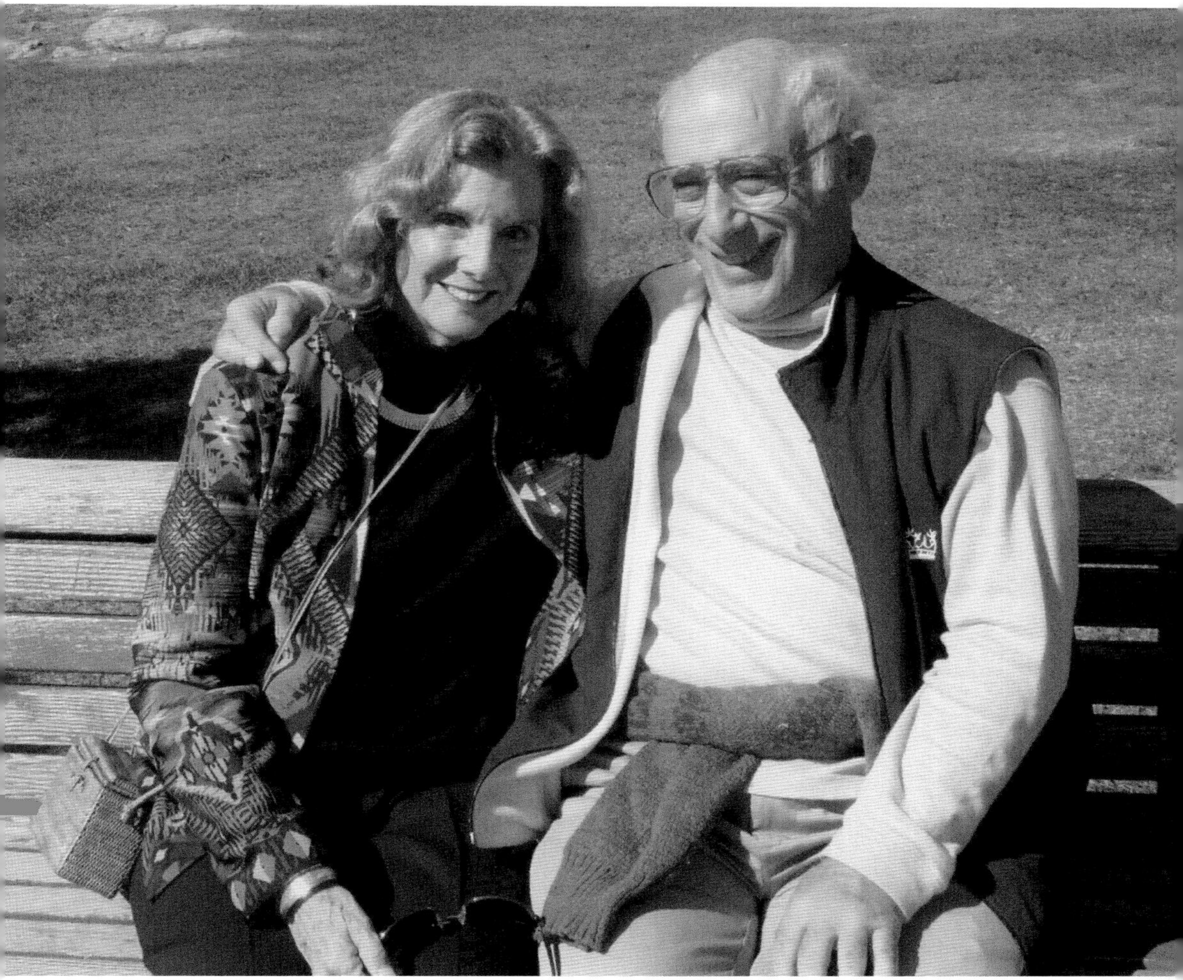

Ruth and Ted Weissberger
Clarity of vision seems to mark everything Ruth and Ted Weissberger do for the town of Yarmouth. Perhaps it has something to do with Ruth's career in psychological counseling and Ted's in photographic research and development.

Successful in their careers in Rochester, New York, the Weissbergers adopted Yarmouth Port as their home and immediately began to contribute to the town's cultural life and historical preservation. Ruth has devoted her energies to the Historical Society of Old Yarmouth and the Taylor-Bray Farm Preservation Association. Among her projects, she organizes costumed walking tours of Yarmouth's historic cemeteries. She is also the author of two books about old Yarmouth.

Ted is involved in historical preservation efforts and the Yarmouth Port Library and has also served on the Yarmouth Finance Committee and Recycling and Solid Waste Advisory Committee and is an accomplished wood turner, selling his wares at various locations around Cape Cod.

The Weissbergers, like many others, visited Cape Cod on vacation, and when the time was right, they quickly made the decision to become permanent Yarmouth residents.

Ted says that Yarmouth Port "was our home before we even arrived." (Courtesy of Ted Weissberger.)

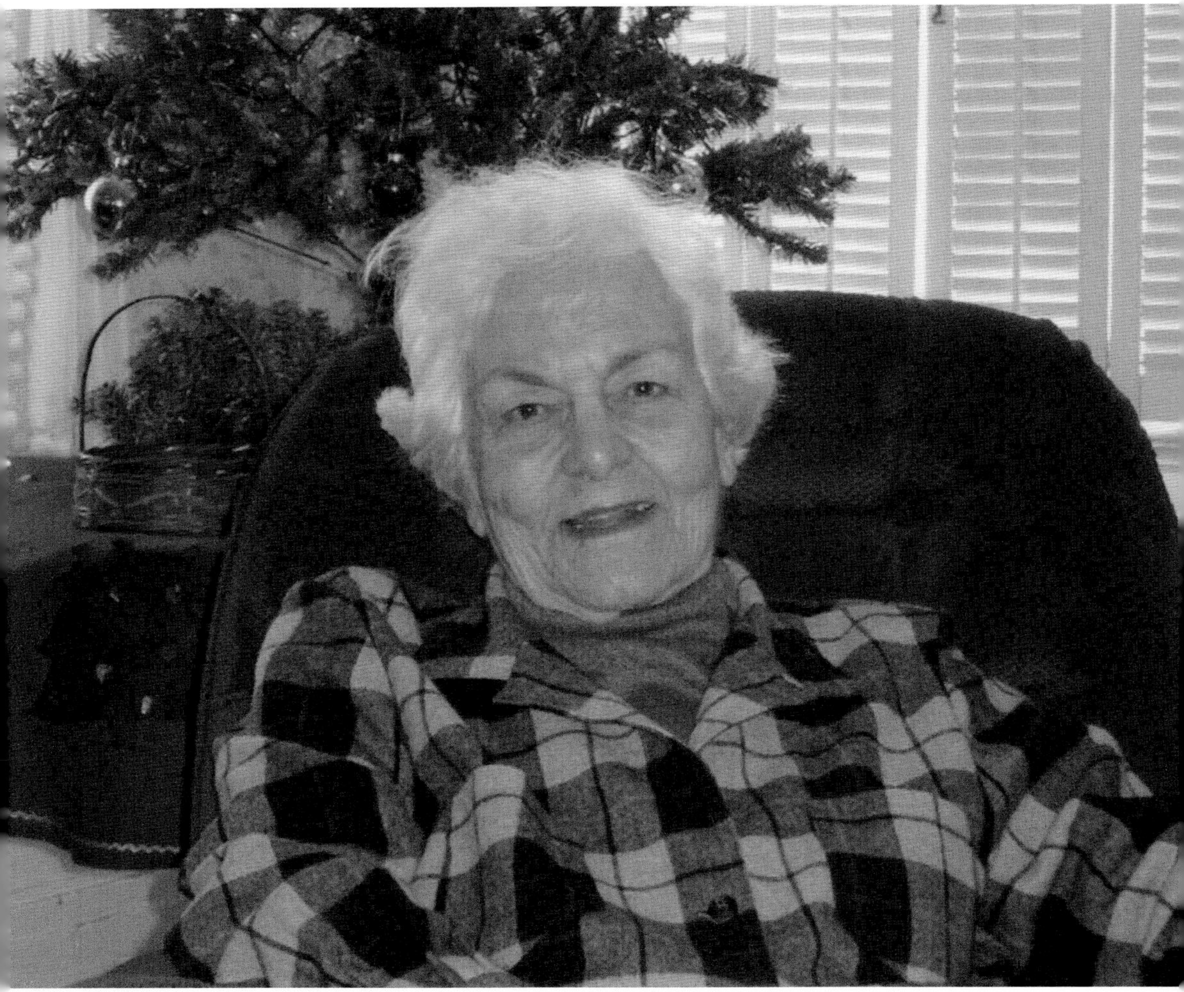

Marge Fallows

Dr. Marjorie Rice Fallows, "Marge" to her hundreds of friends, brought her significant organizing skills to Yarmouth when she and her husband, Alden, moved to town in 1979.

Fallows taught sociology at Berkshire Community College in Western Massachusetts and at the University of Connecticut before moving to Yarmouth and taking a position teaching at Cape Cod Community College.

After her retirement in 1990, as a trustee of the South Yarmouth Library Association, Fallows became a force in town, showing a flair for organizing other volunteers for a variety of projects. During her nine years as a trustee and later as a trustee emeritus, the South Yarmouth Library was always among her top priorities, as she organized the annual book sale, murder-mystery fundraisers, and other events.

In 2006, Fallows began to organize the Cookie Stroll, which quickly became the South Yarmouth Library's signature event. Early each December, a dozen homes in the Bass River neighborhood open their doors and hand out homemade cookies to strollers as a library fundraiser. (Courtesy of the *Register.*)

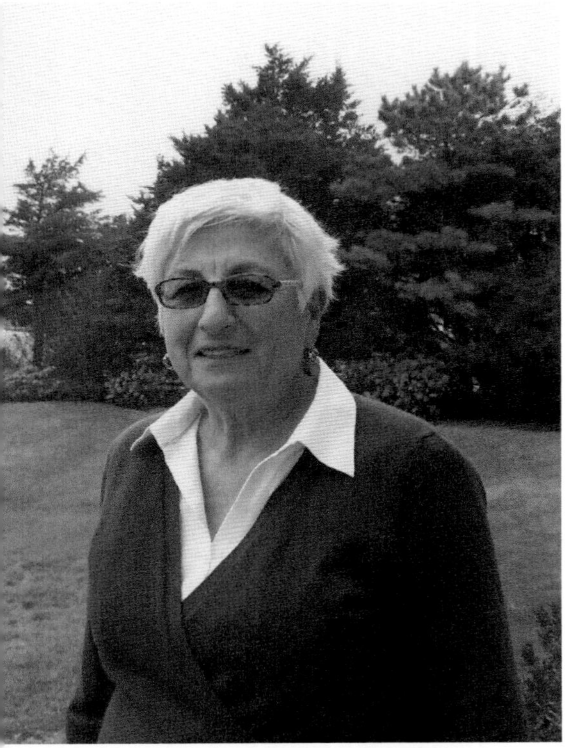

Zabelle D'Amico

Zabelle D'Amico documented the Englewood area of West Yarmouth in her photograph exhibit "Angles along Englewood" in 1995. Her striking black-and-white photographs capture the seaside scene as well as the faces of some of the neighborhood's inhabitants in their home environment.

The photograph exhibit led D'Amico to research the Breed family and resulted in the publication of *The Breeds and the Caretakers of their Englewood Legacy* in 1998 and a house tour of the neighborhood in 2000. (Photograph by author.)

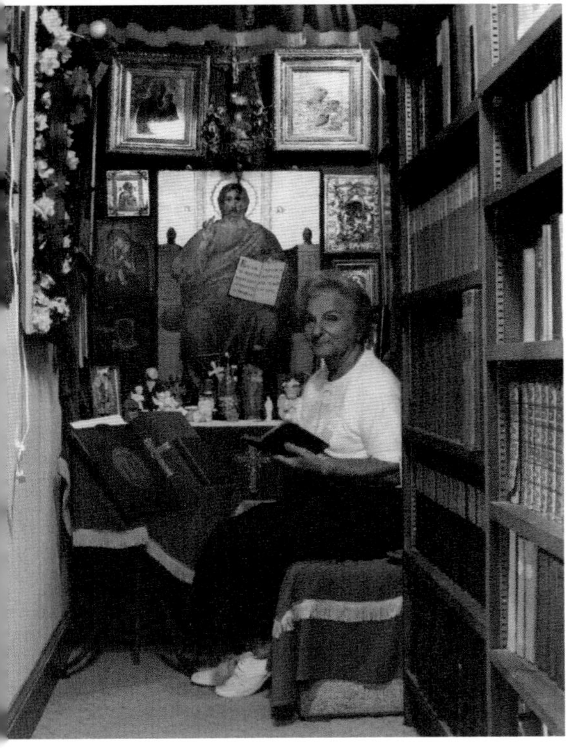

Olga Terpos

Olga Terpos and her husband, Chris, owned a small package store on route 28 and lived in a home filled with books overlooking Lewis Bay in the Englewood Neighborhood.

The diminutive Olga was affectionately known as the "Queen of the Bay." She was devoted to her Greek Orthodox faith and maintained a small shrine in her home.

Her many friends and neighbors remember that as a greeting, she would often extend her arms, give a kiss on both cheeks, and ask, "How are you, darlin'? I'm so glad to see you." (Photograph by Zabelle D'Amico.)

George Breed (1864–1939)

George Breed and his family had roots in Philadelphia but created their beloved family compound called Natoma-Sur-Mer in West Yarmouth on the shores of Lewis Bay.

The Breed family had strong connections to the sea; naval officers abound in the family annals. George graduated from the US Naval Academy and served in the Spanish-American War and World War I. George and his wife, Clara, known as "Missy," bought and developed property in the Englewood section of West Yarmouth and, between 1915 and the mid-1930s, built several houses and cottages fronting the bay, each with a name connected to the sea—the Steerage, the Packet, and Seven Bells were among the names.

The Breeds often hosted musical events and elaborate parties in their summer estate. George's interest in music showed in another way as well. As an electrical engineer, in 1890, he devised and won a patent for what is believed to be the first electric guitar. He also worked on an electric piano and devised a winged kite, which he rigged with a camera and used to take aerial photographs of Natoma-Sur-Mer.

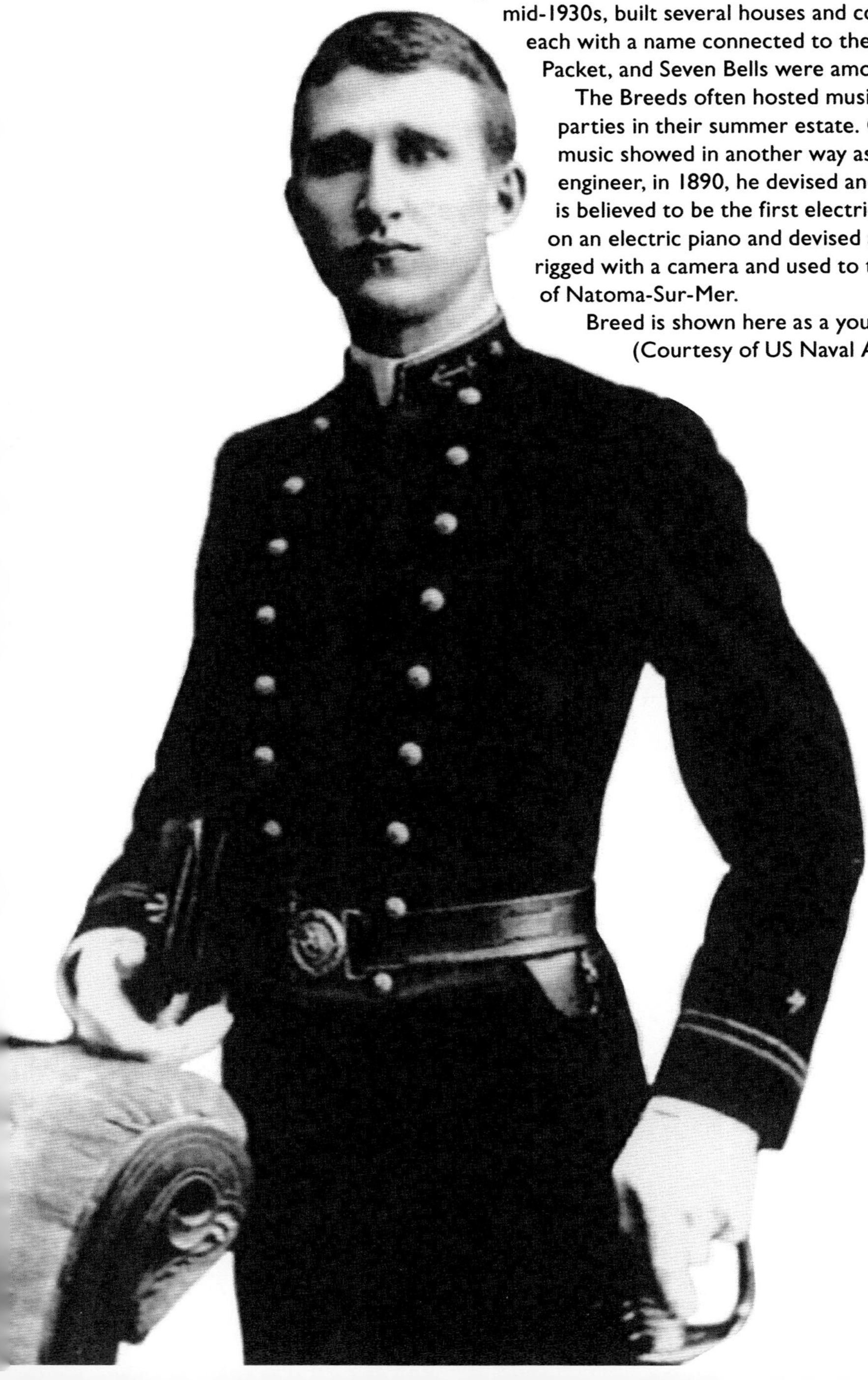

Breed is shown here as a young naval officer. (Courtesy of US Naval Academy.)

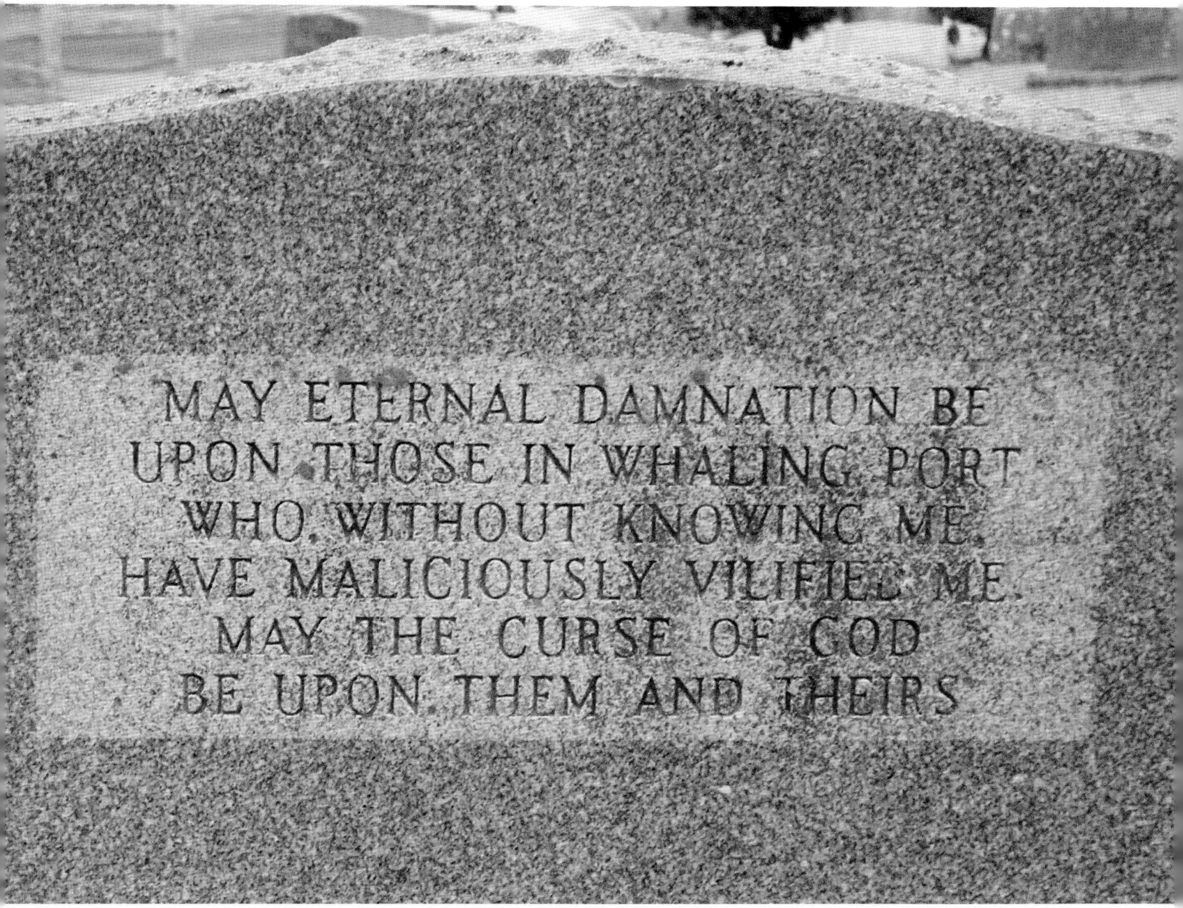

Mary C. Dolencie (1906–1985)
In life, Mary Dolencie was known as a neighborhood character. A well-known cat lady in the Whaling Port subdivision of Yarmouth Port, Dolencie sometimes clashed with her neighbors over what to outsiders may seem like petty issues, like how many cats she had, and her penchant for feeding birds. In death, Dolencie is known as the woman who put a curse on her neighbors. The inscription on her gravestone in Yarmouth's Ancient Cemetery, a short distance from Whaling Port, reads: "May eternal damnation be / Upon those in Whaling Port. / Who, without knowing me, / Have maliciously vilified me. / May the curse of God / Be upon them and theirs."

Neighbors tried to get the stone changed or removed but could not because Dolencie had signed a contract for the grave and stone and paid for both in full before she died. Despite the nastiness of the curse, it does not seem to have had any effect. Whaling Port residents told a reporter in 2013 that they live in a neighborhood where everyone gets along. (Photograph by author.)

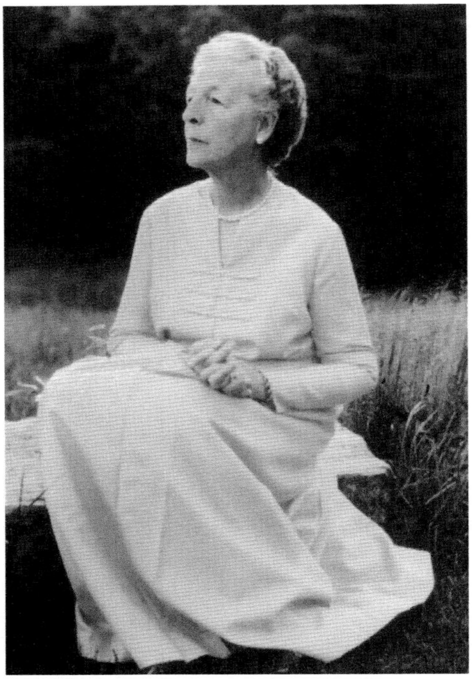

Ann Maxtone-Graham (1899–1991)

Ann Maxtone-Graham was a longtime summer resident of Bass River and her vivid recollections of life in the village in the early part of the 20th century are essential to understanding Yarmouth history.

Her description of the journey by train and boat from her family's home in Orange, New Jersey, gives people a glimpse of how families of a certain status lived. "In our family alone there were Mother, a nurse, three children, at least four maids, the dogs and the cats," she wrote.

Maxtone-Graham's description of arrival in Yarmouth includes a mention of a long-gone railroad station: "The South Yarmouth station itself was an enormous, gaunt building, a most forlorn looking place. We were looking for Mr. Collins, Capt. Charley Brown and his cousin, Capt. Johnny Picket Brown, each in his own particular type of vehicle."

Arrival at the family summer home in Bass River was a ritual: "The moment we swung off the macadam road onto the Sandy Road (now Pleasant Street) was almost more than we could bear. All our houses had long drives made of crushed oyster and scallop shells, and when we turned in and heard the familiar crunch under the wheels, life had nothing better to offer us."

In her memoir, published in 1968 in the *Register*, Maxtone-Graham mentions many of the people who inhabited Bass River and South Yarmouth decades ago. She tells of buying molasses at Reuben Baker's store, "at the south end of Main Street," and a "cold drink parlor" run by Melville Baker. "It was dark and dank and up a short flight of steps from the street," and she was not allowed to go in there.

During World War II, Maxtone-Graham's husband was stationed in London with the Royal Artillery. Sending her children to live with relatives on Cape Cod, Ann Maxtone-Graham moved to London, where she worked with a surgical dressing unit.

After the war, Maxtone-Graham returned to South Yarmouth, where she operated a guesthouse for many years and was active in local organizations. She was elected president of the newly formed Historical Society of Old Yarmouth in 1953 and was involved with the South Yarmouth Library Association, where she was president. She died at 92 in 1991.

A portrait of Ann Maxtone-Graham hangs in the South Yarmouth Library on Old Main Street near the site of her long-ago summer home. This photograph depicts her as many knew her. (Courtesy of the Historical Society of Old Yarmouth.)

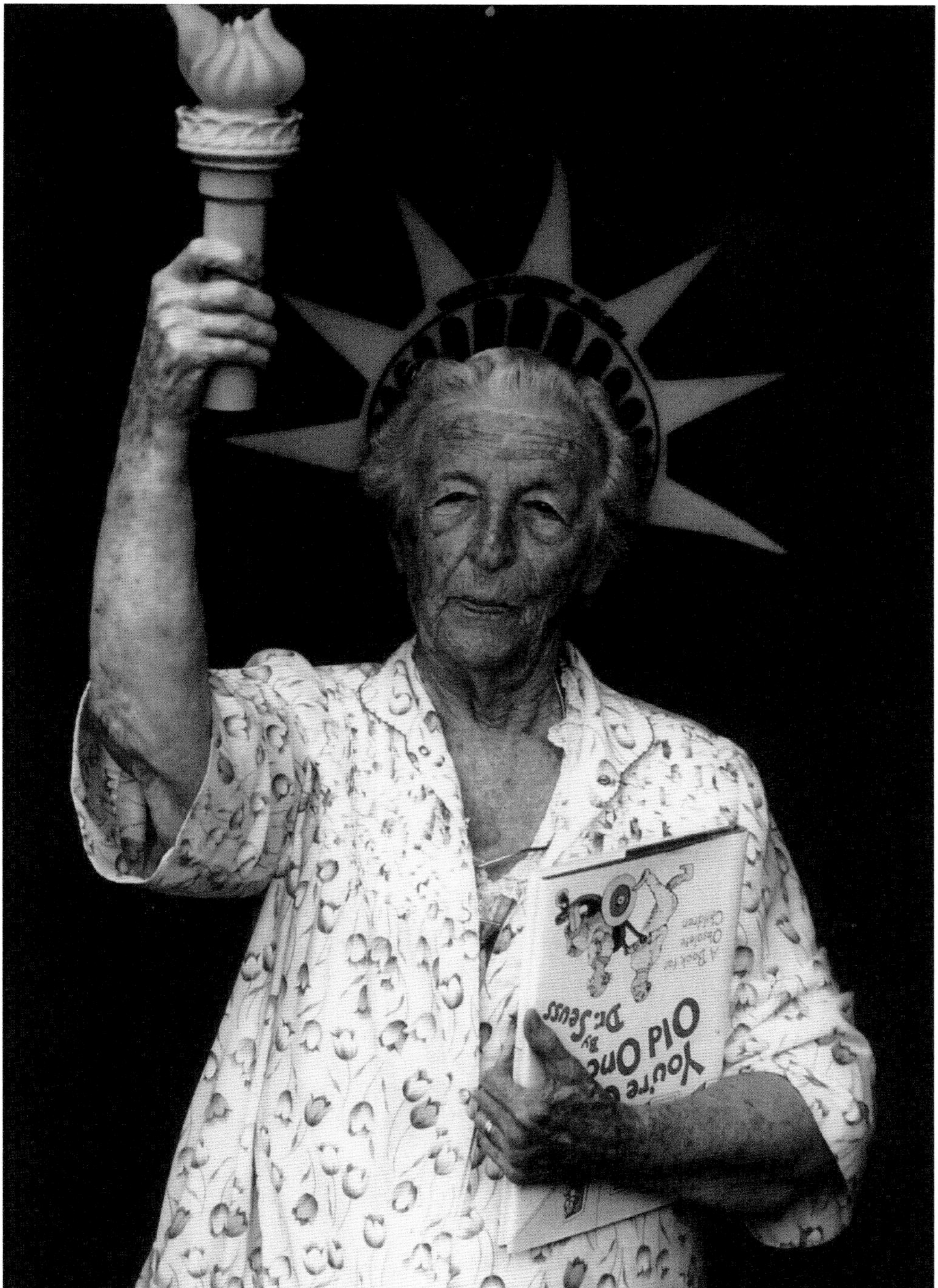

Anne as Statue of Liberty

In this whimsical family photograph, Anne Maxtone-Graham takes the role of the Statue of Liberty. (Courtesy of the Historical Society of Old Yarmouth.)

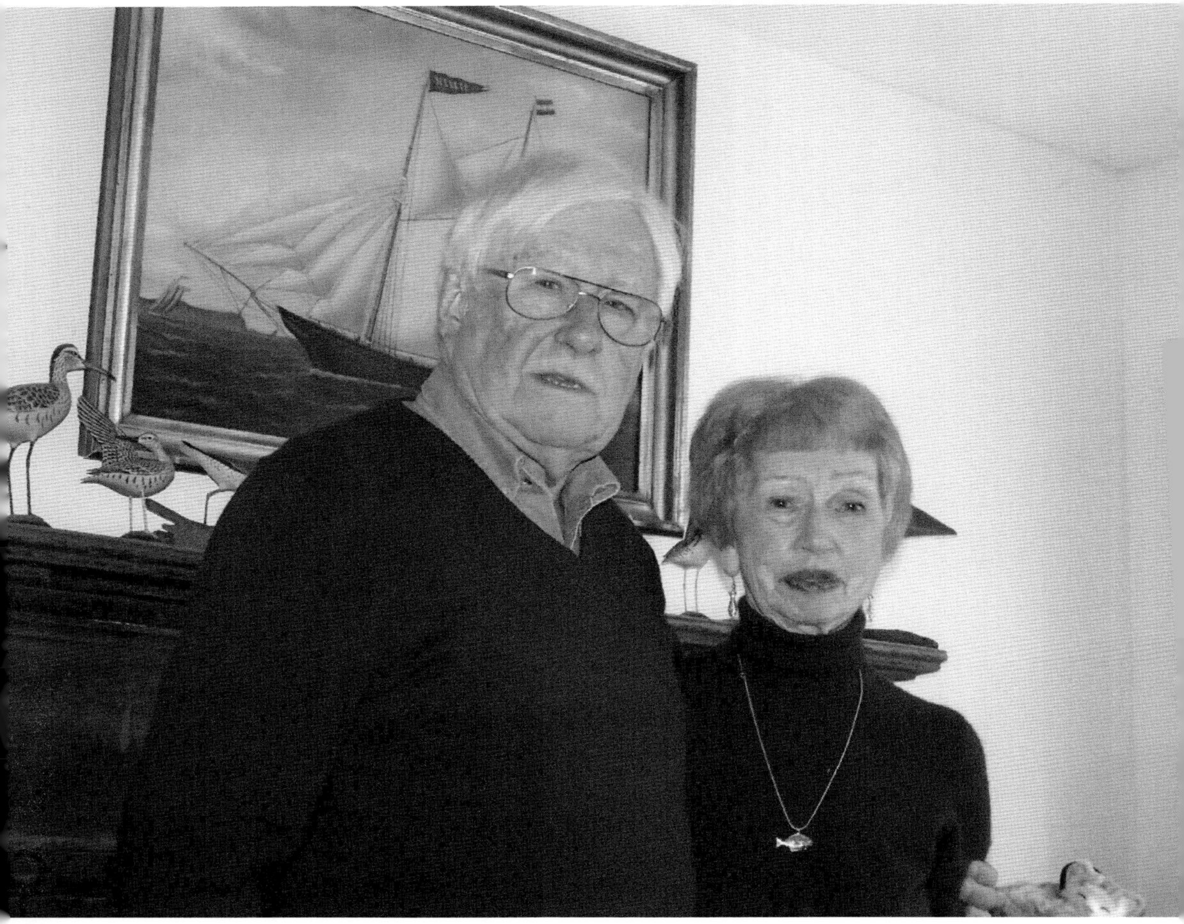

Charles and Barbara Adams

Charles and Barbara Adams are not Yarmouth natives; people just assume they are. The couple has logged more hours volunteering and done more for the town than most people who have spent a lifetime in Yarmouth.

Coming to Yarmouth in 1999 after successful careers in insurance (Charlie) and teaching (Barbara), the Adamses quickly became a valuable part of the local scene.

The following list of organizations they are involved with is impressive: the South Yarmouth Library Association, Cape Cod Antique Dealers Association, Yarmouth Rotary, Cultural Center of Cape Cod, and the Historical Society of Old Yarmouth, to name a few. Various school councils and town boards have all benefited from their volunteerism and financial contributions.

With a longtime interest in antiques (they find time to be antiques dealers) and history, the Adamses are particularly concerned with preserving the past and devote countless hours to Yarmouth's historical preservation. (Photograph by author.)

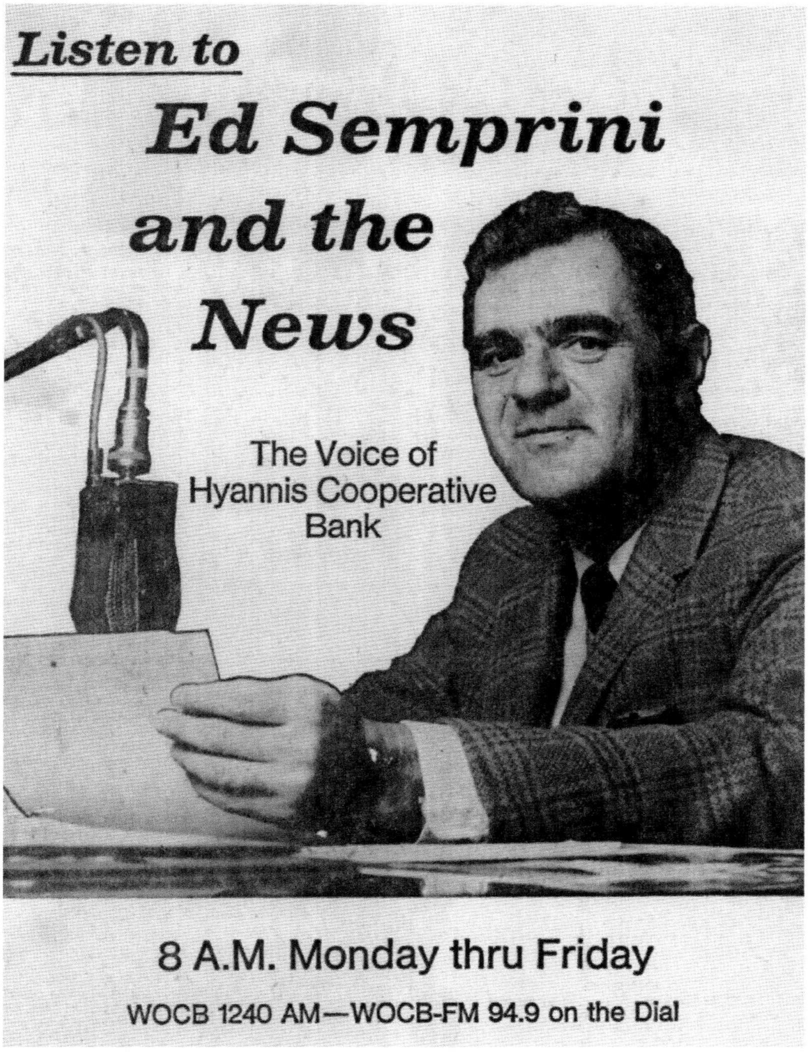

Ed Semprini (1917–2011)
From the 1950s to the 1980s, WOCB, with studios on South Sea Avenue in West Yarmouth, was the top radio station on Cape Cod, and Ed Semprini was a big part of that success.

As a newsman, he had a knack for delivering stories in an authoritative, yet folksy way. Raised in Allentown, Pennsylvania, Semprini found he was discriminated against in his hometown because of his Italian American heritage, so he made his career on Cape Cod in the days when the local radio station was the prime source of information.

Semprini reported every major story on Cape Cod, including the rescue of the crew of the tanker *Pendleton* off the coast of Cape Cod in 1952 and the election of Pres. John F. Kennedy in 1960. Among Semprini's journalistic scoops was his interview with the son of Soviet premier Nikita Khrushchev, who came to Cape Cod as a journalist to interview President Kennedy.

Semprini also was instrumental in making coverage of locals important on Cape Cod.

Later in his career, Semprini moved to WQRC-FM, wrote for newspapers, and even worked in local television, but it was his days at Yarmouth's WOCB, when local news on the radio really mattered, that made him a permanent part of the Cape Cod scene. (Courtesy of Edward F. Maroney.)

Annette Kelley (1886–1980)

Annette L. Kelley was the heart and soul of the *Yarmouth Register* newspaper from 1902 until the late 1970s.

The following is the best description of Miss Kelley, as she was invariably known; it was written by Dana Hornig, who worked at the *Register* from the 1970s to the 1980s as a reporter and editor: "Annette L. Kelley, barely five feet tall and 90 pounds, blue-eyed, blond and strikingly beautiful, born and raised in Yarmouth Port, went to work for the *Register* and its print shop at the age of 16, fresh out of Yarmouth High School. The year was 1902. When I walked into the *Register*, seven decades later in 1973, Annette Kelley was still there."

Miss Kelley performed virtually every job at the newspaper at one time or another. This included operating the linotype machine and the printing press, writing articles, setting type, and mailing the papers. During World War II, she was left alone to run the paper, and she did. (Courtesy of the *Register*.)

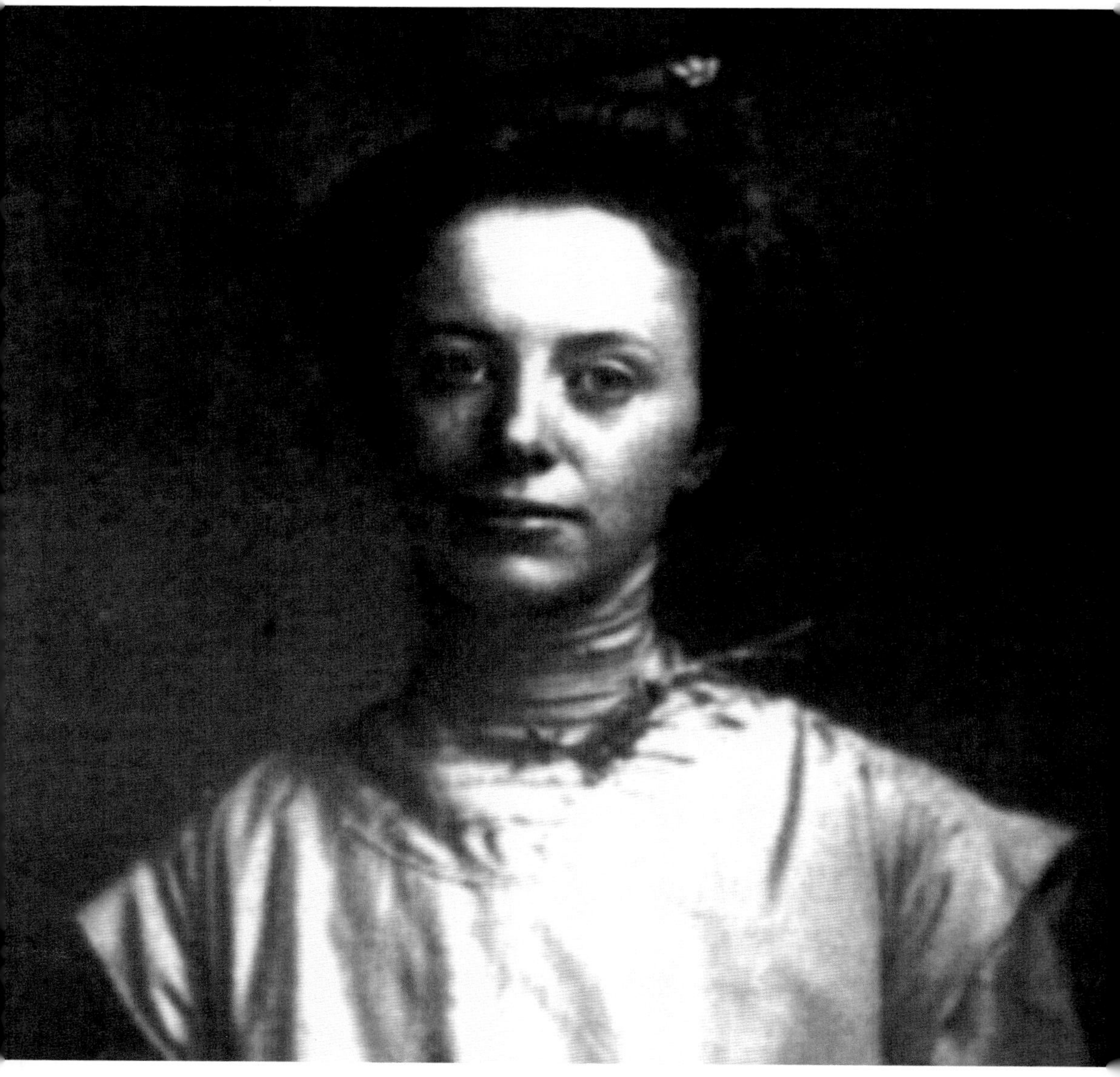

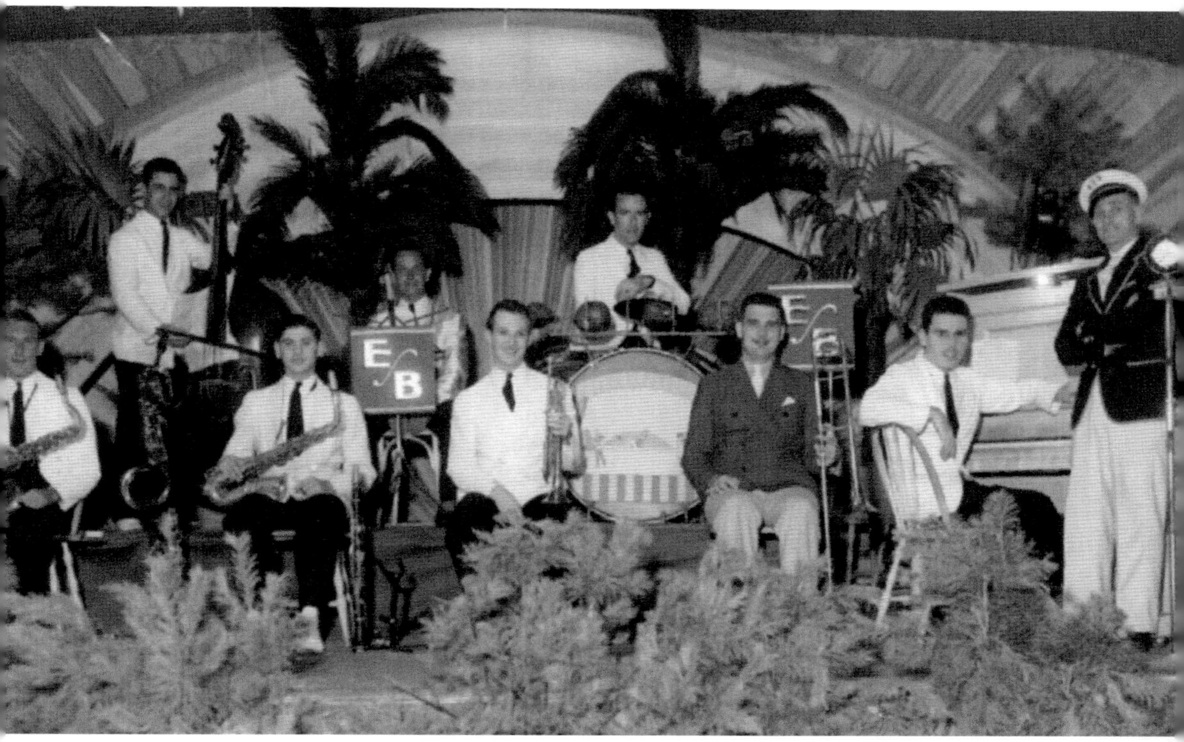

Ernie Baker

Ernie Baker was a musician, gas station operator, businessman, and ballplayer.

The Ernie Baker Orchestra was well known on Cape Cod in the 1920s, performing often at the Mill Hill Pavilion in West Yarmouth, where Ernie was the manager for a time, organizing varied events including dances and basketball games at the popular venue.

As the operator of a gas station near his family home on Old Main Street, Baker knew most people in town. But sometimes, he left the station to play semiprofessional baseball for various teams throughout Cape Cod and beyond as a featured attraction. (Courtesy of John Sears III.)

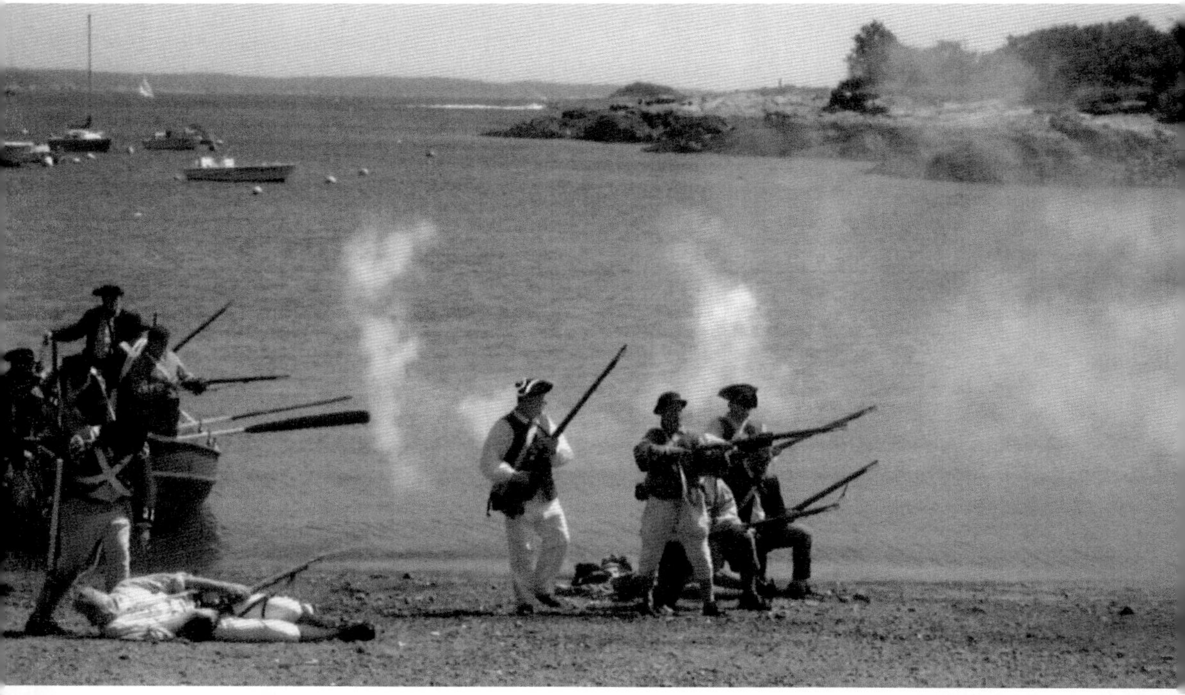

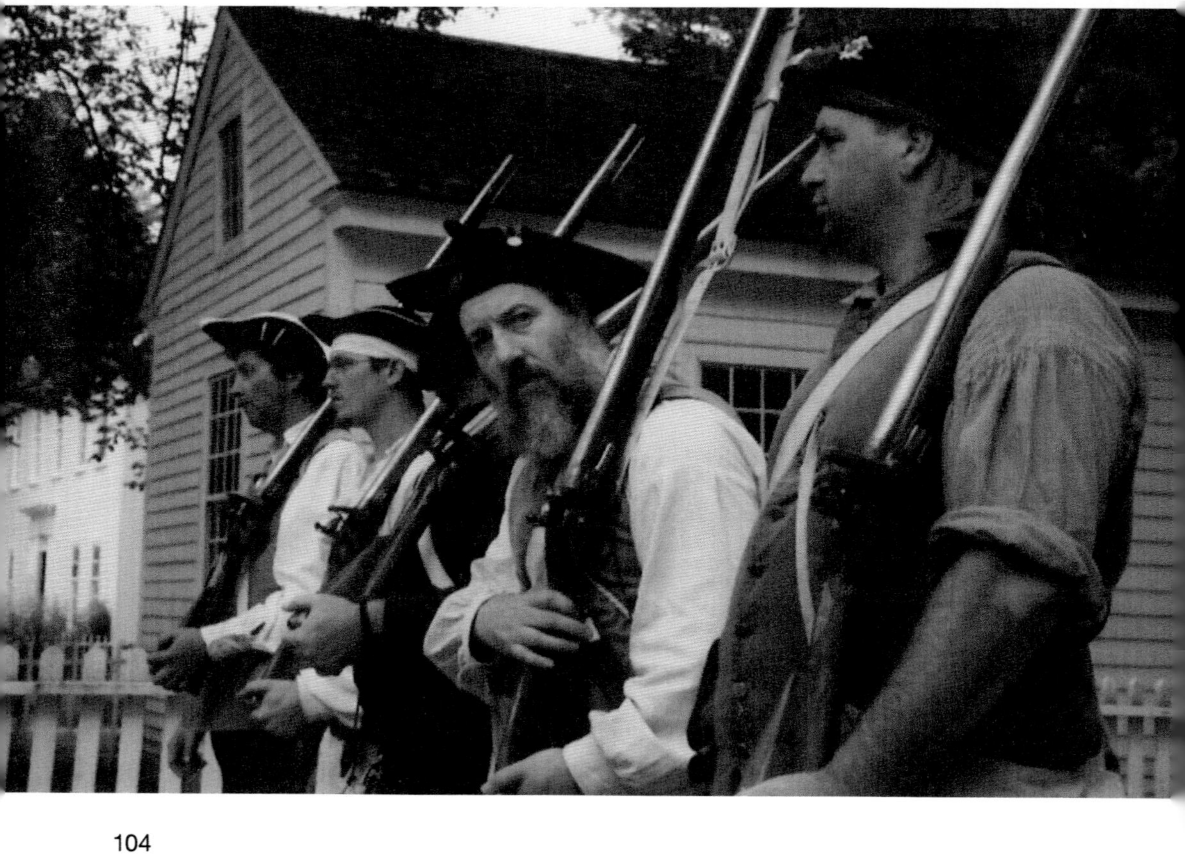

Yarmouth Minutemen (OPPOSITE PAGE, TOP)
Keeping Yarmouth's history alive in a colorful and very public way is the job of the Yarmouth Minutemen. Formed in 1994, the group at any one time has about 20 active members who stage Colonial reenactments, march in parades, and do presentations on Colonial history in schools.

All history buffs, the members of the Minutemen portray civilians and military personnel in Colonial settings. (Courtesy of Yarmouth Minutemen.)

Yarmouth in the Revolution (OPPOSITE PAGE, BOTTOM)
Traveling to historical gatherings in other Cape Cod towns and beyond has become routine for the Yarmouth Minutemen, and they are often seen at Concord Bridge, Yorktown, and other sites vital to American history.

On June 20, 1776, Yarmouth unanimously voted to "declare a state of independence of the King of Great Britain, agreeably to a late resolve by the General Court, if in case the wisdom of Congress should see proper to do it." While the vote was both bold and cautious at the same time, it did predate the Declaration of Independence by weeks.

This move was one in a string of actions taken in Yarmouth in support of independence from England. In 1774, Yarmouth Town Meeting records show that a vote was taken to send funds to the citizens of Boston. In October of that year, a committee of observation and prevention was created, and the following month another committee was formed to see that "no tea is consumed in Yarmouth," as a protest against the British.

In January 1775, Yarmouth chose Capt. Elisha Basset as a representative to the Congress in Cambridge, and in early March, the town created a committee of Seth Tobey, Isaac Matthews, Deacon John Sears, James Baker, and Daniel Taylor to "see that all the resolves of the Continental Congress be adhered to."

In April 1776, Capt. Joshua Gray was named militia captain and was responsible for gathering volunteers who would serve in Boston. Charles F. Swift's history depicts the scene: "Capt. Joshua Gray, who commanded the militia, at once set forth, accompanied by a drummer, to call for volunteers. Every one was ready and willing to go. The night was spent in preparation. In the chamber of the ancient house now standing at the corner of Hallet and Wharf streets, the mothers and daughters spent the night molding bullets and making cartridges, and at early dawn, 81 men, under the command of Capt. Gray, were on the march for Dorchester."

Throughout the Revolution, town records show efforts were made to encourage volunteers to serve in the fight against the British as well as to pay those who enlisted. Yarmouth responded to a call for 23 blankets to be sent to the army and voted funds to help support the families of those who enlisted.

When, in 1778, the British frigate *Somerset* was wrecked off Truro near the tip of Cape Cod, Yarmouth's Col. Enoch Hallet was chosen to march the 480 British sailors taken prisoner first to Barnstable and then to Boston. "This was a good closing up of the year, and though not fraught with results of widespread importance, gave our people some tangible results of the war," wrote Swift more than 100 years later. (Courtesy of Yarmouth Minutemen.)

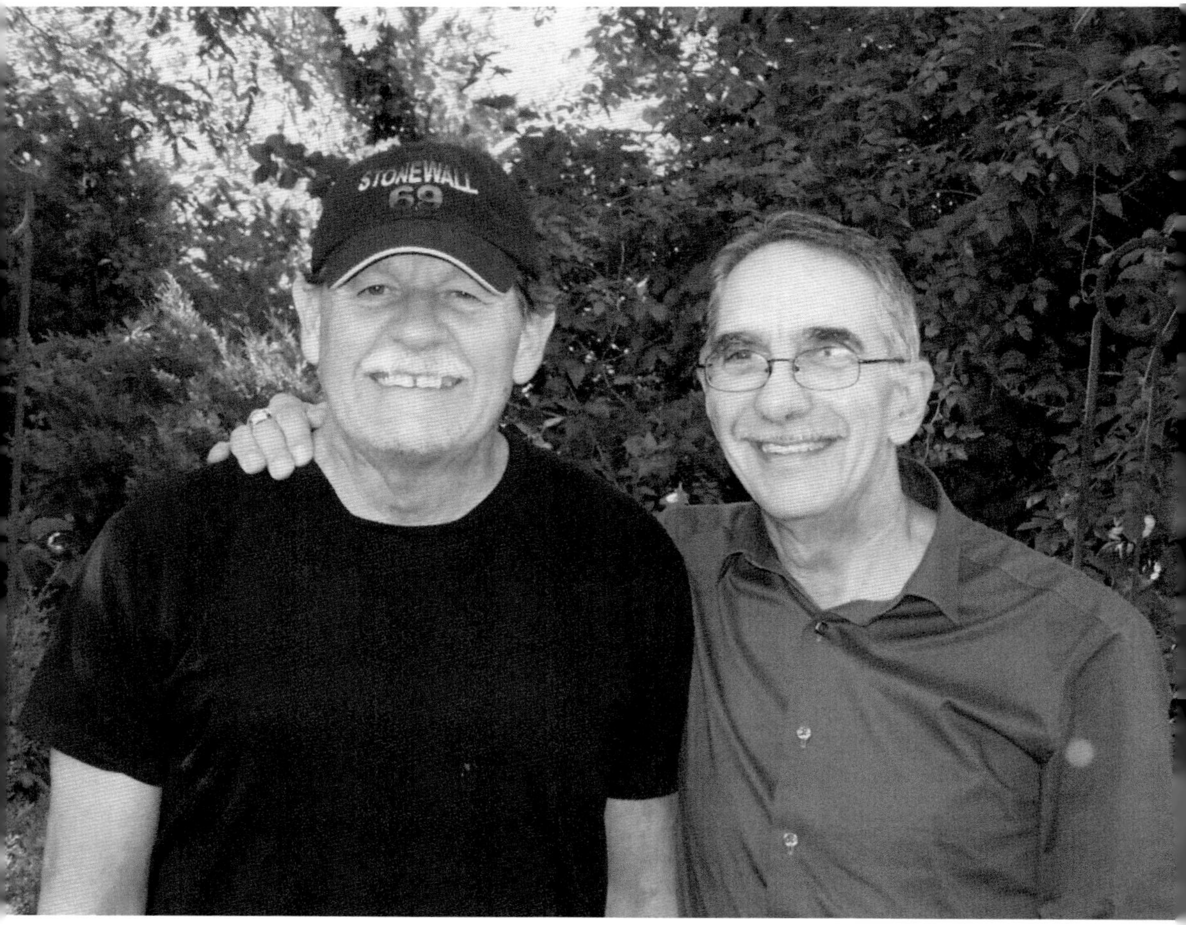

Bob Isadore and David Velasco

Bob Isadore and David Velasco are tireless workers for social justice who took a circuitous route to their adopted home of Yarmouth Port.

Isadore, born in Fall River, Massachusetts, and Velasco, from New York City, met in New York in 1974 and lived in California for many years before returning to Cape Cod, where Velasco had once run an inn.

Velasco, who at various times has been an actor and singer as well as an innkeeper, is a veteran of the Stonewall uprising, a watershed moment in the gay rights movement, in which patrons of a bar in New York resisted police who they believed were harassing them unnecessarily. Velasco has, over the years, become more involved in Stonewall-related issues, often speaking at schools and colleges and serving on the executive committee of the Stonewall Veterans Association.

Isadore has been active in political campaigns and, soon after arriving in Yarmouth in 1994, became chairman of the Cape and Islands Democratic Council, which promotes Democratic candidates. In 2013, he began hosting and producing a television program about gay rights and has served as chairman of the board of the Yarmouth Senior Center.

The two were married in 2004, when Massachusetts became the first state in the nation to legalize same-sex marriage, on the anniversary of the Stonewall uprising. (Photograph by author.)

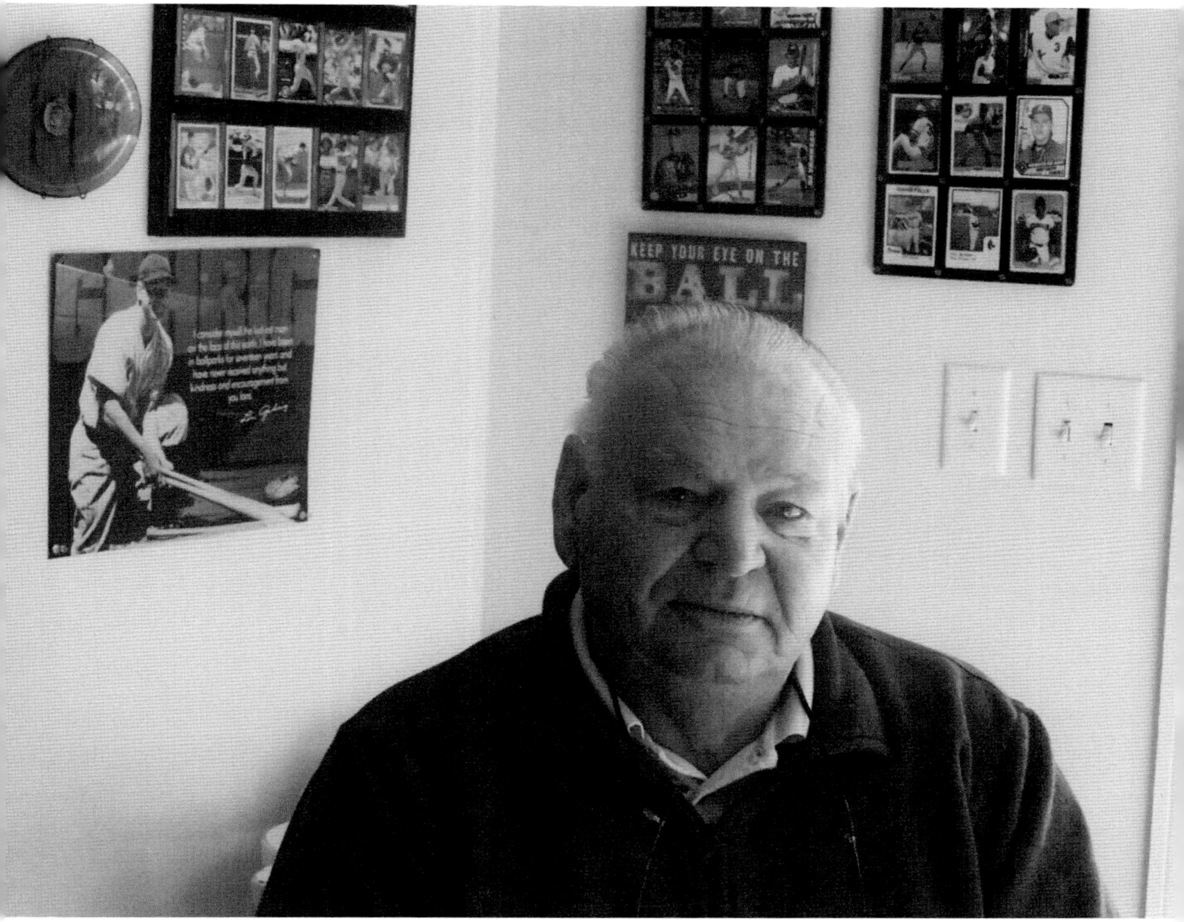

Donald Tullie

Donald Tullie is among the small group of people who kept baseball alive in Yarmouth when the existence of the town team was in jeopardy. Beginning in the late 1970s, Tullie helped to raise badly needed money to assure that Yarmouth could field a team in the Cape Cod Baseball League.

Tullie became the general manager of the Yarmouth-Dennis Red Sox and made the team the first in the league to own its own bus, allowing the players to travel as a unit, rather than in a collection of private cars, to away games.

Tullie helped to guide the team until 1989, when he took a position with the Cape Cod Baseball League administration. He says he is proud of the fact that players who come through the league learn about sportsmanship, competition, and family, whether or not they become Major League players. (Photograph by author.)

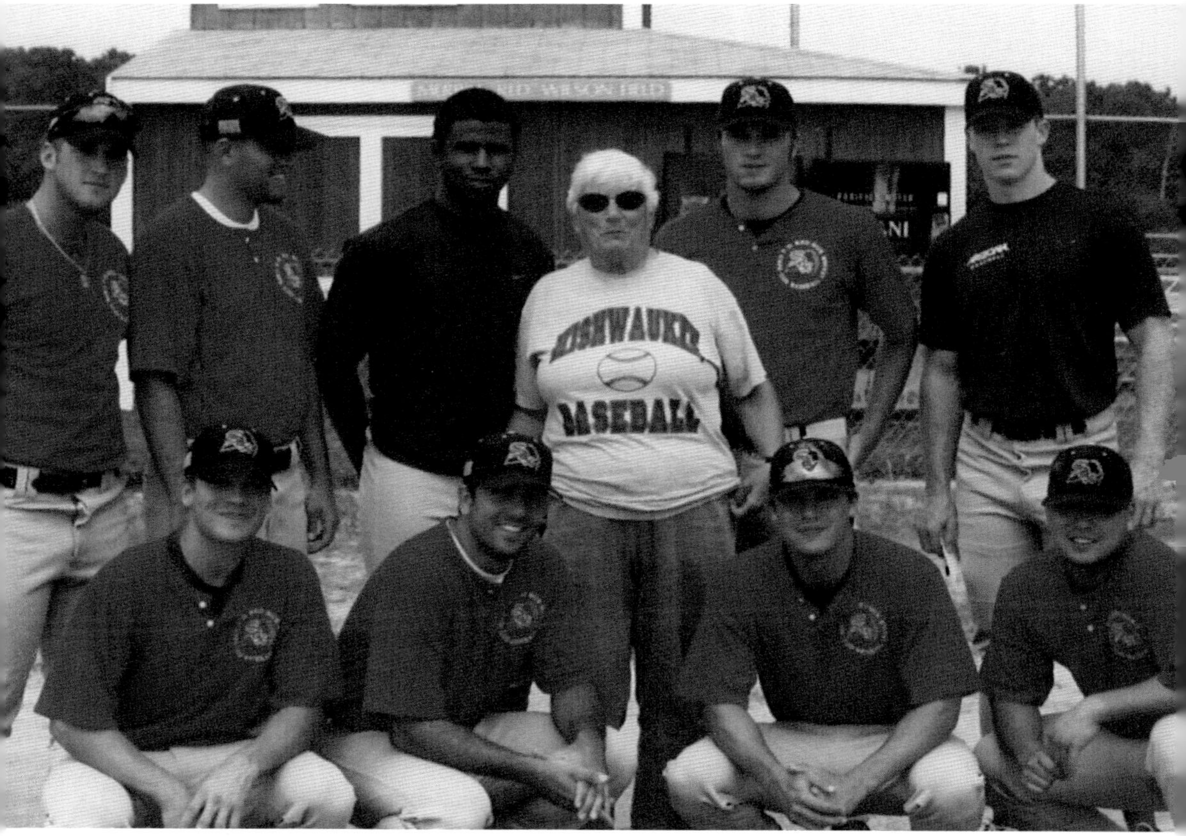

Barbara Ellsworth

Barbara Ellsworth, known as "Mrs. E" to the many Cape Cod Baseball League ballplayers she has housed over the years, is one of many who make the summer league happen.

By opening her home each summer, Mrs. E has provided hundreds of players with a comfortable place to live while they pursue their baseball dreams. Over the years, the Ellsworth family has formed lasting friendships with many of the players on Major League rosters who passed through Yarmouth while playing in the nation's premier summer league for collegiate players.

Here, Mrs. E is joined by a few of the players who have called her house home. (Courtesy of Barbara Ellsworth.)

CHAPTER SIX

Spiritual Life

Yarmouth's religious community began when the town began, in 1639, with the founding of the First Congregational Church of Yarmouth in Yarmouth Port. Establishing a church was essential to those who saw Yarmouth as a place in which they could develop homesteads.

The first church was not without controversy. The first minister, Marmaduke Matthews, was accused by some of what were called "weak and unsafe expressions," and he left town in 1645. Among the town's later religious leaders was Hal Cooper, who came to Yarmouth as a veteran of the Civil Rights movement. Dutch Nelson is credited with being the force that established the Episcopal church in town. David Akin, a former fire chief, became a Catholic deacon, serving his town in a new way once his career in the fire service was over.

As Yarmouth grew and divergent viewpoints emerged, more churches joined the First Congregational. In addition to the original Congregational church, another Congregational church in South Yarmouth, Quaker, Swedenborgian, Baptist, Episcopalian, Methodist, and Catholic parishes have all flourished in Yarmouth and most continue to contribute to the life of the community.

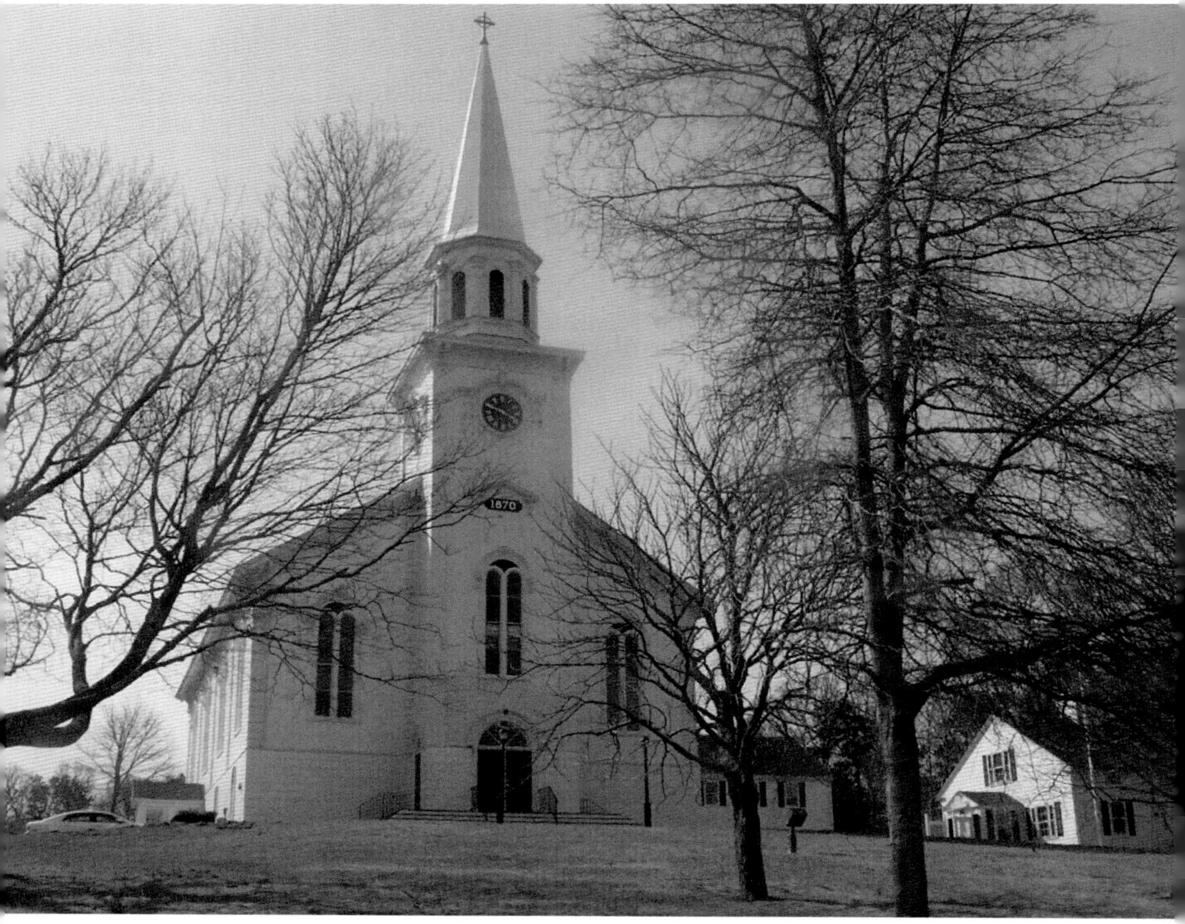

First Congregational Church

Without the First Congregational Church, there would have been no Yarmouth. In Colonial times, a church was central to the formation of a town, and while the earliest records have been lost, it is known that Rev. Marmaduke Matthews, described as "one of the first-comers," to Yarmouth in Swift's *History of Old Yarmouth*, was the first minister.

The first meetinghouse was where Yarmouth's Ancient Cemetery is now located. As the congregation grew, the first meetinghouse was followed by three more; the last one was built in 1870 and is still standing atop Zion Hill, visible from Cape Cod Bay to mariners seeking safe harbor. (Photograph by author.)

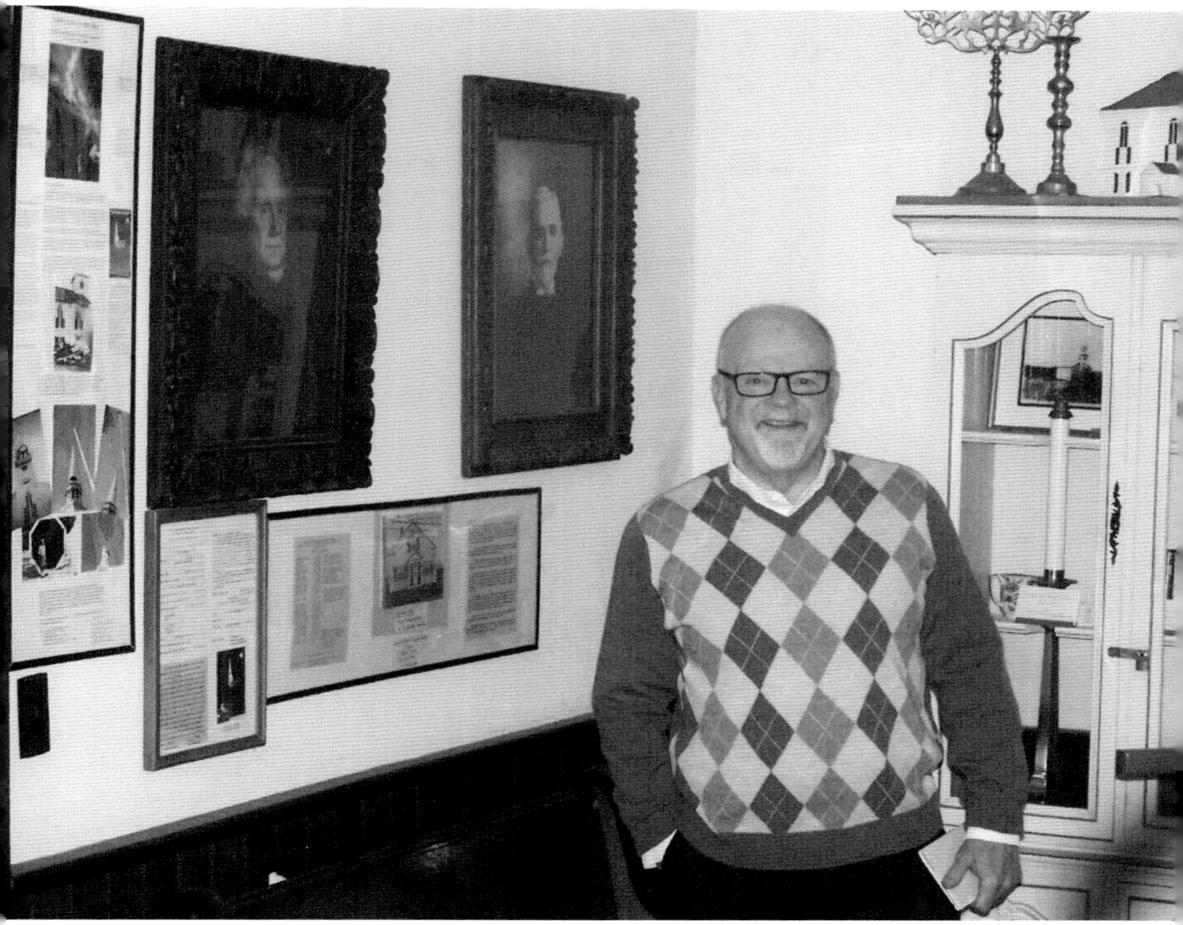

Rev. Phil R. Jackson
Continuing the long line of ministers at the First Congregational Church of Yarmouth is Rev. Phil Jackson, shown here with a collection of portraits and other items representing the congregation's long history. (Photograph by author.)

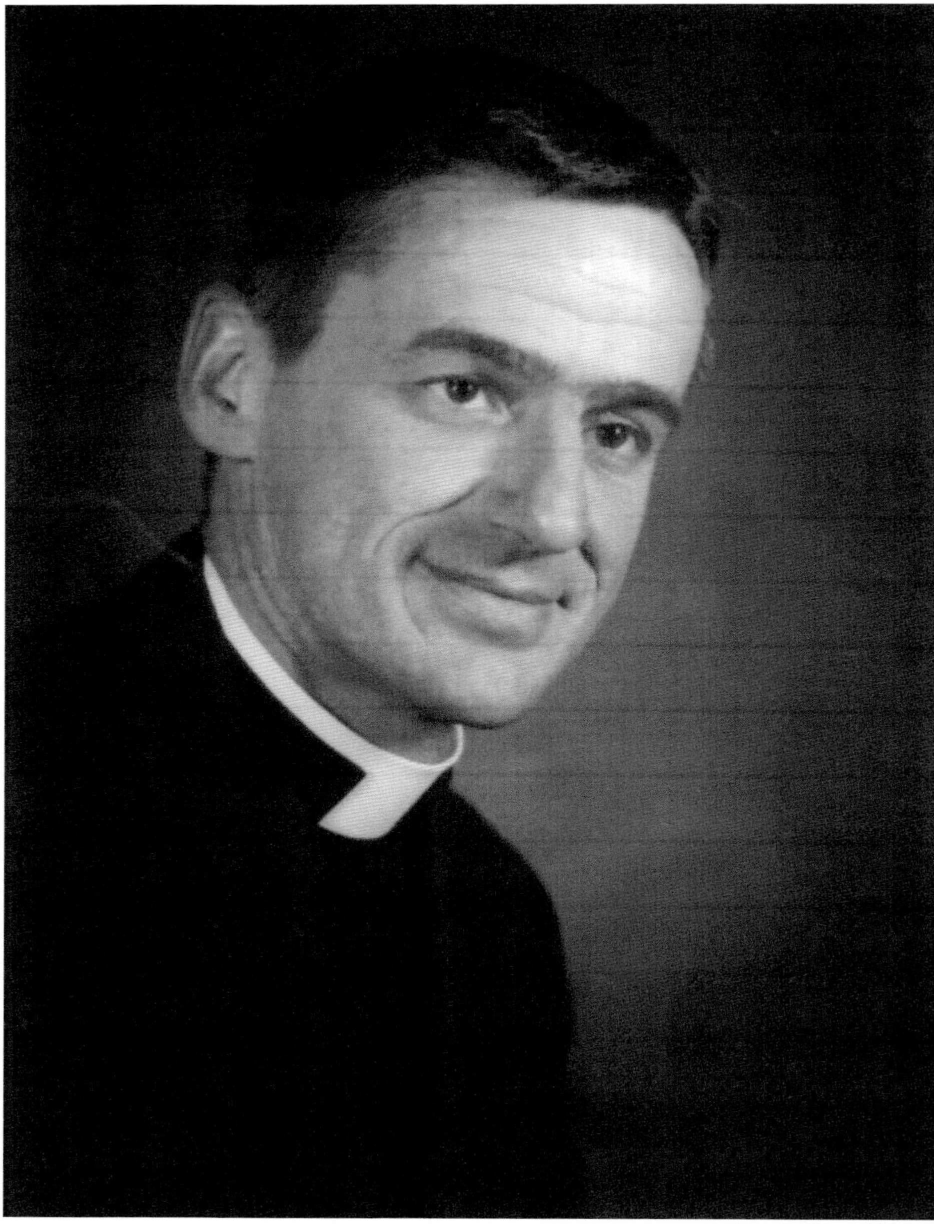

Rev. James Lowell Nelson
"Dutch" Nelson was the first priest of St. David's Episcopal Church and led the congregation even before there was a church building.

In early 1966, about 40 Episcopalians began holding services in the basement of Yarmouth Town Hall. Over the next four years, they built St. David's on Old Main Street in South Yarmouth, and the church was dedicated on January 12, 1970, with Father Nelson leading the service.

A church history says that Nelson was "ideally suited to bring the parish through its beginning years" and that in retirement he remains an invaluable member of the parish. (Courtesy of St. David's Episcopal Church.)

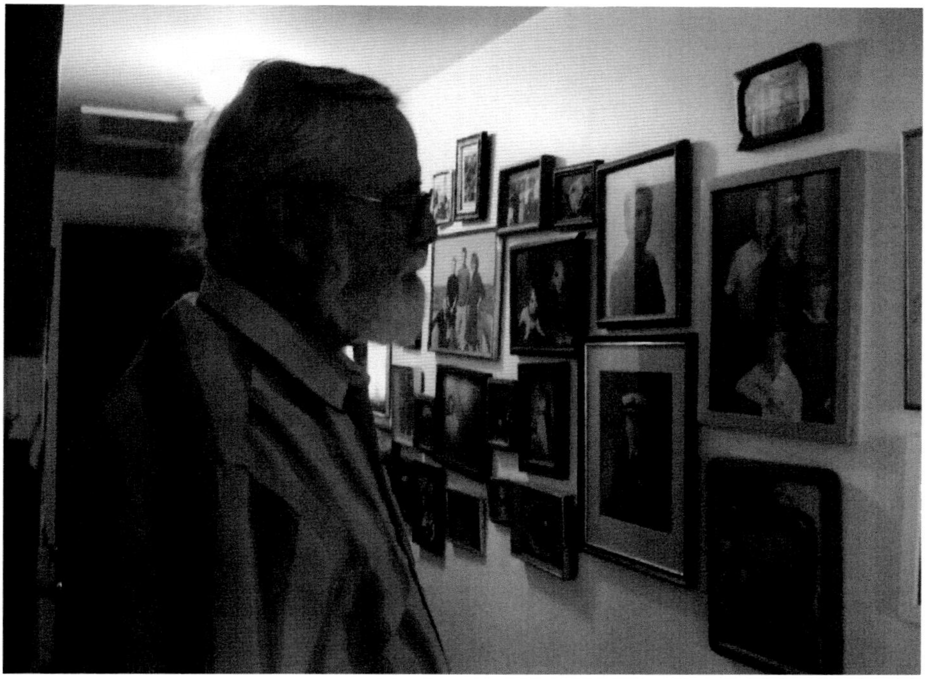

David P. Akin

David Akin has served Yarmouth in two capacities, first as the town's fire chief from 1983 to 1995, and after his retirement as a deacon in the Catholic Church.

Akin, raised on the North Shore of Boston, had no connection to Yarmouth before he succeeded John Clemence as chief, but in an odd coincidence, a street not far from Yarmouth Fire Department headquarters is named for another David Akin, a prosperous businessman. In another ironic twist, on Chief Akin's first day on the job in Yarmouth, he was among the firefighters responding to a horrific traffic accident at the intersection of Old Main Street and Akin Avenue in which two people died. Akin said the fact that the call was at a street bearing his family name convinced him Yarmouth was where he was supposed to be.

Under Akin's watch, the Yarmouth Fire Department grew and increased its presence on the north side of town, with Station No. 2 on Route 6A becoming a more intensively used station particularly for ambulances responding to calls north of the Mid-Cape Highway, which bisects the town.

After his retirement as chief, Akin followed another calling, that of deacon at St. Pius X Catholic Church in South Yarmouth. He says the stress of being fire chief was actually the first step toward his embrace of religion. While his wife, Rosemary, was undergoing extensive treatment for cancer, he made a decision to cut back his work hours to no more than 40 per week. He contends this made him a better fire chief. He also learned that he lived in a "generous community," which he began to look at in a new way.

Working with his mentor, Deacon Joe Stanley of nearby Centeville, Akin, in 1993, began taking steps to become a deacon and was ordained by Bishop Sean O'Malley in 1997.

Akin serves as the chaplain for the Yarmouth Police Department and the Dennis Fire Department next door to Yarmouth. With Rosemary, he serves as a coordinator of the Marriage Preparation Team for the Diocese of Fall River; he is also affiliated with the Dennis-Yarmouth Ecumenical Council to Prevent Homelessness, the Housing Assistance Corporation's prevention program to keep financially stressed families in their homes, and many other community organizations.

In his capacity as chaplain, Akin made two trips to ground zero at the World Trade Center following the terrorist attacks of September 11, 2001. Reflecting on his service there and his time in the Army decades earlier, Akin said, "I never went to Vietnam; I went to ground zero." (Photograph by author.)

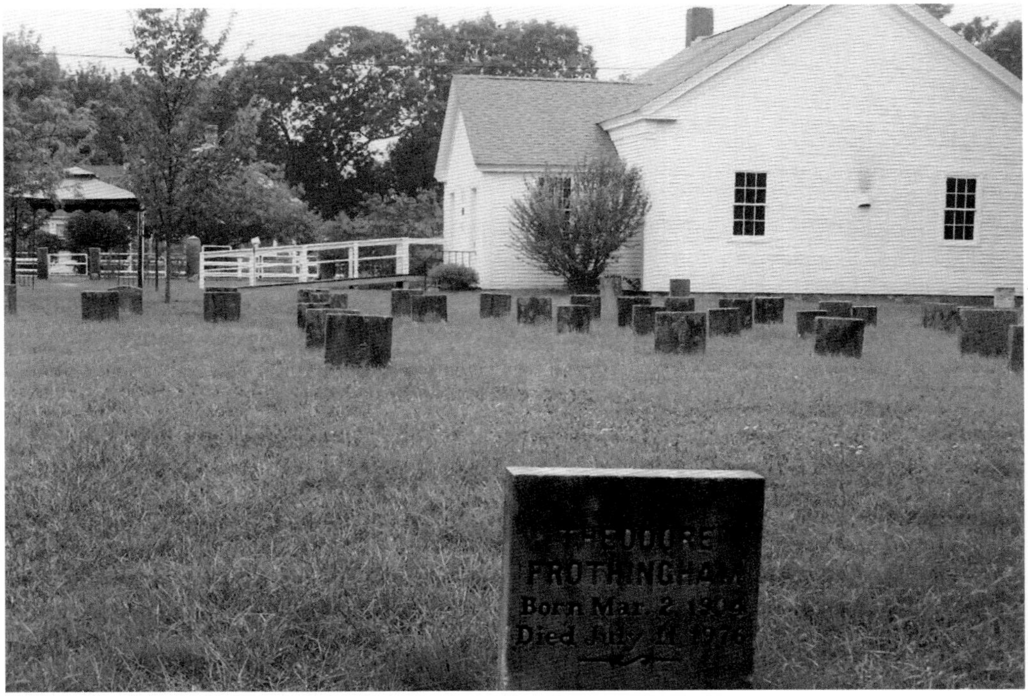

Yarmouth's Quakers

In the 19th century, there was no more important place in South Yarmouth than the Quaker Meetinghouse on North Main Street. Quaker meetings had existed on Cape Cod since the earliest days of English settlement, but the Yarmouth meeting traces its origins to Russell Davis, who preached at first to "bare walls" but soon attracted a following, according to Laurence Barber's *When South Yarmouth Was a Quaker Village*.

The Yarmouth meetinghouse was built in the plain style favored by the Quakers and looks today much as it did when it was the center of life for many in South Yarmouth. Buried in its graveyard are many who were prominent in Yarmouth's early days. (Photograph by author.)

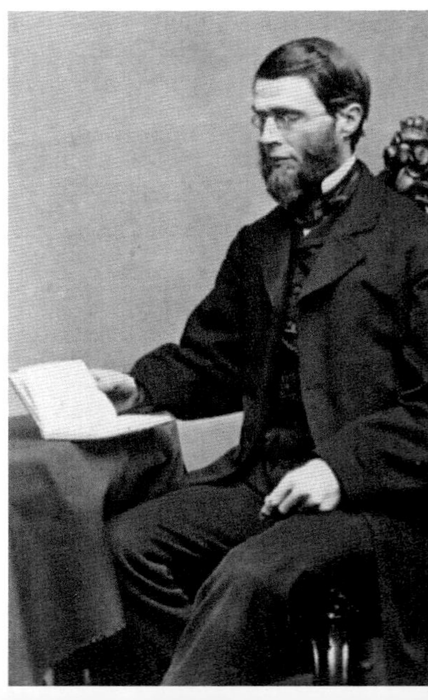

Rev. John Philander Perry (1819–1886)

John Philander Perry occupied a prominent position in Yarmouth as the pastor of the Church of the New Jerusalem. Beginning in 1853, Perry led the then-popular and influential Swedenborgian congregation for 17 years. Shortly after his arrival in Yarmouth Port, he married into a prominent family when Caroline Thacher became his wife. (Courtesy of Lawrence Perera.)

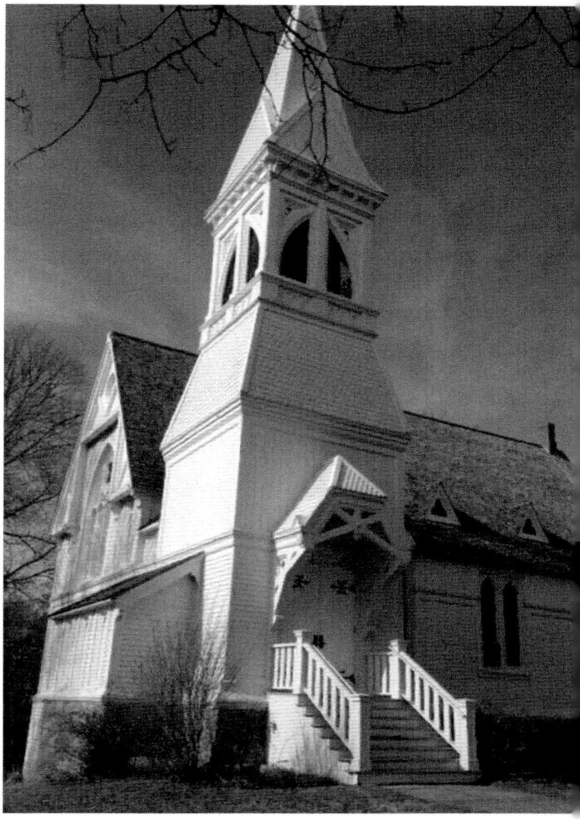

The Church of the New Jerusalem
The Swedenborgian Church had a long presence in Yarmouth; however, for much of its existence, the congregation was small. There was interest in the Swedenborgian doctrine in Yarmouth as early as 1819, when, according to Marion Vuilleumier's history of Yarmouth, Caleb Reed came to town and took with him a copy of Swedish theologian Emanuel Swedenborg's book, hoping to study the religion so that he could convince his brother to abandon it. Instead, Caleb became a convert and began holding meetings. Andrew Hallet began holding meetings at his home in the 1820s, and by 1837, the congregation was meeting in Thomas Thacher's store. That same year, the congregation opened a school. In 1843, the congregation was formally constituted, and in 1858, it moved to the second floor of the building that is now home to Parnassus Book Service.

In 1870, the congregation opened its S.J.F. Thayer–designed church, located opposite the Yarmouth Port Common. The *Register* reported the building was the finest specimen of church architecture in the country. Possible hyperbole aside, the church remains as a classic example of Gothic church architecture. (Photograph by author.)

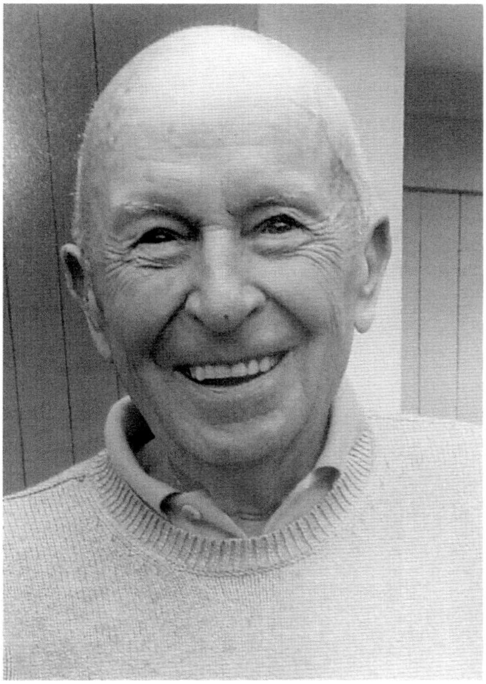

Sherrill Smith (1930–2014)
Sherrill Smith became the pastor at St. David's Episcopal Church in South Yarmouth in 1973, gently educating his parishioners much as he did the readers of his popular "Woodstove" column published in the *Register.*

Smith was a knowledgeable fisheries expert, a fisherman, and lobsterman, as well as a minister.

Working with Sen. Edward Kennedy, he helped to write the 200-mile fisheries limit law.

As a writer, he taught reporters to listen to the people they interviewed and put that knowledge into their stories. His columns, like his sermons, were far ranging and always inspirational. (Courtesy of St. David's Episcopal Church.)

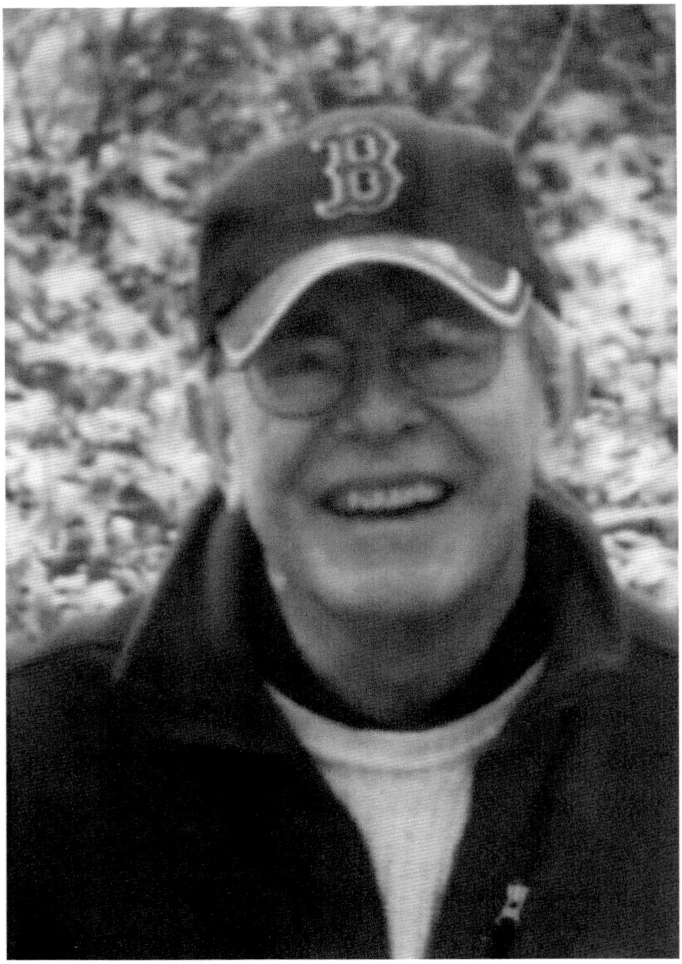

Rev. Harold Cooper (1938–2012)

Sociologist, teacher, civil rights activist, and pastor are all titles that apply to Harold Cooper.

"Hal," as his many friends knew him, was best known in Yarmouth as the pastor of the West Yarmouth Congregational Church; however, his work as a minister was only part of what he accomplished.

Born in Worcester, Massachusetts, Cooper graduated from the University of Massachusetts with a degree in psychology. He followed that with master's and doctorate degrees in sociology before earning his degree in theology.

Cooper returned to the University of Massachusetts as chaplain in the 1960s. It was also during this time that Cooper dedicated himself to civil rights work in the South and to antiwar efforts during the time of the Vietnam War. He was instrumental in developing the black women's studies program at Mount Holyoke College and taught sociology at St. Francis College in Maine and elsewhere.

Only after teaching for years did Cooper pursue his calling as a minister, first in Fall River, Massachusetts, and later, in West Yarmouth, where he would serve as pastor for 19 years until his retirement in 2000. Even after retirement, Cooper was remarkably active in community organizations and was named a Paul Harris Fellow by the Yarmouth Rotary in recognition of his work to improve understanding among people around the world.

Cooper died in 2012, and a year later, his congregation in West Yarmouth honored him by naming the parish center for him. (Courtesy of the Cooper family.)

CHAPTER SEVEN

Competitors

In this chapter, those who have been stars on the playing field are highlighted. Whatever the sport, and whether the stage was local or national, they all set high standards for competition.

Yarmouth has a long history as a member of the Cape Cod Baseball League (CCBL). The Yarmouth Indians were the town team and part of the CCBL before it became the premiere college summer league. Today, the Yarmouth-Dennis Red Sox are made up of top college players from around the nation. Baseball remains a big part of summer life in the town and has produced many of Yarmouth's athletic heroes.

Bobby Valentine, who had a long career as a Major League player and manager, was a standout for the Yarmouth Indians while still a high school student. Mike Bordick, undrafted by Major League teams, shined in a brief stint in Yarmouth and went on to a 14-year big league career. Red Wilson was a player, coach, and mentor to hundreds of young players in a variety of sports. And Yarmouth's Elaine Joyce made legal history challenging golf course customs.

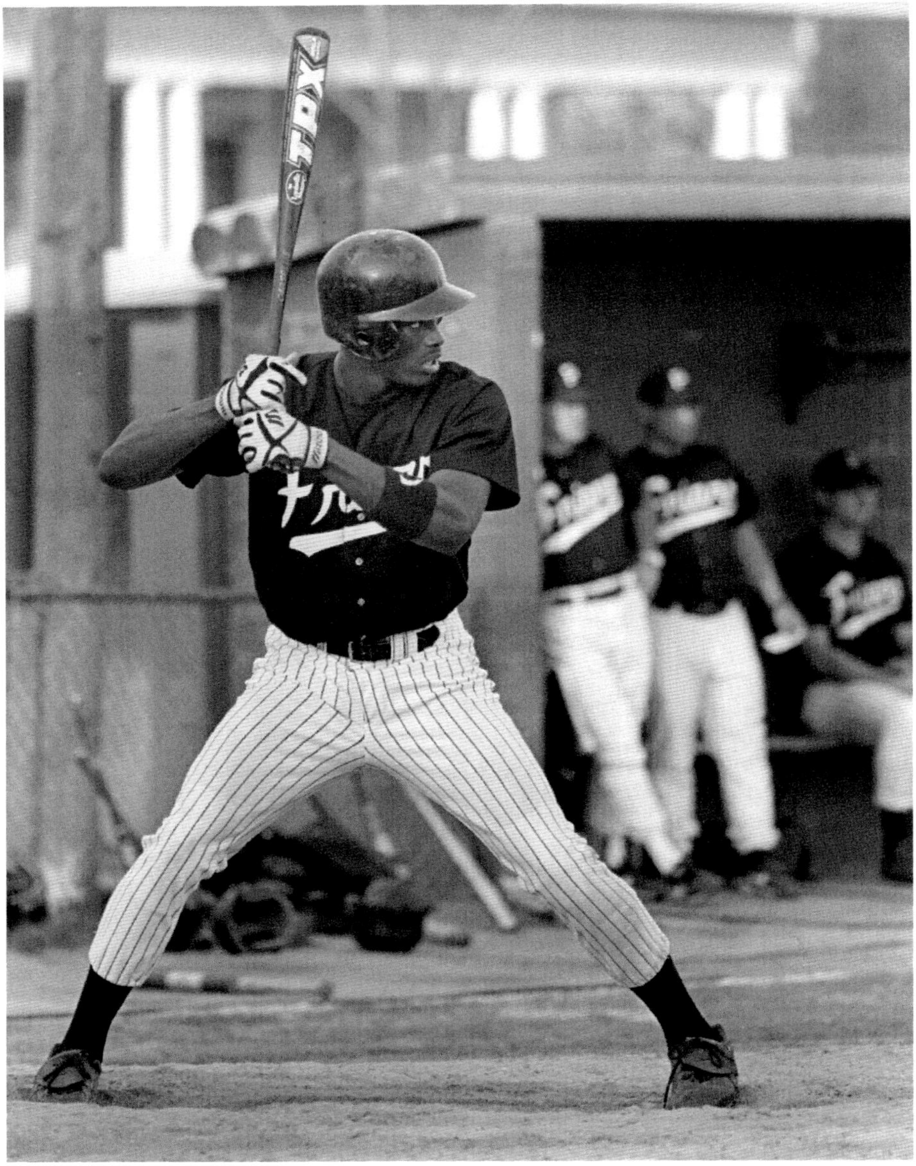

Keith Reed

His time in the big leagues was brief, but Keith Reed is believed to be the only person born in Yarmouth to play Major League baseball.

Reed attended high school in Worcester, Massachusetts, and played college baseball at Providence College in Rhode Island before he was drafted in the first round of the 1999 free agent draft by the Baltimore Orioles. Reed moved up through the Minor Leagues and was called up to the majors by the Orioles on May 11, 2005. He played for just a week for Baltimore, collecting one hit before he was sent back down to the Minor Leagues.

Reed went on to compile solid statistics for Ottawa in the International League in 2006 and with the Newark Bears of the independent Atlantic League in 2007 and 2008, but his baseball career ended without a return trip to the Major Leagues. (Courtesy of Providence College.)

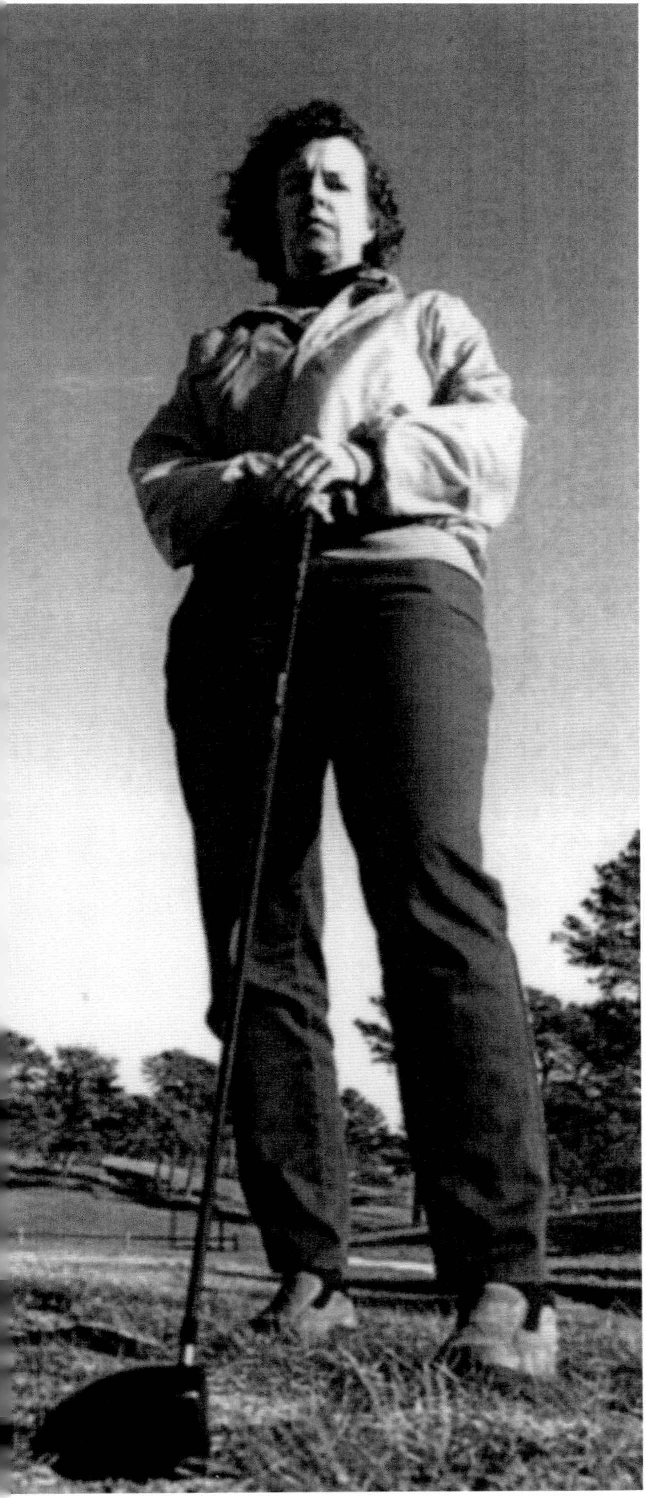

Elaine Joyce
Elaine Joyce has been a champion on the golf course, winning many tournaments. She has also become a champion of another sort, winning a lawsuit challenging the rules at municipal golf courses.

Joyce, who lives in Yarmouth Port and works with computers professionally, is a top amateur golfer. In 2007, she wanted to play in a tandem with her father, in a members-only tournament at a public course in Dennis, where she is a member. When father and daughter were denied entrance to the tournament, Joyce sued the town of Dennis, claiming she was "denied full-citizen status" because men-only tournaments are usually scheduled on weekend mornings, considered a preferred time. In 2011, she won in court; although by then, Dennis had already changed its policy to allow women to play in men's tournaments.

The victory was her second. A decade earlier, she had challenged the men-only policy and gained admittance to the Forty Thieves group at Yarmouth's public courses, which plays at preferred weekend times. (Courtesy of the *Register*.)

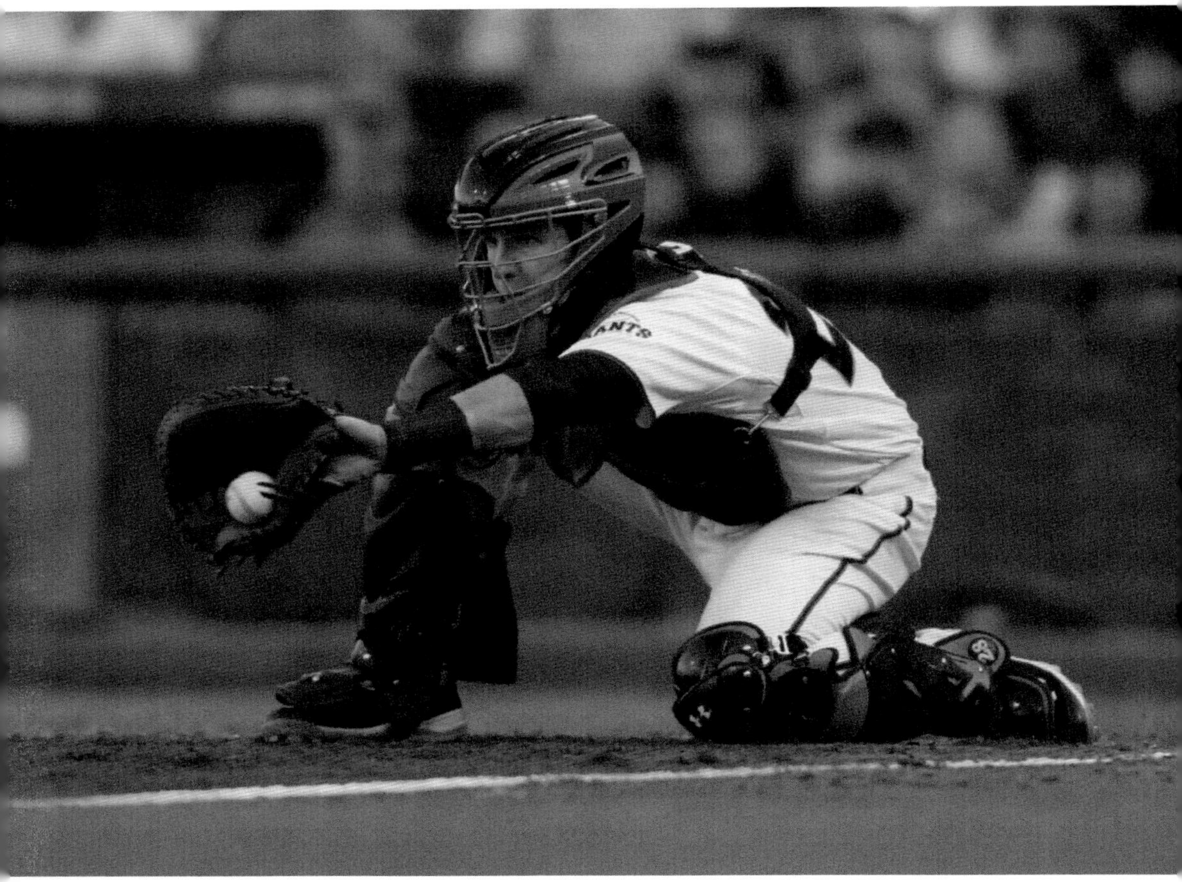

Buster Posey

For two summers, Buster Posey gave fans of the Yarmouth-Dennis Red Sox in the Cape Cod Baseball League a lot to cheer about.

Posey, now an all-star catcher for the National League San Francisco Giants, with Rookie of the Year and Most Valuable Player awards to his credit, helped to lead the Yarmouth-Dennis Red Sox to championships the two seasons he played for them. In 2006 he was a shortstop, but in 2007, he moved to catcher, the position he plays for the Giants. (Courtesy of and © 2013 San Francisco Giants.)

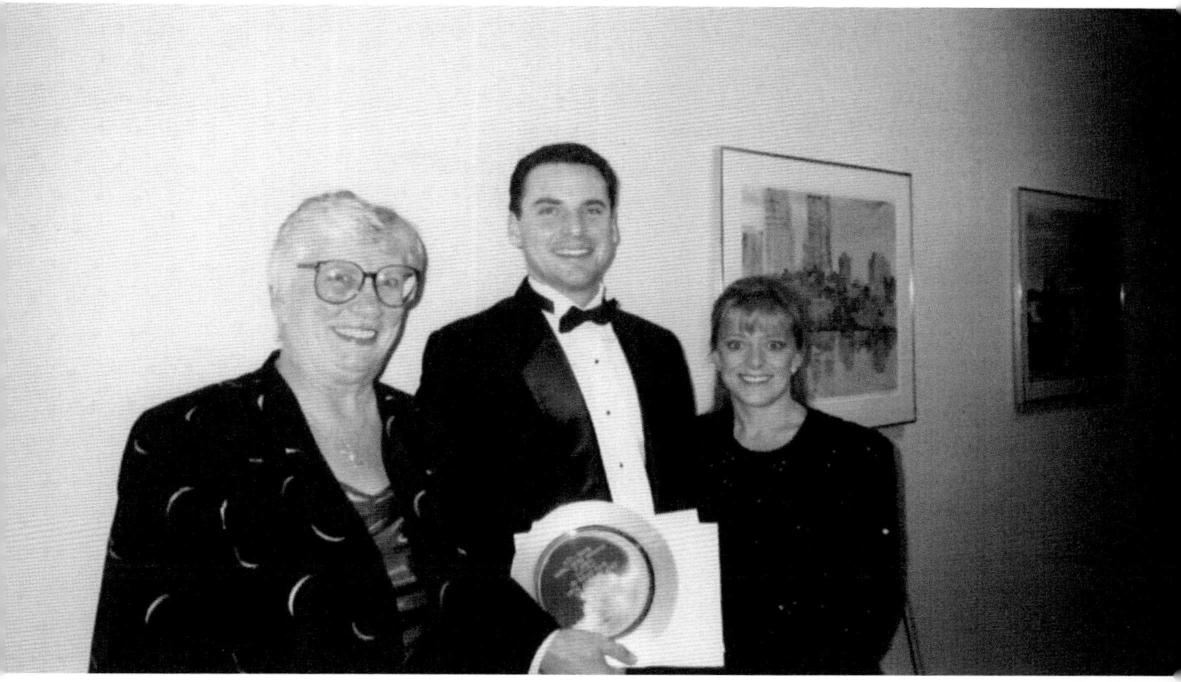

Mike Bordick
Mike Bordick's time in Yarmouth was short, but he made the most of it. He went undrafted by any Major League team after his career at the University of Maine, but it was while he was playing for the Yarmouth-Dennis Red Sox in 1986 that Bordick made an impression on Major League baseball scouts that resulted in him being signed to a contract. He went on to have a 13-year Major League career, and remains in touch with his friends from Yarmouth and with the Cape Cod Baseball League. In 2001, Bordick made a major contribution to help pay for improvements to Red Wilson Field, where he played while a member of the Yarmouth-Dennis Red Sox. Here, Bordick is shown with his Yarmouth host Barbara Ellsworth, left, and his wife, Monica, at the Boston Baseball Writer's Dinner. (Courtesy of Barbara Ellsworth.)

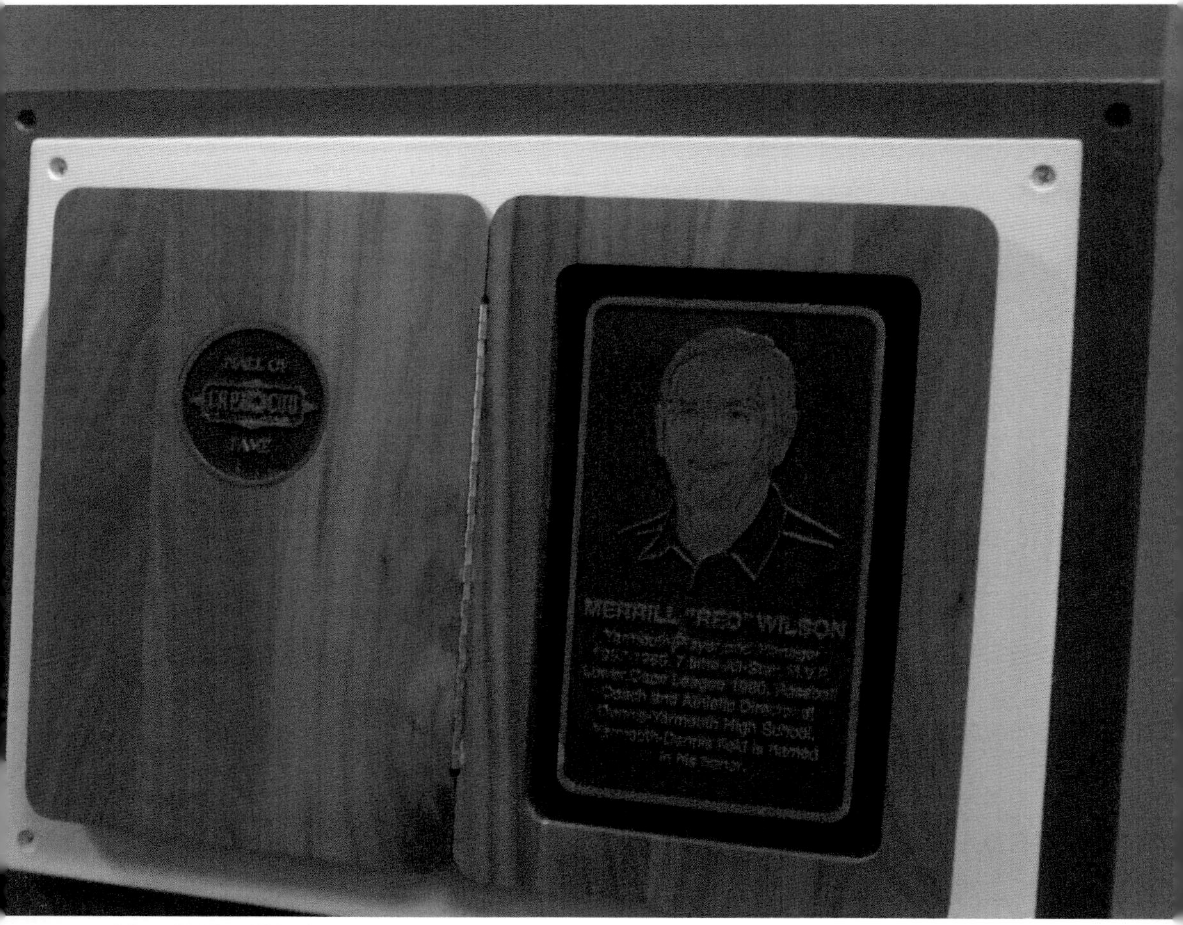

Merrill "Red" Wilson

Merrill "Red" Wilson and baseball are synonymous in Yarmouth.

Wilson was a catcher for and later managed the Yarmouth Indians in the Cape Cod Baseball League in the 1950s, when Cape Cod players competed against one another and before the top college players in the country filled the league's rosters.

As the head of the Physical Education Department at Dennis-Yarmouth Regional High School, Wilson was also the assistant football coach, assistant basketball coach, and baseball coach.

In 1981, he was immortalized when the baseball field at the high school, which also serves as the home field for the Yarmouth-Dennis Red Sox, was named in his honor. He remained with the Yarmouth-Dennis Red Sox until his retirement in 1986.

In 2001, Wilson was among the first inductees into the Cape League's new Hall of Fame. In 2008, he served as the honorary captain of the Yarmouth-Dennis team when, as defending league champions, the team played a benefit game to raise funds for the Hall of Fame. (Photograph by author.)

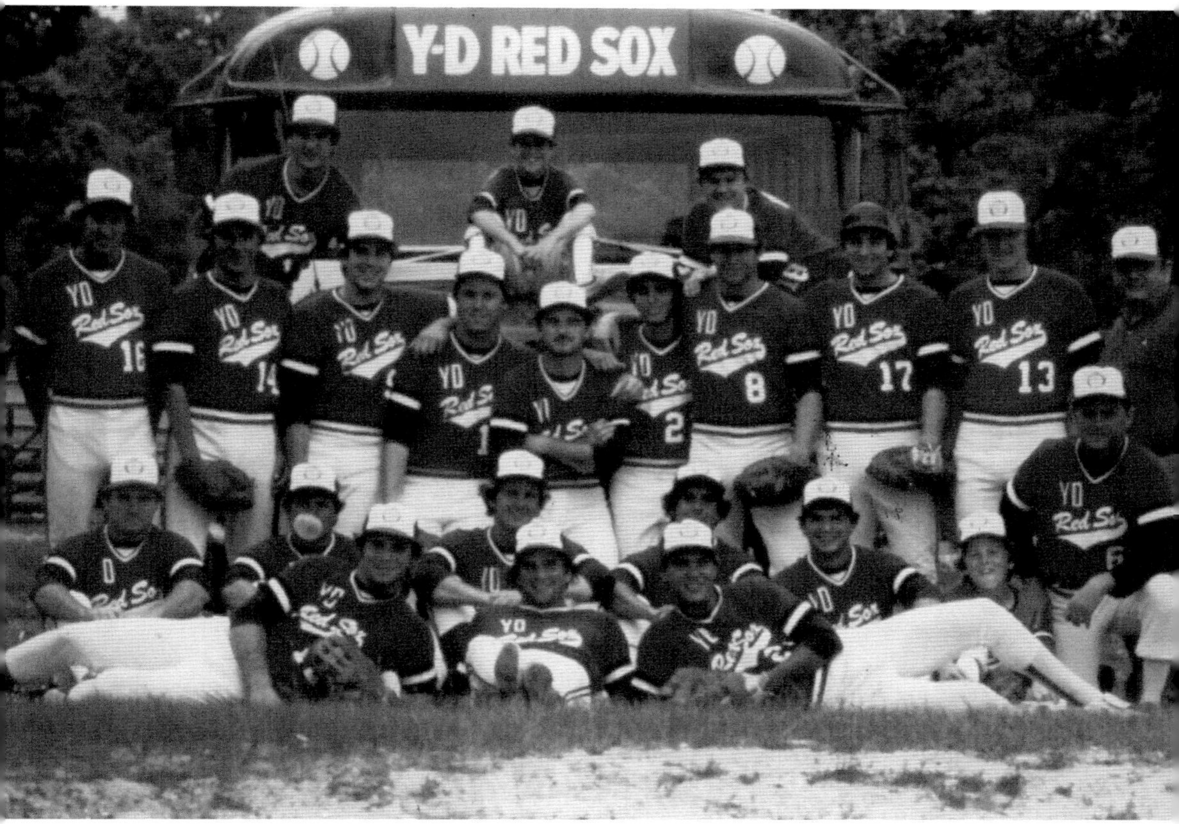

Yarmouth-Dennis Red Sox

This team photograph from 1984 shows the Cape Cod Baseball League champion Yarmouth-Dennis Red Sox. At the far left in the second row is coach Red Wilson. At the far right in the second row is general manager Don Tullie. (Courtesy of Barbara Ellsworth.)

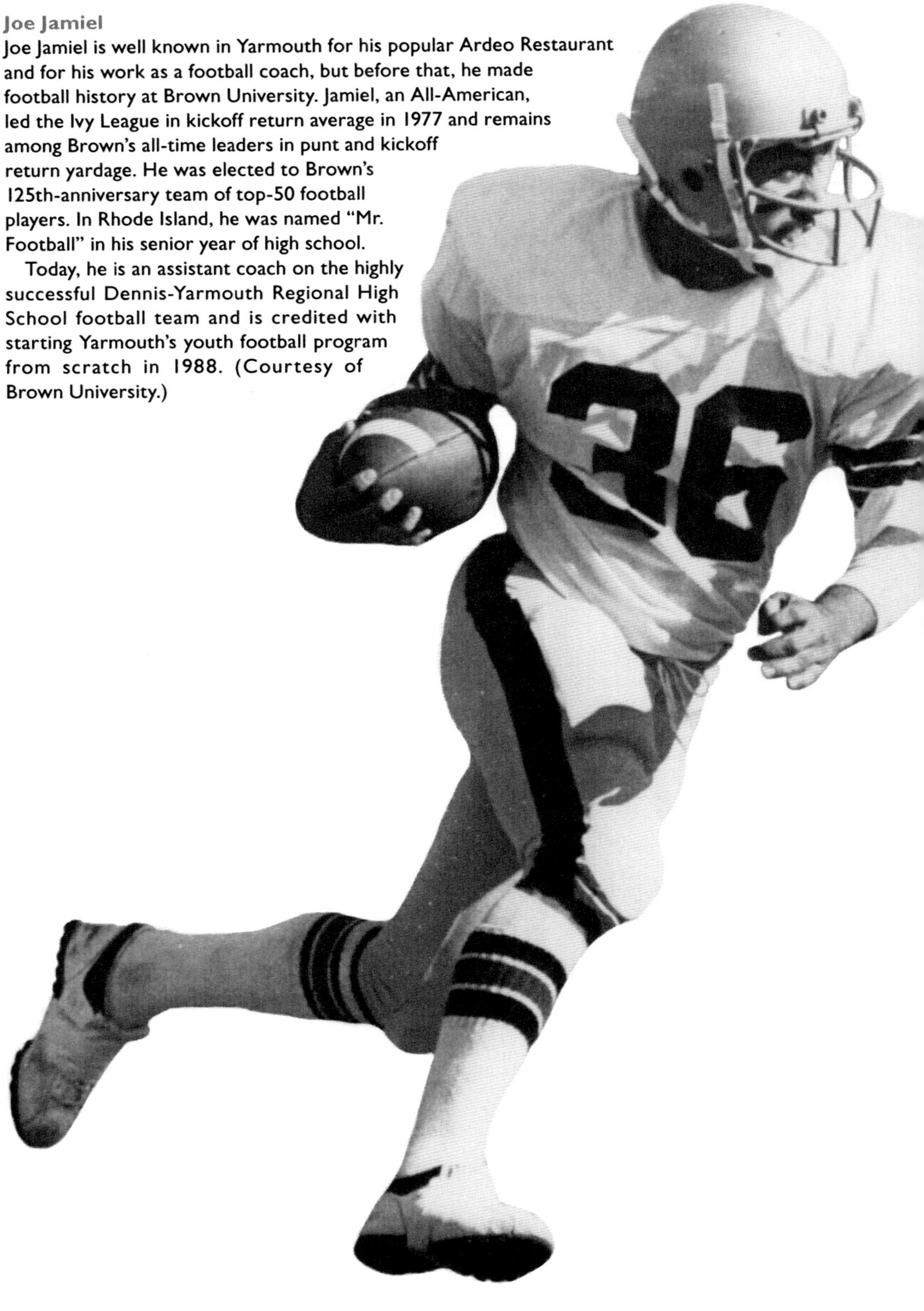

Joe Jamiel
Joe Jamiel is well known in Yarmouth for his popular Ardeo Restaurant and for his work as a football coach, but before that, he made football history at Brown University. Jamiel, an All-American, led the Ivy League in kickoff return average in 1977 and remains among Brown's all-time leaders in punt and kickoff return yardage. He was elected to Brown's 125th-anniversary team of top-50 football players. In Rhode Island, he was named "Mr. Football" in his senior year of high school.

Today, he is an assistant coach on the highly successful Dennis-Yarmouth Regional High School football team and is credited with starting Yarmouth's youth football program from scratch in 1988. (Courtesy of Brown University.)

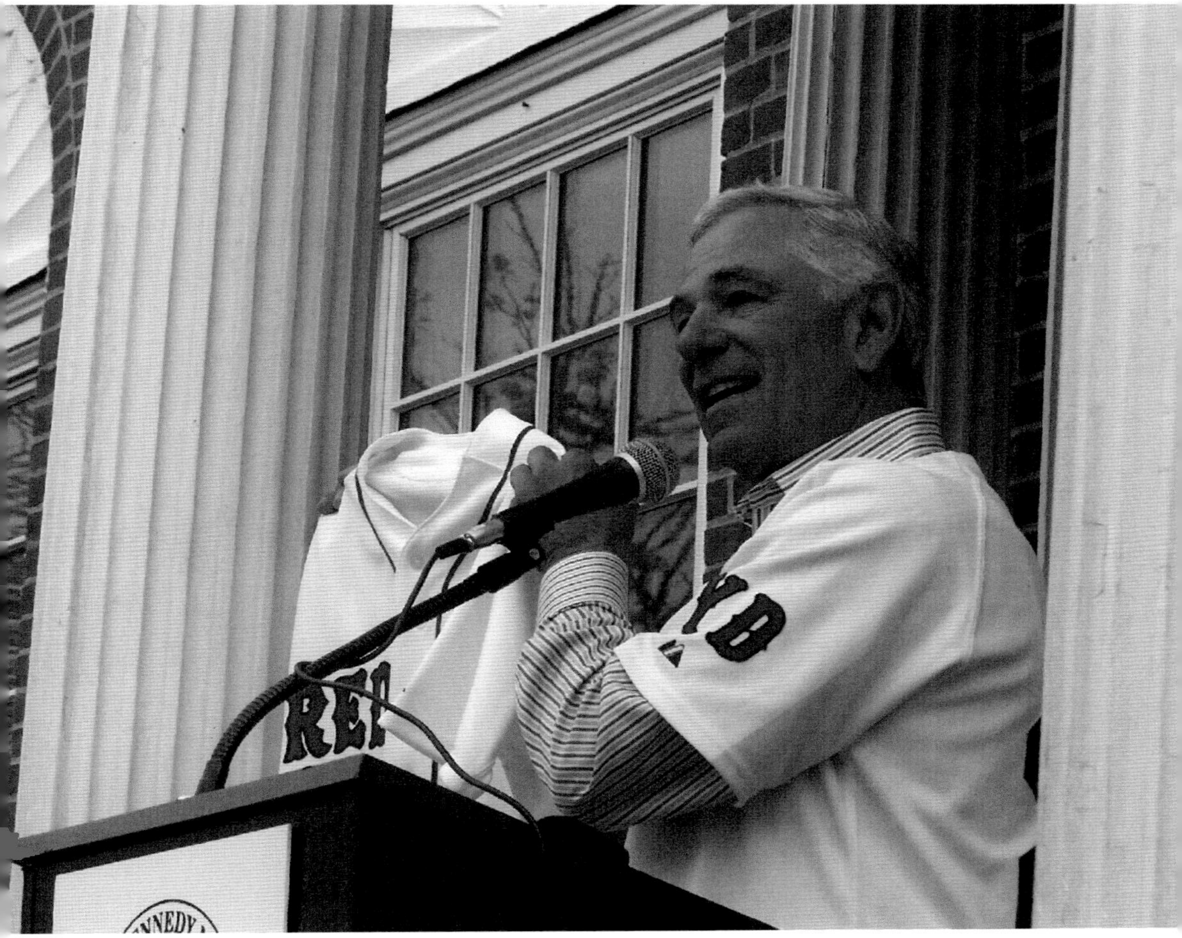

Bobby Valentine

Baseball player, manager, and broadcaster, Bobby Valentine was a star player for the Yarmouth Indians in the Cape Cod Baseball League as a 17-year-old high school junior in 1967.

These were the days before the CCBL was a college league, and Valentine compiled a .294 batting average and led the league in runs scored. A year later, Valentine was among the first players chosen in the Major League draft by the Los Angeles Dodgers.

In 2009, Valentine returned to Yarmouth to see his former manager Lou Lamoriello inducted into the CCBL Hall of Fame. He returned again in 2012 as manager of the Boston Red Sox to donate an autographed Red Sox jersey to the league. (Photograph by author.)

BIBLIOGRAPHY

Barber, Laurence. *When South Yarmouth Was a Quaker Village*. Yarmouth Port, MA: Historical Society of Old Yarmouth, 1988.

Deyo, Simeon L., ed. *History of Barnstable County, Massachusetts*. New York: H.W. Blake & Co., 1890.

Gregory, Priscilla D. and Judy Thomas, eds. *Yarmouth Old Homes and Gathering Places*. Yarmouth Port, MA: Yarmouth Historical Commission, 1989.

Perera, Lawrence Thacher. *The Homestead Saga*. Self-published, 2012.

Price, Christopher. *Baseball by the Beach*. Hyannis, MA: Parnassus Imprints, 1998.

Swift, Charles F. *History of Old Yarmouth*. Yarmouth Port, MA: Historical Society of Old Yarmouth, 1876.

Vuilleumier, Marion. *The Town of Yarmouth, Massachusetts: A History 1639–1989*. Yarmouth Port, MA: Historical Society of Old Yarmouth, 1989.

INDEX